D0786627

Popes and Princes, 1417–1517

EARLY MODERN EUROPE TODAY

Editor: Professor J. H. Shennan

Popes & Princes, 1417–1517 John A. F. Thomson
Radical Religious Movements in Early Modern Europe
Michael A. Mullett

Popes and Princes, 1417–1517

*Politics and Polity in the
Late Medieval Church*

JOHN A. F. THOMSON

*Senior Lecturer in History,
University of Glasgow*

London
GEORGE ALLEN & UNWIN
Boston   Sydney

First published in 1980

GEORGE ALLEN & UNWIN LTD
40 Museum Street, London WC1A 1LU

© George Allen & Unwin (Publishers) Ltd, 1980

British Library Cataloguing in Publication Data

Thomson, John Aidan Francis
    Popes and princes, 1417–1517.
    – (Early modern Europe today).,
    1. Papacy – History
    2. Popes – Temporal power – History
    I. Title   II. Series
    262'.13'09024   BX970   80–40514

    ISBN 0–04–901027–1

Set in 10 on 11 point Times by Inforum Ltd, Portsmouth
and printed in Great Britain
by Biddles Ltd, Guildford, Surrey

Preface and Acknowledgements

This book was originally completed in 1974, but its appearance was delayed by the economic difficulties of the first interested publisher. The publication of it in the present series involved some revision, but it was possible to make only minor changes to refer to work which has appeared since that date. To my knowledge, however, there is no reason to modify the broad lines of the argument which follows. As the policy for the series has been to exclude footnotes which do not contain matters of substance, I should be pleased to answer questions on points of detail from anyone wishing to pursue particular topics further, and to provide fuller references to the sources.

Such errors as remain are, of course, my own responsibility, but I should like to acknowledge help in eliminating others which I have received at various stages from colleagues and other friends who have read the work in whole or in part. I should particularly wish to thank Professor Lionel Stones, Professor Denys Hay, Dr Michael Clanchy and Dr Antony Black, who read it in draft, and the general editor, Professor Joe Shennan, who gave invaluable assistance in making the book more suitable for the series. Miss Mary Brodie has prepared the typescript of various versions to make it suitable for the press, and the staff of Glasgow University Library, especially those concerned with inter-Library loans, have done much to make my task easier. My wife has given assistance with the index, in addition to the encouragement which she has provided throughout times when work was not going well and support when it was. To her, in gratitude, the book is dedicated.

J.A.F.T.

Early Modern Europe Today

In introducing a new historical series it is difficult not to begin by offering some justification for its appearance. Yet if we accept that History is ultimately unknowable in the sense that our perception of the past as distinct from the past itself is forever changing, then no apologia is required. That is certainly the premise on which this series is posited. In the last several decades the changes have been particularly rapid, reflecting fundamental shifts in social and political attitudes, and informed by the growth of new related disciplines and by new approaches to the subject itself. The volumes contained within this series will seek to provide the present generation of students and readers with up-to-date history; with judgements and interpretations which will no doubt in turn form part of the synthesis of future scholarly revisions. Some of the books will concentrate on previously neglected or unconsidered material to reach conclusions likely to challenge conventional orthodoxies in more established areas of study; others will re-examine some of these conventional orthodoxies to discover whether, in the light of contemporary scholarly opinion, they retain their validity or require more or less drastic re-assessment. Each in its own way, therefore, will seek to define and illumine some of the contours of early modern Europe, a coherent period at once remote from our own world yet crucial to an understanding of it. Each will combine considerable chronological range with thematic precision and each, finally, will be completed by a significant bibliographical chapter. It is hoped that this last, prominent feature, which will make the series especially distinctive, will be of value not only to readers curious to explore the particular topic further but also to those seeking information on a wide range of themes associated with it.

Contents

Introduction

The outbreak of the Great Schism in 1378 marked a watershed in the history of the papacy. For two centuries, from the election decree of the Third Lateran Council in 1179, which had laid down the requirement of a two-thirds majority of the cardinals to elect a pope, the threat of schism had been virtually removed from the Church. In marked contrast to the previous century, these two saw only one schism, that of 1328–30, and the weakness of the imperially appointed Nicholas V, whom Christendom disregarded as a serious force, only serves to emphasise the stability of the electoral system, which did much to strengthen the authority of the pope at the head of the church. The only danger of it was that conclaves might be deadlocked, and there were some prolonged vacancies as a result, but these were eventually filled. These centuries also saw the consolidation of papal bureaucracy, which continued to develop during the Avignon period, and there is little doubt that on the eve of the Great Schism the institutional strength of the papacy appeared virtually impregnable. Although there were problems – criticisms of curial corruption, disputes with secular rulers over a range of issues, such as provisions to benefices, taxation of the clergy, and the demarcation of jurisdictional rights and even challenges to the theoretical supremacy of the papacy from men such as Marsilio of Padua or William of Ockham – these hardly touched the heart of papal power. The opponents of Boniface VIII may have defeated him politically, but the full claims of the bull *Unam Sanctam* were still incorporated in the *Corpus Juris Canonici*. Although this mattered little in practical terms, it reflected an attitude within the Church to the rights of the papacy which left it without any serious rival.

It was this recognition of its supremacy by churchmen which gave the papacy its basic strength in its dealings with the secular rulers of Christendom. However delicate the balance which the clergy had to preserve between the claims of the pope and those of their secular lord, there were few who would be willing to deny the former's headship if challenged to do so. As Vicar of Christ, with the power to bind and loose souls, the pope was hard to attack, and although individual popes might be criticised, the institution appeared secure. This strength of the papacy was shattered by the schism of 1378. Its seriousness lay in the fact that it arose within the Church, where the popes appeared strongest, and was not imposed externally by some secular opponent. The circumstances of the election, in which some elements of force were present, could provide a pretext for the cardinals who were opposed to Urban VI to turn against him, and the pope's aggressive and unpredictable conduct was not calculated to recover their loyalty. After their revolt, they immediately sought lay support, and the political interests of the European princes rapidly determined their loyalties and drew the lines between the Roman and Avignonese obediences. The internal problem of the Church became one of European politics. The secular rulers quickly saw that this rivalry for the papacy gave them new opportunities to exert pressure on the Church, which could no longer speak with a single voice, and throughout the whole period of the schism the princes were able to take a strong line towards their clerical subjects and towards the popes. The most drastic lay action during this time was the French withdrawal of obedience from Benedict XIII without any transfer of obedience to his Roman rival, because this would imply that the Church could exist on a purely territorial basis without having a single administrative head.

In general, however, men continued to believe in the need for Church unity; the difficulty lay in how it could be attained. Naturally the rival popes were reluctant to admit that their rivals might have a stronger title, and their supporters were also unwilling to abandon a man from whom favours had been received, lest these might be annulled after a change of obedience to the rival pope, who might argue that this showed an admission of his stronger title. Such attitudes stood in the way of any settlement based on concession or compromise, and the even political balance between the rivals ruled out force as a practicable method, although attempts to use it left a legacy of secular political involvement in Italy which played a part in the problems of the fifteenth-century papacy. The possibility of a general council to end the schism was suggested at an early date, but was slow to win general acceptance. The reason for this delay was in part procedural, because there was no obvious way of calling together an assembly embracing both obediences, as the normal person to convene a council was the pope. More serious was the problem of authority, since the rivals were unwilling to submit themselves to the judgement of a body to which they regarded themselves as superior, a view which was shared by many of the leading figures in the Church. It was hard for these to abandon traditional ideas of papal supremacy, and it was only when it proved impossible to end the schism in any other way that they accepted the council as an ineluctable solution. This is well seen in the attitude of Jean Gerson, whose sympathies, originally conservative and papalist, became strongly pro-conciliar under pressure of events, as he saw Church reunion being prevented by the unwillingness of the rivals to come to terms. By the time of the Council of Constance he was one of the strongest exponents of conciliar doctrines.

Merely calling a council did not end the schism, as was shown clearly by the meeting at Pisa which created a third rival to the existing two popes but failed to secure the unanimous support of Christendom for him. Such support could be obtained only through the action of the secular rulers, who could enforce on their subjects an acceptance of conciliar actions in deposing the earlier contenders and appointing a successor. The Council of Constance succeeded in ending the schism where its predecessor at Pisa had failed largely because the princes were willing to work with it rather than to take advantage of the Church's problems by playing off the existing popes against the conciliar nominee. The council may well have recognised the need for lay support, because it made no move to elect a new pope until it was clear that virtually all of Christendom had abandoned the rivals of the schism. This secular support was bought at a price, because the end of the council was marked by a series of concordats between the papacy and the lay powers, in which a number of concessions were made to the latter on matters of ecclesiastical government. Perhaps even more important than the contents of the concordats was the fact that they were agreed at all, because this shows that the papacy was willing to regard the princes as equals with whom to negotiate rather than as subjects to command. This reflects the gains made by the lay power during the schism and foreshadows its attitude towards the papacy during the next century.

The balance of power between the papacy and the princes was further affected by the fact that the former no longer had its old unchallenged authority within the Church. The decrees *Haec Sancta* and *Frequens* of the Council of Constance had respectively asserted that the pope was bound to obey the council and laid down a method by which councils could be called regularly in future even against the wishes of the pope. The council's success had made conciliarism a respectable doctrine of Church government among leading ecclesiastics. It had shown that it could solve the problem of unity, and men might hope that further councils could provide solutions to some of the Church's other difficulties. Men who desired the reform of the Church in head and in members could see in a council with such supreme authority a weapon for over-ruling papal resistance. Others, with a less disinterested concern for the Church's good, realised that a council could be used to bring pressure to bear on the popes in purely secular matters. In consequence, it was vital for the papacy to reassert its position within the Church if it was to recover its authority in the affairs of Christendom, and unless and until the conciliar challenge was defeated it would always be vulnerable to such pressures. The price which had to be paid was high, that of coming to terms with the secular rulers on matters of Church government in return for lay abandonment of the conciliar weapon.

At the same time, the popes of the Restoration period, particularly Martin V, could not escape from the fact that their own position depended on the actions of the Council of Constance, which had to be regarded as lawful. As will be shown, even their own supporters had to qualify assertions of papal superiority, while their opponents could take a strong line in favour of conciliar claims. There were now many churchmen, instead of only isolated individuals as there had been before 1378, who were both critical of papal power and willing to take positive action to enforce their ideas. Previously critics of papal power could not offer an alternative method of Church government and could only support individual secular rulers who were opposed to the reigning pope; now they were sufficiently numerous to act collectively and provide such an alternative, knowing that it might well be more acceptable among churchmen than a return to the old style of papal monarchy. The conciliarist challenge to the papacy was more fundamental than any which the lay power might produce, because it attacked the whole monarchical basis of papal power, whereas the actions of the princes were concerned rather with the practical applications of this power in governmental matters. Compromise was possible between the popes and the princes, because the issues at stake were less ones of principle than those in dispute between the popes and the council. If the papacy had to make concessions, and its weakness after 1417 made this inevitable, it had at least the power to choose where these could be made. Political circumstances were liable to change, so complete consistency of action was impossible, but in general there was more common ground between the secular rulers and the popes than between the popes and the conciliarists. There was a common desire to strengthen monarchical authority, and in this they could provide each other with mutual support, the princes by renouncing recourse to councils and the popes by strengthening royal influence over the Church in individual countries. In practical matters few, if any, monarchs can really have favoured conciliar action; at the simplest level it was easier for them to negotiate with one man than with an assembly for favours in ecclesiastical matters, and most were prepared to leave the papacy with the appearance of power and to acquiesce in its claim to confer benefices and graces, provided that they were the recipients of these favours.

As long as some conciliar threat persisted, the papacy needed allies and, even after the extremism of the later stages of the Council of Basel had done much to discredit ideas of conciliar superiority, the threat was not entirely removed. Secular rulers might raise the spectre of a council to apply political pressure, and within the Church there was still the unresolved question of the powers possessed by the cardinals and the extent to which they could limit papal actions. As it had been a revolt by the college which had caused the Great Schism, it is hardly surprising that later relations between the popes and the cardinals were at times difficult, and the danger of an alliance between a secular ruler and a group of rebel cardinals was something which the popes could regard with considerable apprehension. In practice, however, this was to occur only once, when Louis XII of France joined with some rebels from Julius II, who tried to summon a council to Pisa to condemn the pope. Julius, however, was able to defeat his enemies by political means, and before long the French were willing to come to terms, in the realisation that more could be gained from co-operation than from opposition.

PART ONE

Theories of Authority in the Fifteenth Century

CHAPTER 1

Papal and Conciliar Authority

When Martin V was elected pope at the Council of Constance, the papacy, as an institution, was left in a dilemma. On the one hand, there remained its traditional claims to *plenitudo potestatis*; on the other, there was the harsh reality that, without the action of the general council and of all who had been involved in it, the Great Schism would not have been ended and there would have been no reunited Church of which Martin could have become head. One contemporary observer, the Bourgeois of Paris, writing in his Journal, had no doubts of where the effective power lay; 'At Martinmas 1417 a cardinal called Martin was made Pope by the consent and agreement of all Christian kings . . .' Even for those who saw the ending of the schism as an ecclesiastical rather than a secular act, there was the problem that within the Church papal power had been challenged by the meeting of the Council of Pisa, and the validity of the actions of the Council of Constance depended to some extent on the recognition of the earlier assembly and of the line of popes originating there. Could Martin claim that he was the legitimate pope without admitting the right of the cardinals to withdraw their allegiance, to sit in judgement on the pope and to negotiate with the secular powers of Christendom, so that they too would throw their support behind the man whom the council had chosen? How lawful were the councils which met under the circumstances of the schism? Should they be regarded as true general councils, or merely as exceptional bodies exercising extraordinary powers to solve an extraordinary problem? Had the popes of the schism period, or some of them, the right to be regarded as lawful occupants of the see of Peter?

On this last question, no explicit declaration was made, and clearly any such could have raised serious difficulties, both with the secular powers which had adhered to a pope whose title might be questioned and, more seriously, with those cardinals who had derived their titles from such a pontiff. By implication, however, the Restoration papacy seems to have regarded itself as the successor of the Pisan line of popes from the schism period and to have regarded the Roman line as legitimate until the deposition of Gregory XII at Pisa. The Avignon line, on the other hand, appears to have been dismissed from the start as one of antipopes. Fifteenth-century versions of the *Liber Pontificalis* take this point of view, and Platina's *History of the Popes*, written later in the century, includes those of the Pisan line. Documents issued by the Council of Constance and by Martin V also suggest that the Pisan popes were lawful, although in the forty-third plenary session, on 21 March 1418, Martin appears to have regarded the status of all the popes since 1378 as uncertain.[1] This point of view could explain why various documents, including the concordats with the German and English nations, concluded at Constance, contain revocations of grants made since the death of Gregory XI.

The historian may safely assert that when the Council of Constance enacted the decree *Haec Sancta* in 1415 no one was certain who, if anyone, was the true pope. Any other view derives from later theological rather than historical assumptions. However, it is clear that by the end of the fifteenth century the papacy accepted both the Roman and Pisan lines as lawful and regarded itself as successor to both. In 1484 Cardinal Cibo's assumption of the title of Innocent VIII represented an acknowledgement that Innocent VII had been a legitimate pope, and Rodrigo Borgia's adoption of the name of Alexander VI would presuppose the validity of the title of the first Pisan pope. Indeed, even after the Council of Trent it was still possible for Cardinal Bellarmine, who described the Council of Pisa as *nec approbatum nec reprobatum*, to recognise Alexander V as a lawful pope. By contrast, when Giulio de' Medici took the title of Clement VII in 1523, he implicitly branded Robert of Geneva as an antipope.

The recognition of the Pisan popes did not necessarily give the council undisputed status as a lawful general council, as Bellarmine's description shows. Among contemporaries, there was a natural division between the supporters of the popes whom it deposed, who denied its oecumenicity, and those who upheld conciliar ideas, and held that it was lawful. Such a division persisted until the Reformation, without any clear line of thought emerging. There was a similar division of opinion about the Council of Constance, and particularly about its claims to authority over the pope, as expressed in the decree *Haec Sancta*. Even the pope himself seems to have accepted certain actions of the council, and one may note that Martin V was willing to adhere to the timetable for future councils contained in the decree *Frequens*.

The question of ultimate superiority in the Church was closely linked to that of the lawfulness of the Council of Constance, and clearly there was no agreed doctrine of the Church acceptable to all contemporary opinion. In the decree *Haec Sancta*, which affirmed conciliar supremacy over the pope, there were ambiguities, which can be explained by the fact that it was essentially an *ad hoc* measure to meet a particular crisis. Martin V's attitude was uncertain, and although he declared that he would 'inviolably observe ... everything enacted *conciliariter* in matters of faith by the present Council', and stated that it was necessary for all the Christian faithful to accept the definitions of the council concerning faith and the salvation of souls, he also forbade any appeal from the pope to a future general council. This distinction between doctrinal definition and jurisdictional authority provided a basis on which the popes could rebuild their power, and it is certain that Martin's ecclesiology saw the position of the papacy as a lofty one.[2]

Yet immediately after the council, its validity had to be accepted, as the only way to avoid reopening the wounds of the Great Schism. There may have been men among the council fathers at Constance who genuinely believed in the claims to supremacy, which were later to be developed at Basel, but if there were, they were in a minority compared with those whose concern was with restoring unity in the Church, and with its reform. It was when the issue of authority between pope and council was renewed at Basel that the theoreticians began to argue about the legitimacy of the earlier assembly. Torquemada's *Oratio synodalis de primatu* of 1439 drew distinctions between different phases of the Council of Constance: the first when it represented only obedience of John XXIII, the second following the adherence to it of that of Gregory XII, and the third after the addition of that of Benedict XIII. Only after all sections of the Church were united could the council be truly described as general. This view was followed by later papalist writers, notably Cajetan in the early sixteenth century, who pointed out that while the partisans of the rival factions were not united until the twenty-second plenary session, the decree *Haec Sancta* had been approved at the fifth, when only supporters of John XXIII were present. Lively disagreements persisted on this question through the late fifteenth century and into the Reformation period, and it is worth emphasising that in the sixteenth century supporters of the oecumenical character of the Council of Constance included Luther's antagonist, John Eck, and the Cardinal of Lorraine, speaking at the Council of Trent.

The actual meeting of councils worried the papacy less than where they met. In the century between the election of Martin V and the start of the Reformation, three councils met in Italy under papal auspices, Pavia-Siena, Ferrara-Florence and the Fifth Lateran. But a council meeting outside Italy was less liable to be amenable to papal wishes and therefore more likely to encounter Roman opposition. Eugenius

IV's statement in a bull of 26 June 1432 that he was prepared to transfer the council from Basel to Bologna, and the indication of the latter's advantages by the papal ambassadors to the council on 7 March 1433, were certainly tactical manoeuvres against the fathers at Basel, but they also show that the pope was willing to work with a council, provided he could do so on his own terms. This, of course, he was eventually able to do with the Council of Ferrara-Florence.

The fact that Basel lay beyond the bounds of the pope's political influence was certainly one factor in the lengthy struggle between him and the council. Rome's remoteness from Bohemia meant that the pope was less concerned with the Hussite question, the most important issue to the Emperor Sigismund and to the Germans at the council, than with his own rights, and explains why he was prepared to dissolve the assembly in the autumn of 1431, when its early discussions suggested that it would not be subservient to his wishes. This initial papal hostility raised the question of authority in an acute form, when the council resisted the dissolution and sought to justify its action by reference to the decree *Frequens*. The crisis between Basel and Eugenius was the more acute because there was no question of the pope having a suspect title from a dubious election, as had been the case with the rival claimants at Constance, and because the council itself has been lawfully summoned. The critical issue was whether the pope could dissolve or translate the council without its own consent. Although attempts were made by various interested parties, notably by Sigismund, to bring about agreement between the rival powers, it is probably true to say that even after the pope revoked his dissolution relations between them were always tense, and that the council became increasingly a rallying point for Eugenius's enemies. After a protracted struggle the conciliar revolt culminated in the proclamation by the council as a matter of faith that the council was superior to the pope, and that the pope had no power to transfer it.

This was a far more revolutionary claim by the conciliar faction than any which had been put forward at Constance, but one must be careful not to assume that all who adhered to the council supported it in this. This is most clearly seen in the attitude of Sigismund, probably the strongest lay ally of the council, whose secular interests, notably the question of Bohemia, were a far greater influence on his actions than any wish to strengthen the Church. Indeed, his desire was to exploit the tensions in the Church to his own advantage, his support for the council was based on political and tactical motives, and he took up no clear position on the fundamental issue of conciliar superiority. If he had, it might well have been hostile, as the conciliarism of Basel had anti-authoritarian overtones which could not appeal to him. Likewise the German princes made no attempt to decide on the issue of principle when they declared their neutrality between the pope and the council in 1439; instead they appealed to the two parties to end the schism, affirming that they did not wish to withdraw from the obedience of either the council or the Apostolic See.When the German Church reached a tentative agreement with Eugenius IV, shortly before the latter's death in 1447, the conciliar principle was upheld, albeit in ambiguous terms: 'We accept, embrace and venerate the General Council of Constance, *Frequens* and its other decrees, as we do other councils representing the universal Church militant and their power, authority, honour and eminence.'[3] However, when a more definitive settlement was reached in the following year by the concordat of Vienna, no reference was made to the question of conciliar authority. This did not mean, however, that the Germans had agreed to accept the idea of papal authority, because assertions of conciliar rights continued to be made in the second half of the century.

The most vigorous of such assertions came from churchmen, and can be found most clearly in the proceedings of the Council of Basel. In a disputation of 1433 between Cardinal Cesarini, the president of the council, and the papal orator, the archbishop of Spalatro, the former denied the right of the pope to dissolve the council without its own consent. His arguments rested firmly on the decrees of the Council of Constance, notably *Haec Sancta*, and he asserted that the pope was subordinate to the council, which could therefore take legal action against him. Even more noteworthy, the papal orator himself was prepared to acknowledge the authority of the earlier council, although he argued that there was a crucial difference in the circumstances, in that Eugenius was an uncontested pope, whereas at Constance the council had been faced with rival claimants. A further argument was that Eugenius had not sought the dissolution of the council, but only its transfer, which was a less drastic action. In general the legate did not contest Cesarini's views, but merely asserted the papal superiority.

In 1434 the council renewed the decree *Haec Sancta*, as it had done early in its meetings, and in the following year it put forward arguments against another papal envoy, who had affirmed the primacy of the see of Peter and called for unity in obedience to papal authority. Confident that it was in the right, the radical wing of the council, after its break with the moderates, proceeded to depose the pope and create a new schism in 1439. The debate before this took place showed that there was by no means agreement at the council about the correct course of action or about the issue of superiority. The Archbishop of Milan, Francesco Piccolopasso, the ambassador at Basel of Duke Filippo Maria Visconti, worked hard to defend Eugenius, and the great canonist, Niccolò Tudeschi (Panormitanus), also resisted the resolutions arguing that the pope was liable to deposition as a heretic. The attempt to show that the pope was a heretic was an obvious tactical move, as heresy was the one crime for which he could be judged by a council in canon law. On the other side, the most eloquent speaker was John of Segovia, who argued that the pope's disobedience to the Church made it justifiable to regard him as an unbeliever. When Panormitanus stated during the debate that the pope was ruler of the Church, John countered sharply that he was its servant.

Even among churchmen there was uncertainty about the relations between the two powers in the Church. This is clear from the way in which writers sympathetic to the pope admitted certain limitations on papal power, and rights of papal superiority were acknowledged by men normally associated with the conciliar party. A man's allegiance is sometimes less easy to establish than appears at first sight. A notable example of this is Panormitanus himself, probably the greatest canonist of his day, whose writings are inconsistent on whether or not the council was superior to the pope. It is perhaps unfair to judge his views by his actions, which are rather a reflection of the political views of his master, Alfonso V, and of the latter's more immediate secular interests, though it is worth noting that Panormitanus adhered to Basel in 1436 and later supported the council's antipope, Felix V, despite his reservations about the proceedings against Eugenius. His writings, perhaps a better guide to his opinions, show that he accepted the traditional view that the council could depose the pope for heresy and was prepared to extend this power of judgement to occasions when the pope altered the state of the Church, commanded something sinful, or was guilty of incorrigible crime. In a disputed election, the council was superior, and he declared that the pope did not have power to depose all other bishops. Elsewhere he argues in favour of the papal plenitude of power, admitting that the pope had power to dispense from all laws, even the dispositions of a general council, and stating that the council could not meet without papal authority. To Panormitanus, it was the whole Church to which Christ had promised inerrancy, and if the true faith were preserved only by an individual, this need not be the pope. He might assert that the council was superior to the pope in matters of faith, but he also accepted that the council itself could fall into error. This uncertainty in his writings reflects doubt as to the ultimate source of authority in the Church, a doubt which others shared. It should be remembered, too, that his works continued to circulate and could influence learned opinion even in the latter part of the century, because his *Tractatus de Concilio Basiliensi* was printed at Venice in 1479.

Panormitanus remained loyal to the council until the end, but others altered their position as the actions taken at Basel became increasingly extreme. Cardinal Cesarini, appointed as legate to the council by

Martin and confirmed as such by Eugenius, vigorously defended the oecumenicity of the council and resisted the pope's attempts to dissolve it. The cardinal accepted that a council was superior to the pope on matters dealing with heresy, schism and Church reform, regarding it as traditional doctrine, which had been an article of faith since the Council of Constance. Even when the opposition of the hard line conciliarists to the translation of the council, to enable negotiations for union with the Greeks to be held, led him to rejoin Eugenius, he still was willing to defend conciliar superiority in public, and the fact that the pope allowed him to do so suggests that such views were still regarded as compatible with orthodoxy, provided that they did not diminish the universal jurisdiction of the pope on the doctrine and life of the Church.

The attitude of the extremists at Basel also played a large part in leading men such as Nicholas of Cusa and Andrew of Escobar back into the papal camp, although in his *De Concordantia Catholica* (1432–4), the former had argued for conciliar superiority, both jurisdictionally and doctrinally, as the pope was more likely to be fallible than a general council. Even then, however, he recognised that the pope should normally call a council and that his representatives, if present, should preside. Later, when he had joined the papal party, he still held that there should be curbs on potential papal excesses, and that the Church could disobey a pope who abused his powers, with the council acting against him unanimously if he were working against the Church's interests. The stress which Nicholas laid on the necessity of unity in the Church provides the key to his actions, because it was the action of the Council of Basel in creating a new schism, where the Council of Constance had healed one, that led him to conclude that right remained with the pope. In Escobar's thought, the need for reform in the Church was vital and this could be accomplished only through the action of a council and, although this should not normally meet without papal authorisation, it could under certain circumstances summon itself.

Cesarini, Cusa and Escobar had all been present at Basel and participated in the arguments over policy which resulted from the desire to implement theories of conciliar authority. Perhaps an even better illustration of intellectual uncertainty over these questions can be found in the assumptions of the English canonist, William Lyndwood, whose *Provinciale* was completed in 1430, the year before the opening of the Council of Basel and the consequent emergence of the papal-conciliar struggle. The issue of authority is mentioned only incidentally – in writing his gloss on the customs of the English Church, it was not of prime concern to him – and it is clear that he represents the mainstream of canonist thought of his day, accepting the right of the council to judge the pope for heresy, and extending this to cover cases when the Church was scandalised by the enormity of the pope's offences, if after frequent warning he refused to amend his ways. But Lyndwood gave no indication of who could determine when the Church was scandalised and, therefore, when a council could take action. On the crucial question of right of summons, he supported the claims of the pope, and while he was willing to say that the pope had a moral obligation to obey the law, he still regarded him as *legibus solutus*. Basically Lyndwood was papalist in sympathies, although his views were clearly modified by his experience of conciliar action in the exceptional circumstances of Constance and the need to comprehend this in his ecclesiology. He clearly did not envisage the possibility of a conciliar challenge to a pope whose title was undoubtedly lawful.

This recognition of occasions when the council could act against the pope is found also in other pro-papal writers, one of the most significant of whom was Antonio Roselli of Arezzo. As a consistorial advocate, he may well have drafted the bull in which Eugenius attempted to dissolve the Council of Basel, and he continued to occupy this position after the writing of his treatise *Monarchia sive de potestate imperatoris et papae* a few-years later. In this he attacked the radical theses put forward at Basel, but at the same time was prepared to justify the councils of Pisa and Constance in condemning the popes of the schism for failing to carry out the renunciations which they had promised to make. He recognised Constance as a lawful council, and was prepared to regard the decree *Frequens* as binding on the pope, at least if the Church would suffer from a failure to observe it. While in general the pope was superior to the council, there were three occasions when it was lawful for the council to act against the pope, and for it to meet without a papal summons. These were when there was an issue of heresy, one concerning the good of the universal Church, or where its condition was desolate. In this, one sees a backward glance, both at earlier canonist writing and at events of Roselli's own time, because he clearly could not forget how Church unity had been re-established after the long crisis of the schism, Possibly more immediate events, particulary the Hussite problem, were reflected in his emphasis on conciliar responsibilities in doctrinal matters. and in his affirmation that the pope could not dissolve a council without its own consent, when it was dealing with a matter concerning faith, such as the extirpation of some heresy scandalising God's Church. A similar acceptance of the actions of the Council of Constance, as the only way to heal the divisions of the Great Schism, is to be found in the *Dialogus de remediis schismatis* of Rodrigo Sánchez de Arévalo, one of the more rigorous pro-papal writers of the mid-fifteenth century.

Even the man regarded as the strongest advocate of papal authority against the council, Juan Torquemada, recognised some limits on the former. In his *Oratio synodalis de primatu* of 1439, delivered to refute the claims of Cesarini, the assertion that general councils could teach something contrary to the faith, if this lacked final papal confirmation, was modified by the reservation that if only the pope contradicted something asserted as a truth of faith by the fathers of a general council as a whole, the synod and not the pope must be followed, as the judgement of many was worth more. In the later *Summa de Ecclesia*, he broadened his view on the question of summoning a council against papal wishes, acknowledging that a pope could be compelled by the cardinals, prelates and princes to call one in an emergency and that, if he refused, the right of summons passed to the cardinals. Similarly, if there were two popes in office, both regarded as lawful by the faithful of their obedience, each should summon their own to constitute a council to resolve the dispute. If they failed to do so, the right devolved, first to the cardinals, and later to the other prelates or the emperor, as in cases of necessity the lesser powers could supplement the deficiencies of their superiors. Obviously Torquemada wrote this in the light of the events at Constance, and even he felt it necessary to allow to general councils some powers beyond the traditional right to act against a pope guilty of heresy.

In the crisis between Eugenius IV and the Council of Basel, there were three options open to contemporaries: allegiance to one party or the other, or neutrality between them, and it was primarily political factors which determined their decisions. On matters of belief it was harder to draw clear dividing lines between the supporters of the rival parties, and even a small modification in a man's opinions might involve a change of allegiance, as can be seen in the cases of Cesarini and Nicholas of Cusa. One can no more say that all adherents of Eugenius IV in the 1440s were rigorous conservatives than see all supporters of the council as revolutionaries. Men who had returned to the papal side could still see the possibility of the council playing a vital part in Church life. In a *Tractatus de potestate papae et concilii generalis* of 1446, Heimericus de Campo, professor of theology at Louvain, tried to persuade Eugenius to resolve his dispute with Basel through a new council. He saw in the nature of the Church two elements, the 'catholic' or totality of individual members, and the 'apostolic' or hierarchical structure leading up to the pope. A council included both the pope and the faithful, and was superior to either taken separately. He suggested that conciliar and papal power were complementary aspects of the Church and could not be opposed to each other any more than body and soul.

Clearly men found it hard to resolve the issues between rival parties, and different men might in good faith end up on opposing sides. This

was recognised in a treatise emanating from the University of Köln,
possibly written by Laurence of Groningen, one of the younger
masters who in 1448 resisted the papal legates seeking university
recognition for Nicholas V. This work displays a toleration rare in this
period, in its affirmations that in time of schism it was not heretical to
say that one or other of the contenders was not pope, and that it was
rash to assert that all adhering to one party, or remaining neutral, were
suspected of being outside the condition of salvation. It was safe to
offer tacit obedience to either party and, however dubious one side
was, it savoured of heresy to assert that the sacraments of the other
were invalid. Equally it was rash to assert that it was unlawful to hear
the masses of the opposite side, or to communicate with them. Most
striking of all the propositions was that it was possible for some persons
in the right party to be schismatics and some in the wrong party not to
be, because schism would be determined by the motives of the individual. The author's aim seems to have been to stress a sacramental
unity in the Church, which was of more account than jurisdictional
unity. He did not concern himself with the issue of authority, which his
contemporaries were arguing, and it is well to remember that such
issues could be left unresolved.

The critical fact in this situation was that there was no authoritative
doctrine of the Church, in which the position of the council was clearly
defined, comparable to that established for some four hundred years
by the Council of Trent, and opponents of the papacy were able to
exploit the uncertainty. The assertions and counterassertions of the
years of crisis were left unresolved, with the conciliarists tending to rely
on the decrees of the Council of Constance and on legal concepts of the
corporation, while the papacy relied on its historic past and on mystical
notions of a hierarchical universe. John of Segovia took the saying of
Christ that the man who wished to be greatest should be the servant of
all as an indication of actual forms of Church government, and
described the pope as 'first servant' of the Church. The supporters of
the council saw it as an autonomous body, existing on its own authority, and the pope as an elected *executor*, accountable to it, The relation
of pope to council was seen as parallel to that of *rector* and *universitas*.

At the time of the short-lived reunion with the Greek Church at the
Council of Florence, the papacy was able to assert its claims to authority in the definition of papal primacy contained in the decree of the
union. While this clearly was a matter affecting the Greeks, and while
the issue of the primacy had been one of the most critical issues in the
union negotiations, the uncompromising nature of papal claims could
hardly have been lost on the pope's rivals in the Western Church also,
even although no mention was made of the claims of councils in the
decree, which naturally was more concerned with the immediate issues

discussed at Florence. The very absence of reference to conciliar ideas may be seen as a tacit dismissal of them as irrelevant to the powers of the pope as head of the Church.

The papacy did not, however, merely assume that the strength of its case would defeat the conciliarists without argument, and the theoreticians of papal power were vigorous in defence of authority. Roselli based his arguments on the idea that there must be only one Church, founded by Christ, and developed the idea of perfection and supreme good being found in unity. It was Peter alone whom Christ had commissioned, and this power passed to Peter's successor. To deny this would be to deny the one holy Catholic and Apostolic Church, and this would be heretical. Contrary arguments, based on the equality of the apostles, are discussed and contradicted and the Petrine primacy is seen as the basis of unity in the world. The same principles underlay the most comprehensive and formidable of the pro-papal writings, Torquemada's *Summa de Ecclesia* of 1449. He uses all the traditional texts in support of papal primacy against conciliarist claims, and although he gives quite a fair and lucid outline of his opponents' arguments, quoting their justificatory texts, he then dismisses the objections to the pope's monarchical power. Central to the whole work is his emphasis on the essential unity of the Church, which he declares early in the first book and reconsiders at the beginning of the second. This unity is secured by the primacy of Peter, and he attacks conciliarist claims that the apostles were equal, and even more the idea that the power of governing the Church lay in its members. In the third book, where he considers the subject of councils particularly, he stresses the need for papal authority to summon them in normal circumstances, and also the necessity for the pope or his legate to preside.

Much of the work is couched in general terms, but Torquemada does refer, sometimes explicitly and sometimes by implication, to the claims put forward at Basel, and it is noteworthy that he is far more hostile to the Council of Basel than to that of Constance, although he restricts the period when the latter could be truly regarded as a general council to the time after the three contending obediences were united. The concluding chapters of the book deal with some of the practical issues which had arisen at Basel: to which party a Christian should adhere if there was a division in the council, and the right of the pope to transfer or dissolve a council which had been lawfully summoned. Torquemada accepts few limitations on the pope: there was the traditional canonist case of a pope who lapsed into heresy, and an acceptance that in abnormal circumstances when the Church was in danger and the pope refused to call a council the right of summons devolved on the cardinals. Against a bad pope the council had no power beyond that of exhortation, and although he should observe certain decrees *de hones-*

tate he could not be compelled to do so. The distinction between moral obligation and legal compulsion is drawn at another and very revealing point, when the author is discussing whether, in order to restore unity in a time of schism, even a true pope can be made to resign. He denies that the pope can be compelled to do so, but does affirm that if the false claimant has overwhelming strength, the right action for the true one is to give way. Here, as clearly as anywhere in the work, the importance of unity in the Church is made plain, nor is this surprising when one remembers the effects of disunity in the Church during Torquemada's earlier years.

If one examines the views held about the authority of the Council of Basel in the latter part of the century, one can see how the papacy had recovered its position, despite the persistence of some conciliar claims. Some men changed their views, such as Domenico de Domenichi, who held in 1456 that the council had been a lawful assembly of the universal Church, but took the opposite view five years later. The normal attitude of the pro-papal party was that the council had been valid until the time when the pope translated it, but that thereafter its title had become illegitimate. This view seems to have been generally taken in the sixteenth century, as at the Fifth Lateran Council, and by writers such as Cajetan and Bellarmine. These views did not go completely unchallenged, and Matthias Ugonius was still prepared to uphold the claims of Basel.

In the second half of the century, the conciliar threat to papal power was latent rather than active, but did not disappear. In 1449, the German Carthusian, Jakob of Jüterbogk, still saw the council as the means for carrying out Church reform, and attacked papal claims to dissolve or translate councils. He claimed that the pope could be corrected by the Church, and had no doubt that he was inferior to the council. By this date, Nicholas V was recognised as the sole pope, but Jakob hoped that he would not abolish the decree *Frequens*, because it could heal the wound which Eugenius IV inflicted on the Church in his decree *de superioritate Papae supra Ecclesiam*.[4] In 1451 a tract calling for a general council was nailed to the door of the papal legate, ironically the former conciliarist, Nicholas of Cusa, at Mainz. In 1454 Aeneas Sylvius Piccolomini wrote, 'Christianity has no head whom all wish to obey. Neither the Pope nor the Emperor is rendered his due. There is no reverence, no obedience.' This suggests that the victory of the papacy over the councils was still rather hollow, that its authority had not acquired any measure of popular acquiescence, and that to many men the site of final authority in the Church was uncertain. Six years later, Aeneas, now Pope Pius II, attempted to rectify this by establishing an undoubted papal headship, when in the bull *Execrabilis* he forbade appeals from a pope to a council. This, in one sense, was the most notable assertion of extreme claims by the fifteenth-century papacy, but at the same time, its text does not appear to have been widely circulated throughout Christendom, nor did the papacy employ it often in later controversies. Pius himself used it twice, against Sigismund of the Tyrol and Archbishop Diether of Mainz; there was a vague reference to it by Sixtus IV in 1483, during the war with Venice, and it was formally cited by Julius II in 1509, when he declared that the bull possessed enduring validity. However, on other occasions when appeals were made to a council, the popes did not allude to the bull, although in 1476, when Louis XI threatened to appeal to a general council, Sixtus IV reaffirmed the papal attitude by declaring: 'The authority to will or not to will a council is fixed solely in the Roman pontiff.' Nor did Pius himself regard *Execrabilis* as his last word on the subject; he reiterated his position in 1463 in another bull, *In minoribus agentes*, addressed to the University of Köln. Near the end of this he wrote: We have never heard of an approved council that assembled without papal authority when there was an unquestioned Roman pontiff; the body of the Church is not without a head and all power flows from the head into the members.

Even here it is possible to see some compromise with conciliar tradition. Pius may have affirmed that there was one head and ruler in the Church because the peace of the people depends upon one ruler, and plurality of rulers breeds discord, but he also said that he recognised the power and authority of a general council as it had been defined at the Council of Constance. No reference was made to the precise terms of the conciliar decrees, and the omission, almost certainly deliberate, left the position ambiguous. Even the clause in the bull *when there was an unquestioned Roman pontiff* emphasised the dependence of the restoration papacy on the Council of Constance, because it implied that when there was a dispute about the occupancy of the papal throne extraordinary measures would be permissible to resolve it, including the summons of a council in a manner which would in normal circumstances be regarded as irregular.

What was the significance of these measures? It would be dangerous to assert that they marked the end of effective opposition to the papacy, as a final clarification of the doctrines of Roman authority. Rather they were polemical statements, asserting the papal point of view, and it is perfectly clear that they were not generally accepted throughout Christendom. There was still uncertainty about the nature of the Church, and the respective roles of the papacy and the council.[5] In practice, men opposed to the pope continued to appeal to a council, and theoreticians still asserted its authority, despite the papal bull. Indeed, the issue of *Execrabilis* was followed by conciliar agitation, which produced a war of pamphlets, in the course of which it was

clearly assumed that the issue of authority had not been finally resolved. Charles VII of France protested to the pope that he should
summon a free council in France, and George Podebrady of Bohemia
promised to cause the assembly of a general council in a German city
on the Rhine. Above all, two specific crises in Germany led to demands
for a council. These were the troubles in the diocese of Brixen between
its bishop, Cardinal Nicholas of Cusa, and Duke Sigismund of the
Tyrol, and the disputed election at Mainz between Diether of Isenburg
and Adolf von Nassau-Wiesbaden. Diether had been excommunicated
for failure to pay the services demanded for the grant of the pallium
and had appealed to a future council. Even when he was prepared to
come to terms, the pope determined to make an example of him, and
provided Adolf in his place. In both cases the appeals to a council were
made in defence of private interests and as a protest against papal
interference. Both Sigismund and Diether employed as a polemicist
the jurist, Gregor Heimburg, who himself incurred violent opposition
from the pro-papal writers as a result, and was excommunicated in
1460 for his part in the appeals made by the Duke. The arguments in
these depended on the decrees of the Council of Constance, and their
renewal at Basel, with emphasis being laid on the affirmation that the
council held its power immediately from Christ, and on the fact that
over ten years had elapsed since the last meeting of a general council.
Heimburg asserted that the councils were the successors of the apostles, that they had power to correct the errors of the popes, and
attacked Pius's denial of conciliar superiority, with the affirmation that
the world was greater than the city. Despite *Execrabilis*, he held that
appeals to a council were still valid. Diether also rejected *Execrabilis*,
which he mentioned specifically in his defence against the papal sentence of deposition, as being contrary to all divine and natural law, and
claimed that if no one could appeal from the oppression of a pope to a
future general council, the pope could deal with everyone according to
his whim, and no one could resist.

These hostile writings naturally provoked a reaction. In Spain
Arévalo produced a treatise, *Tractatus de expedientia, utilitate et con-
gruentia congregationis generalis concilii*, in which he claimed that
there was no need for a council at this particular time and that it could
endanger lawful ecclesiastical authority. In Germany, the distinguished theologian Gabriel Biel, who had left his position as cathedral
preacher at Mainz because of his opposition to Archbishop Diether,
laid stress on the obligation to obey the commands of the Holy See,
unless these were categorically rejected by scripture, divine law or
natural law, and affirmed that uncertain matters in this were to be
referred to the pope for decision. In his writings he never pronounced
clearly on the issue of conciliar authority, but he did stress the papal

plenitudo potestatis. He accepted the validity of *Execrabilis*, as did a contemporary Italian defender of the papacy, Teodoro Laelio, Bishop of Feltre, whose writings, more remarkable for their rhetoric than for their reasoning, were specifically directed against Gregor Heimburg. The latter's reply was no less rhetorical in character, and did little more than reiterate the basic positions taken up by the pope's earlier antagonists.

The theoretical issues were not settled at this time, and even when Diether of Isenburg submitted to the pope in 1463, the settlement dealt purely with the practical issues, and his submission did not include any formal recognition of papal supremacy in accordance with the terms of *Execrabilis*. Similarly, when Sigismund of the Tyrol was absolved by a papal legate, after both Pius II and Cardinal Nicholas of Cusa were dead, all he did was to make an ambiguous declaration that he had never harboured any evil intent against the pope, but had merely wished to maintain his position as a prince. Heimburg alone remained unforgiven and, despite his earlier denials of Laelio's charges of heresy, including a reminder that it had been the Council of Constance which had condemned Wyclif, Hus and Jerome of Prague, moved into the service of George Podebrady of Bohemia. It is likely that demands for a council from this quarter in the later 1460s may have resulted from Heimburg's influence as well as from the king's policy.

These events suggest that the bull *Execrabilis* cannot be seen as the final victory of the papacy over the conciliar movement and the challenge to papal authority which had continued since the Great Schism. Although attempts to appeal to a council had no practical effect, there was no general acquiescence in the papalist point of view. Political circumstances were unsuitable for the secular rulers, who alone could have brought a council into existence when there was an undisputed pope, to take any practical action. The question of authority was dormant rather than dead, and the failure to resolve the theoretical issues meant that conciliar claims could be revived in the future when circumstances changed. The pattern of events in Germany in the early 1460s, when conciliar theory was employed essentially for tactical reasons by men with a grievance against the pope, represented one form of conciliarism which survived into the following century. It was basically political in character, and was essentially a weapon which a secular ruler might use in his dealings with the papacy, a stick with which he could threaten the pope to secure his own ends. This was very different from the older type of conciliarism, which in origin and essence represented the idea of the universal Church, as supranational in character as the papacy. At the theoretical level, the older tradition was able to survive longer, but its supporters were unable to shake the effective power which the popes had established.

This survival appears most notably among the canonists. For example, Francesco Accolti must have been recognised as anti-papal by his contemporaries, for when in 1482 Andrew Zamometic, titular archbishop of Krania, made his futile attempt to revive the Council of Basel, his advice was sought *pro concilio*, and his *Consilia seu responsa iuris* was published at Pisa in 1482 and again at Pavia in 1494.[6] His writings illustrate the survival of conciliar ideas and in these views he did not stand alone. Two important canonists at the Curia in this period were Felinus Sandaeus and Giannantonio Sangiorgio, the latter of whom was made a cardinal by Alexander VI in 1493. Both of these accepted that a council could meet without the pope, although Sangiorgio limited the powers which it could exercise, by denying that it had the power to depose a pope – all it could do was to caution him, and call in the secular arm. Furthermore, there was also support for the idea of a council if it had been summoned by the pope for the reform of the Church. This idea was put forward in a sermon during the papal vacancy of 1484.

The secular use of the conciliar weapon was most obvious in France, where the kings regularly threatened a council in their struggles with the papacy, and where in consequence conciliarism developed a strongly Gallican character. During the Great Schism, the University of Paris had been a stronghold of conciliar thought, and from 1438 the assertion of conciliar superiority was included in the laws of the kingdom, for the Pragmatic Sanction of Bourges, adopting the reform decrees of the Council of Basel, was promulgated by royal authority. In 1449 a council of the French Church at Lyons declared that the decrees of Councils of Constance and Basel should be inviolably observed, and should be promulgated in provincial councils and episcopal synods. In 1464 the Milanese ambassador in France wrote in a letter to his master that there were men saying that the pope should not be allowed to govern the world in his way without a council for a long time.[7] In 1476, when tension had arisen between Sixtus IV and Louis XI, three ordinances were approved on ecclesiastical matters, the first of these recalling the decree *Frequens*, affirming that it had never been more necessary for a council to meet, and asking the pope to summon one. When reports of this reached Sixtus, he was clearly alarmed, and wrote to the King of Hungary asking him to see that nothing was done contrary to the apostolic see.

Conciliar ideas were still propagated theoretically also: in a glossed edition of the Pragmatic Sanction, published by Cosme Guymier at Paris in 1486, the author declared that there were three occasions when the council was superior to the pope: when it condemned and deposed him for heresy, when it was acting to end a schism, and when it was acting to reform the Church in head and in members. The last of these occasions had the most radical implications, for it would give the council a right to freedom of action far beyond the traditional cases when its superiority was recognised. Within the French Church, however, one can distinguish between the attitudes of various groups, and whereas some men might associate conciliar ideas with an assertion of Gallican liberties, others did not. For example, the reforming party in the Church, led by men such as Jean Standonck, was concerned with asserting Gallican liberties as a defence against the abuses of the Curia and as a means to obtain reform, but it did not appeal to the council against the Holy See. On the other hand, the University of Paris and the chapter of Paris were prepared to do this in order to attack Roman claims to authority, as in 1472, when the latter was resisting the papal provision of a royal protégé to the cathedral, and attempted to ward off censures in the papal bulls by appealing to a better informed pope or to the next general council.

Even in France, however, the papacy found defenders. During the Council of Basel, Pierre de Versailles was prepared to write a moderate defence of papal superiority and to plead the pope's case, albeit without success, before the Bourges assembly which approved the Pragmatic Sanction. His attitude to councils was a moderate one, and in 1441 he was prepared to argue that a new council was necessary to reinforce papal power. Nothing was to be feared from a council under papal control, but it would be dangerous for the pope to refuse to call one. The principal supporters of papal claims were the friars, a number of whom fell foul of the University of Paris, which remained a firm opponent of such opinions throughout the fifteenth century, as the theology faculty was alert to censure them.[8]

The theory of conciliar superiority was of comparatively little importance as long as the pope could prevent the council from meeting. The real danger came when the threats to call one were translated into action. The circumstances which gave rise to serious renewed conciliar agitation were the outbreak of the Italian wars in 1494 and the resultant political struggle between the papacy and France. Early in 1498, when the French were considering a renewal of their Italian campaigns, the king sent various questions to the Paris theology faculty concerning the summons of a council. Clearly the king's motives in inquiring were purely political but this does not necessarily mean that the theologians' replies were also politically inspired. In view of the faculty's past attitude to the papacy, one may reasonably assume that the answers reflected the views taught and held in the university. Four questions were asked: was the pope bound to call a council every ten years; in view of the disorders in the Church, was he bound to do so at that time; if he refused to call a council after ten years, did secular and

ecclesiastical princes have the right to do so themselves; if this were
done by some notable part of Christendom, such as the kingdom of
France, but other countries did not come to such a council, was it
possible for France to hold the meeting in the absence of the others?
The faculty answered all the questions in the affirmative.

In the next few years conciliar rights were again asserted in appeals
made both by the university and by the Paris chapter. In 1500, during a
crisis over taxation, the university appealed from the pope, when
ill-informed, to him when better informed, to the Holy See when better
informed, and finally to the holy general council. This series of
authorities suggests belief in a hierarchical structure, with the council
as the highest power. The concept of conciliar authority appears more
explicitly in the chapter's appeal in 1502, against a papal tax: 'There is
not, nor cannot be in the Church a greater authority, strength or power
than when it is assembled in Holy General Councils under the direction and guidance of the Holy Spirit.' Not even the Roman pontiff had
power against it, and he was bound to obey its sentences. The university denied the validity of the censures imposed on the chapter for its
refusal to pay the tax. Later the matter was brought before the royal
courts as a plea against the papal legate, and in the pleadings
references to a council and to the liberties of the French Church were
closely intermingled.

This tradition of appeals lay behind the most notable assertion of
conciliar doctrines in the French interest in the immediate pre-
Reformation period, that which took place during the *conciliabulum* of
Pisa. This represented the last serious attempt by a council to proceed
against a pope, and although it failed, its importance should not be
minimised, because it drew together the theoretical-canonist tradition
of conciliar thought and the political-nationalist adoption of this as a
weapon against the temporal concerns of the papacy. Even before the
cardinals revolted against Julius II in 1511, French hostility to the pope
had been developing conciliar characteristics. A meeting at Lyons in
June 1510 had reasserted the principles of the pragmatic and the
limitation of papal authority, and on 21 July Machiavelli, then at Blois,
wrote to Florence that there were plans to withdraw obedience from
the pope and summon a council against him. It seems that then the
council which was envisaged was one of the French Church, though it is
clear that this was seen as a forerunner of something more. On 30 July
a royal letter summoned the French bishops to Orleans for 15 September, and the plans for the meeting are reported in a further letter
from Machiavelli to Florence on 18 August. He wrote that the council
would withdraw obedience from the papacy, and that if agreement
could be reached with the emperor and the King of England a new
pope would be created. This would be followed by an invasion of Italy

in the spring of 1511. Machiavelli seems to have regarded the deposition of the pope by international action as a practical possibility. That so acute an observer of affairs should think this is an eloquent comment on the practical weakness of the pope, and on the ineffectiveness of attempts to reassert papal authority.

When the French council met, the king submitted a number of articles to it for discussion. These did not deal with the basic issues of authority between pope and council, but with the relations between the pope and the king, and the latter's right to defend himself against threatened papal encroachments by a withdrawal of obedience or a disregard of sentences against him. Not surprisingly the king obtained all the answers which he wished, but one should note that the gathering suggested as a course of action that ambassadors should be sent to the pope urging him to desist from his proceedings, and that if he refused to hear them, they should appeal for the summons of a free council, in accordance with the decrees of the holy Council of Basel. This appeal to a council was suggested as though *Execrabilis* had never been issued, despite the fact that Julius II had declared its enduring validity in the bull *Suscepti regiminis* little over a year earlier.

Such was the background to the situation which developed when a number of the cardinals revolted against Julius II in the following year. When they called a council to Pisa, Louis XII and the Emperor Maximilian I gave them support, although some people had reservations about the cardinals' right to act in this way. In an undated letter, perhaps from September 1511, Maximilian's daughter, Margaret of Austria, warned him against involvement in the council, because its summons rightfully pertained to the pope. In another letter she mentioned that the English king had also advised against such involvement, although one may suspect that Henry VIII was more moved by political considerations than by any scruples about the right of summons.

This crisis produced the last great debate about the authority of pope and council before the Reformation, and the works written during it show clearly that the issues contested between the papacy and the Councils of Constance and Basel could still provoke fierce debate. The writings varied in character; some were frankly apologetic for the council and dealt with immediate issues, others looked more broadly at the problems of authority. Among the apologists one of the most notable was the abbot of Subasio, Zaccaria Ferreri, who played an influential part in the assembly at Pisa. In his *Apologia Sacri Pisani Concilii*, he was concerned with the immediate question of the council's validity, in the light of papal attacks on it and of the papal summons of the Fifth Lateran Council. He claimed that the council had the right to withstand the pope, as Paul had withstood Peter and as Baalam's ass had contradicted its master, and he deplored the abuse with which the pope had attacked the council. His rebuttal of Julius's charges was, however, a work of rhetoric rather than of logic.

Another defender of the council was the jurist, Filippo Decio, who wrote two works on its behalf. In the first, his *Consilium . . . habitum pro ecclesiae auctoritate*, he began by affirming his past connection with the papacy,which he had served as an auditor of the Rota and as a papal chaplain, to which dignity he had been appointed by Innocent VIII. He then raised four questions, which he discussed later: whether the pope could be accused if he persisted obstinately in an offence from which the Christian religion suffered scandal; whether the pope was bound to keep promises which he had confirmed by oath and not to absolve himself; whether in such cases the general council could judge the pope, and how the general council should be summoned in these circumstances. After characteristic scholastic presentation of both sides of the case, Decio put forward his own view that in five cases the pope could be judged by a council, including the problematical one of when he was guilty of incorrigible crime, because by his persistence in it he incurred suspicion of heresy. Although under normal circumstances the pope may be judged by no one, this rule does not apply when he is guilty of scandalous crime. On the question of an oath being binding, Decio held that the pope could not break a vow which he had taken as a cardinal, because only unlawful oaths, or those extorted by force, could be broken. He then applied the general rule to the particular case. The general council was the judge on those occasions when the pope was accused, even although it did not generally have this power. The fourth question, concerning the procedure for calling a council, raised particular problems in view of the circumstances. Not only did Decio have to argue away the normal right of the pope to summon the council, which he did by acknowledging that the majority of the cardinals could act when the pope had failed, but he also had to face the fact that the cardinals who had rebelled against Julius II and called the council were only a minority of the college. He justified their action with considerable ingenuity, suggesting that when the head was suspect, those who followed the head were likewise suspect, and that therefore the power of summons pertained to those cardinals who were not with the pope and therefore not under his influence. He renewed his defence of the council in a sermon which he gave after it had been transferred from Pisa to Milan, in which he criticised the pro-papal arguments, and claimed that the papal council could not be free. There is, however, little new in this work.

Outside Italy, it was hardly surprising that the protagonist of conciliar claims was to be found in the University of Paris. Its Gallican tradition, combined with French political support for the rebel cardinals, made it an obvious ally to which the council fathers could look for theoretical justification of their actions, when these had come under attack from the most forceful of the pro-papal writers, the Dominican master-general and future cardinal, Cajetan. Under royal pressure, the faculty of theology named a young master, Jacques Almain, to reply to Cajetan's work, and this he did during the summer of 1512. He emphasised that authority pertained to the whole Church and not only to the pope, and stressed that whereas the council could not err in matters of faith, papal decisions had been known which were affected by heresy. A council could depose a pope for heresy, or if his conduct were threatening to ruin the Church, and it could assemble on its own to judge him. Although Almain was a theologian by training, his work has a somewhat juristic tone, which reflects the links between political and religious Gallicanism at Paris. The clearest distinction between the attitudes of Almain and Cajetan can be seen in their conclusions: the latter said that he would always accept 'the correction of the Holy Roman Church', and the former that he would submit 'to the judgement of the universal Church'.

The vigour of this debate shows the openness of the issues, but in the final analysis the writers' views are hardly surprising, considering the relation of each to the council which was then meeting. But about the same time there was a more surprising piece of conciliar writing in Giovanni Gozzadini's treatise *De electione Romani pontificis*. That he should write in favour of the council is surprising both because he was an official of the Curia and because, despite his dislike of Julius II, for whose deposition he was clearly wishing, he remained on the papal side during the meetings of the assembly at Pisa. His views on the issues of authority may therefore be regarded as perhaps more disinterested than those of the other writers and, in consequence, as a better illustration of how far conciliar ideas had persisted through the period of the papal restoration. He wrote that though the plenitude of the power was given by God to St Peter, and then to his successors by election, this power was given so that it could be independent of any creature and that it might depend on the Church. The Church was inerrant, perpetual and irremovable, whereas the pope was errant, temporary and removable. Behind this affirmation lay his belief that the Church in council was not merely a political body, but also a mystical one: had it been political, it could err, deceive, and be deceived, and would not resemble the Church of which Christ was the head. Gozzadini had no doubt on the question of appeals, declaring that though they were unlawful from the pope to any man, because the pope had no earthly superior, an appeal to a council was lawful, as this represented the universal Church, which was greater than the pope, and an appeal may be made from a lesser power to a greater. By the same token, appeals could not be made to the pope from a council. Ecclesiastical power is in the Church *fundamentaliter* but in the pope only *ministerialiter*. For this reason power could not be taken from the Church, but it could be taken from the pope, if he were *scandalosus vitiosus, incorrigibilis vel haereticus*. This affirmation extended the rights of the Church over the pope beyond the recognised canon law provision that he could be deposed for heresy. If the council does not have to concern itself with the position of the pope, its appropriate means of summons is by papal action and authority, but although such authority is expedient for the calling of a council, it is not essential, because the council can meet without it.

Gozzadini did not shirk the problem posed by the papal decrees against the claims of councils, Pius II's *Execrabilis* and Julius II's *Suscepti regiminis*, a problem which the apologists for Pisa had omitted to mention. He declared bluntly that the prohibition of appeals from a pope to a council was unlawful, because the pope did not have the power to make such a prohibition. That which he had made was of no value, because it was contrary to divine and natural law, and the decrees of the Councils of Constance and Basel, which had been issued with universal consent and by the Spirit and Providence of God, should not be destroyed by the will of only one or two men. Nor was Gozzadini the only writer of his time who stressed the superiority of natural law to the pope, and saw it as something which invalidated *Execrabilis*: Matthias Ugonius held the same view, and also claimed that a council could be held without papal summons, and that papal censures on those who summoned it were inefficacious.

All these early sixteenth-century writings suggest that for all the strength of the papal reaction, and despite papal efforts to eliminate the challenge from conciliar ideas, the question of final authority in the Church was still regarded as one open to free theological discussion. Gozzadini indeed protested that he had not written anything against the Church, the Holy See or the papacy, and the fact that he presented his work to the College of Cardinals suggests that he believed that it would be acceptable, if not to the pope, at least to some men in the higher ranks of the Church. It is worth noting also one of the measures taken at the Fifth Lateran Council: on 10 December 1512 it approved a bull, which annulled the acts of the assembly at Pisa. In one way this may be seen, and rightly, as marking the victory of the papacy over its rival, but it also suggests that the pope took the activities of the schismatic assembly seriously. Even if he had no doubts about the legality of his own position, this view was not shared by the whole of Christendom, and the fact that the bull against the actions of the rebel council was itself given conciliar approval of a kind may be seen as a demonstration to the supporters of Pisa that the actions of their assembly were of no account. The effects of this may be seen when in August

1513 Henry VIII of England wrote lettters of defiance against James IV of Scotland, asserting that he was resisting 'the Malice of all Scismatiques and theyr adherents, being by the General Counsell expressly excommunicated and Interdicted.' It is surely not a mere accident that the king referred to the condemnation by the lateran council rather than to any papal sentence.

Even among men who were undoubtedly papalist in sympathy there were still traces of conciliar influence. Giles of Viterbo accepted that the pope could command all and was obliged to obey no one, nor did he seem to have thought that under normal circumstances the council could challenge papal authority. He did, however, seem to recognise that if there were contending popes, a council could have the right to depose them. The same circumstances were acknowledged by Cajetan as so exceptional as to warrant a general council assembling itself and taking the action it deemed necessary, even against the wishes of the pope. Nor was there any specific condemnation of *Haec Sancta*, although this may have been inplicit in the whole conduct of the council, and this may suggest that the pope did not wish to risk a rebuff from men who would not follow him to an extreme position.

There is no doubt that in its dealings with the *conciliabulum* of Pisa the papacy secured a political victory, but this did not prevent the re-emergence of conciliar ideas at later dates, sometimes in surprising quarters. No one need be surprised when the Gallican party in France upheld conciliar traditions in its resistance to the concordat of 1516, with the Parlement affirming that the pope could not reject the canons of general councils, and calling for a general council, and the University of Paris making an appeal *ad futurum concilium*, for this was fully in accord with the traditions of French opposition to the papacy. But it is unexpected to find the claims of councils being upheld in a letter from Sir Thomas More to Thomas Cromwell on 5 March 1534, when he was already a prisoner in the Tower of London. Two excerpts make More's position clear; 'As for generall counsailis assembled lawfully, I never could perceive, but that in the declaration of the trewthis it is to be byleved and to be standen to, the authorite therof owght to be taken for vndowtable' . . . 'ffor albeit that I have for myn awne parte such opinion of the popys primatie as I have shewed yow, yit neuer thowght I the Pope above the generall counsaile . . .' The first excerpt might still have allowed for papal superiority, with the reference to the lawful assembly of councils, but the second is explicit in its affirmation of conciliar claims, and may help to clarify what More meant earlier in the letter.

At first sight this would seem to run contrary to More's beliefs, as expressed in his declaration on the scaffold that he died the king's good servant, but God's first, and also in his refusal to swear to the succes-

sion in terms which implied a repudiation of the pope's spiritual
authority in England, the act which was the direct cause of More's
execution. But if one considers his thought in its wider implications,
this utterance about general councils falls into place. Above all, he was
internationalist in sympathy, and the affairs of Christendom mattered
to him as much as those of England. An account of a conversation with
his son-in-law, Roper, told in the latter's life of him, emphasises the
point. 'Now would to our Lord, son Roper, upon condition that three
things were well established in Christendom, I were put in a sack, and
here presently cast into the Thames.' When asked what the three
things were, he replied; 'The first is, that where the most part of
Christian princes be at mortal war, they were all at universal peace.
The second, that where the Church of Christ is at this present sore
afflicted with many errors and heresies, it were settled in a perfect
uniformity of religion. The third, that where the King's matter of his
marriage is now come in question, it were to the glory of God and
quietness of all parties brought to a good conclusion.' The peace of
Europe and the peace of the Church were of as much concern to him,
probably of more, as was the pressing matter of Henry VIII's divorce.
When he resisted the king in the name of the pope's spiritual rights in
England, it was less the opposition of a strong papalist than that of an
internationalist to the rising power of the territorial prince. At the time
when More's letter to Cromwell was written, the powers of a secular
ruler *vis-à-vis* the international Church were a practical issue of politics, whereas those of a general council *vis-à-vis* the pope were not.
More's conciliarism was abstract and theoretical, but it also reflected
how far conciliar ideas had penetrated the minds of the leading intellectuals of the early sixteenth century.[9] Indeed, one may describe
More's outlook as anachronistic, in that his conciliarism was unaffected by the nationalist feelings which were so marked in other
writings of the period, and which played so large a part in modifying
conciliar thought in France. He did not, however, stand alone, and
there were contemporary writers in Spain who blamed the evils of the
Church on the fact that the pope would not obey a general council.

   More was a humanist who accepted conciliar ideas, but not all
humanists shared his sentiments. In late fifteenth-century Germany,
Rudolf Agricola, in an oration congratulating Innocent VIII on his
election, declared that all men owed faith and obedience to the Roman
Church and its head. Early in the sixteenth century Jakob Wimpfeling
was as conservative. Even while he stressed the need for the reform of
the Church in head and members, he still looked to the pope to carry it
out, and when in 1510 the Emperor Maxmilian expressed an intention
of following the example of France in the pragmatic sanction, Wimpfeling cautioned him against doing so. In 1511 he attacked the *con-*

ciliabulum of Pisa, affirming that only the pope, with the help of a council, could reform the Church. Clearly he saw the role of the council as subordinate to that of the pope.

This was the opinion of one German, expressed within a decade of the outbreak of the Lutheran controversy, but it was not the only point of view. The University of Erfurt, where Luther began his studies, had a tradition of opposition to papal power in the fifteenth century, having adhered to the Council of Basel after other schools had returned to the papal fold. Two of its leading figures, Jakob of Jüterbogk and Johann of Wesel, were notable for their anti-papal views, though it is uncertain how far their opinions influenced Luther. The latter's ideas at the outset of his career as a rebel against authority are not clear, and his impulsive reactions in the debate against Eck at Leipzig in 1519 probably fail to show his considered opinions. In the early stages of the debate, Luther asserted that the papacy existed by human right, but under pressure from Eck was provoked into saying that councils could also err. This did not, however, prevent him from making an appeal to a council at a later date.

In 1520 Ulrich von Hutten urged the calling of a council, and republished a conciliarist tract dating from the time of the Council of Basel. He attacked Leo X for calling an appeal to a council a crime, and denounced the bulls of Pius II and Julius II. As the Reformation crisis developed and he aligned himself with Luther, he renewed his attack on the papal ban on appeals to a council, particularly in his glosses on the *Bulla Decimi Leonis, contra errores Martini Lutheri*. This was the bull *Exsurge, domine* of 1520, in which Luther had been condemned and where the conciliar theory had again been rejected, on the basis of the earlier bulls *Execrabilis* and *Suscepti regiminis*. When in 1521 Luther was called to Worms, there were many who looked to a council as the only means of settling the crisis, as was reported by the papal legate, Aleander, and his colleague, Raffaele de' Medici. A memorandum preserved with the acts of the diet shows strikingly how far conciliar ideas had taken root: 'A council alone is in a position to ascertain whether Dr Martinus has written against the faith; he has appealed to a Council and thereby tied the Pope's hands. Pius II's and Julius II's prohibitions are invalid, because they are at variance with natural and divine law, as well as with the decrees of Constance, and they have not been recognised by the University of Paris.' Two points in this merit particular attention, the reference to natural law as a limitation on the pope, which invalidated the bulls of prohibition, and the mention of the University of Paris. The former shows that the ideas expressed by theorists such as Gozzadini and Ugonius were held more widely, and that papal attempts to recover absolute power had not won popular acceptance. The latter indicates the teaching authority which the university could exercise, even in an age when national sentiment was bulking more largely in the formation of men's opinions. Its conciliarist tradition, which had persisted from the period of the Great Schism to the sixteenth century, made it a natural ally to which those who desired a council could look for support.

Throughout the century which elapsed between the end of the Great Schism and the outbreak of the Reformation, adherents of the conciliar tradition maintained a peristent challenge to papal claims to authority within the Church. The crisis of authority which had come to the fore in the councils of the early fifteenth century was not fully resolved, because to those who held that ultimate power lay with a general council bulls which forbade appeals or affirmed papal supremacy could not be accepted as binding. The question of final authority remained unresolved, and although in practical terms the papacy was victorious – only one council met which had not been summoned by the pope, that of Pisa in 1511 – this victory was not decisive. This council's failure was due less to strong moral support for the papacy than to the lack of adequate secular assistance for the pope's opponents. French adherence to it merely meant that France's enemies were prepared to throw their influence on the pope's side and accept his council rather than the one meeting at Pisa. But this did not guarantee that the same political support for the papacy would be forthcoming on another occasion if circumstances were different. The success of the Fifth Lateran Council in undermining the position of its rival could not diminish the fear which the papacy had of an assembly which it could not dominate. This meant that when a new crisis struck the church after Luther's defiance, the papacy was reluctant to accept demands for a free council in German lands, lest such a gathering might resurrect the conciliar claims, which had wide support throughout Christendom.

The uncertainty of the papacy about its authority played a part in determining its policies. French support for conciliar doctrines in the Pragmatic Sanction of Bourges influenced relations between successive popes and kings, and affected negotiations over the immediate administration of the French Church. In order to recover power, in theory as well as in practice, the popes had to come to terms with the secular rulers of Christendom, with whom they had much in common, as conciliar curbs on the pope were similar to the restrictions which some subjects were trying to enforce on their princes, and against whom the princes were struggling to establish their sovereignty.

CHAPTER 2

Nationality and Sovereignty

During the fifteenth century, the secular rulers of western Europe had considerable success in increasing their authority and in identifying their own position with the rights and traditions of their lands. Nationalism and sovereignty were not necessarily associated, but one can see such an association becoming increasingly common, with the two giving each other mutal support: national sentiment strengthened princely power, while the prince served as a focus for an identification of land and people. National feeling of a kind was not new, and had appeared as early as the twelfth century over a wide area of Christendom, but at this stage it does not appear to have involved any particular stress on the postion of the monarch. By the fourteenth century, however, the Italian jurist, Lucas de Penna, had propounded the idea that a moral and political marriage was contracted between the king and his *respublica*. Comparable to this idea is the application of the term *corpus mysticum* to the nation, a usage found in France in the early fifteenth century, in the works of Gerson and Jean de Terre-Rouge, and in England in 1430, when it was employed in a sermon at the opening of Parliament by William Lyndwood. In France the term was still being used in the sixteenth century by Claude de Seyssel and Guy Coquille. The idea of the mystical body of the State, the head of which was the prince, is found in the treatise *De ortu et auctoritate imperii Romani* of Aeneas Sylvius Piccolomini, written in 1446, and while this work is not specifically absolutist in outlook – indeed the author declared that the prince was obliged to sacrifice himself for the State – the emphasis on the prince's headship could clearly be given an autocratic twist.

In practical matters one can see a development of this nationalism connected with royal authority in some of the negotiations between Casimir of Poland and Urban V in 1363, which led to the original foundation of the University of Cracow. In the petition for the foundation of a *studium generale* the king laid particular stress on the establishment of a faculty of law, just at the time when he was concerned with the codification of customary law in his realm. One can see a similar attitude behind the foundation of the other fourteenth-century universities in eastern and central Europe, at Prague, Pecs and Vienna.[1] The fifteenth century saw a continuation of this stream of new university foundations, and in a number of cases the local prince seems to have taken the first steps towards obtaining the bull. This is most notable in Germany, where the local princes, ecclesiastical as well as secular, played an important part in foundations at Trier, Mainz, Ingolstadt and Tübingen, but one can see a similar action of Christian I of Denmark in the establishment of the University of Copenhagen. Elsewhere the initiating force might be the local bishop, as can be seen in the three Scottish universitites and at Upsala in Sweden.[2] In all cases, however, one is left with the impression that possession of at least one university was coming to be regarded as a normal characteristic of a territorial state, indeed that it was almost necessary to have one in order to maintain a proper dignity for the state.

Certainly by the time of the Church reform councils of the early fifteenth century a clear consciousness of nationality had developed. This can be seen at the Council of Constance, where an artificial division by nations was employed for procedural purposes, to prevent the voting being overwhelmed by the large number of Italians present. Despite the artificiality of the division, the nations developed a chauvinistic aggressiveness towards each other. There were disputes between the English and the Aragonese over rights of precedence, claims from the French that the English should not rank as a separate nation, and counter-claims by the English that they possessed all the characteristics of an authentic nation. In this last one can see some attempt being made to formulate a theory of nationhood, because the English suggested that to be a nation involved a habit of unity, a blood relationship, or peculiarities of language. On the other hand, nationality was not identified with unified royal dominion; lands might be part of a nation without acknowledging obedience to a particular prince. In the years after the end of the council, the Bohemian revolt was strongly influenced by popular national feeling, and this may well have provoked the superior tone adopted by Eugenius IV in a letter to the Emperor in May 1432: 'by the grace of God there are no heresies in Italy, for the extirpation of which it is necessary to toil; but the Italians are true and good Catholics, as they ought to be.'

One way in which a consciousness of national identity could develop into a manifestation of national pride lay in claims to precedence between the representatives of different powers. Indeed such claims could give rise to diplomatic incidents. In 1434 the ambassadors of the Duke of Brittany to the Council of Basel were involved in a dispute on this matter before their formal incorporation as members of the council, while towards the end of the century there were at least two incidents involving Scottish representatives in Rome. In 1487 the ambassadors of the Scottish and Hungarian kings were both excluded from the papal chapel after a dispute and, what is more indicative of the nature of national feeling, the former protested afterwards about the insult to their king. In 1490 another Scots envoy was upheld in the place he claimed after a dispute with the Neapolitans.[3] Above all, one sees a touchiness to real or imagined slights. In 1464 the Milanese ambassador to the French court reported that there was ill-feeling against prelates who spoke of the French king as though he were merely a minor vassal of the Church. The ambassador, in fact, was quite sympathetic to the French grievances.

Contemporary with this growing awareness of national identity, was also the growth of a concept of nationhood, expressed in juridical terms. This tended to stress monarchical authority, and it was probably the lawyers who made the most marked contribution to the growth of royal claims within a national framework. The most obvious manifestation of this was the formula *Rex in suo regno imperator est* which goes back to the twelfth century, and upon which the glossators of the following centuries commented. From about 1250 the views of civil lawyers on this subject were conditioned by local circumstances, and even supporters of the empire admitted that *de facto* the kingdoms of Christendom were not subject to the emperor, whatever the latter's title was *de jure*. This period saw the same formula being used in France. In the fifteenth century the canonist, Roselli, in one of his few references to the actual State system, said bluntly that it was clear that the King of France did not *de facto* recognise any superior.[4] More theoretically Panormitanus argued that even the most intrinsically imperial prerogatives could be obtained prescriptively by kings, if there had been papal intervention, although normally a king could not obtain certain imperial powers. One feels that here the writer is attempting to force a political reality into the rigid structure of his theories. While it would appear that such a claim was directed primarily against the universal claims of the emperor or the pope, in practice its importance, in France at least, lay in asserting royal authority over those princes within the realm who claimed that the king was only *primus inter pares*.[5]

The intellectual questions over the issue of authority in the period of the reform councils were applied in the secular as well as in the ecclesiastical spheres. The papal counter-attack against conciliar doctrines played a part also in the development of monarchical theory. The idea of a hierarchical society was not new, and the pope's victory in his earlier struggle with the emperor had, by emphasising the superiority of *sacerdotium* over *imperium*, confirmed the idea of a hierarchy with a spiritual peak. But with the virtual cessation of the conflict between pope and emperor, the theorists became more concerned with the relations of ruler and subject in both the spiritual and secular spheres, but the hierarchical concepts were maintained. Piero da Monte, about 1450, drew parallels between the heavenly hierarchy and that of the Church Militant, and went on to assert that in secular government also power descended from the head to the members. Similar views were held by Juan Torquemada in his *Summa de Ecclesia* and by the Austrian, Thomas Ebendorfer.[6]

At the same time as this growth of theories of royal power, there was also an increase in monarchical authority in practical matters, and on occasions the theories were used to justify a political action. In France, such a growth took place throughout the fourteenth century and the extension of the king's power included ecclesiastical matters. Royal intervention in Church affairs became more common from 1340, and was intensified in the period of the Great Schism, particularly when the kingdom withdrew its obedience from Benedict XIII. When the schism was ended by the Council of Constance, an appeal to Rome by the University of Paris, made without royal permission, led to proceedings against the latter, in the course of which the problem of authority was vigorously brought to the fore. The king's advocate, Guillaume Le Tur, affirmed, *'que le Roy est empereur en son royaume, qu'il tient de Dieu seul, sans recognoistre souverain seigner terrien . . .'*[7] The same formula was used to justify royal supremacy at later dates. In 1443 the king's advocate asserted his master's power over everyone in the kingdom, in effect affirming the territorial nature of the State, and in 1464, when the Duke of Bourbon had ventured to speak of his sovereignty, the king's proctor retorted,*'En ce royaume il n'y a que ung roy, une corone et une souverainete*. The practical implications of such nationalism were reflected in royal legislation, as in letters patent of Charles VII in 1432, which laid down that no one should be appointed to a benefice in the realm unless he were a native of it. By the reign of Lous XI, it is clear that the crown was attempting to replace the older contractual bonds of vassalage by the idea of the obedience owed by a subject to his lord. This was not merely a matter of words, and in the case of Brittany brought about a bitter clash over jurisdictional rights, because Louis held that, as the Duke of Brittany and the Bishop of Nantes were both his subjects, litigation between them pertained to the royal court. This view was not shared by Pope Pius II, not admittedly an impartial witness, who wrote in his *Commentaries* that as the king was emperor in his kingdom, so the duke was king in his duchy. Louis' concern was with the substance of power rather than with appearances – in his relations with Brittany he was prepared to abandon claims of liege homage as opposed to simple homage, presumably because he regarded such distinctions as having little real meaning.

Royal claims to sovereignty could be buttressed by an emphasis on nationality. This popular sentiment in France can be traced back to at least the twelfth century, where it is notably expressed in the term *la douce France* in the *Chanson de Roland*, and in the period of the schism one finds Nicholas de Clamanges referring to *nostra Gallia*. Shortly afterwards, Jeanne d'Arc's phrase, 'the holy realm of France', shows that the sentiment still persisted despite the political divisions of the kingdom. The strength of the feeling was recognised by outsiders, as in 1435 when Sir John Fastolf stated, as a matter of course, that the French people naturally loved Henry VI's adversary more than him. One probably sees here not merely nationalism, but also a loyalty to the monarchy. Two cases before the Parlement of Paris, in 1437 and 1441, illustrate how the idea of nationality was developing, so that it was held justifiable to over-rule private interests on public grounds. In the first case an Englishman requested permission to marry a French girl to whom he was betrothed. There was no canonical impediment, but the Parlement held that a change of nationality *durant la guerre* was a criminal matter – the case is contained in the criminal and not the civil register of the Parlement – and that the state of war between the two countries was a bar to the marriage. The second case concerned a Parisian girl, married to an Italian merchant from Lucca, who had followed the English to Rouen after their withdrawal from Paris. She had obtained a safe-conduct and rejoined her husband, but as they were regarded as rebels at Paris, their goods were forfeited. The girl's mother put forward a plea that she was bound by divine and canon law to follow her husband, but Parlement took the contrary view that she was not bound to follow her husband into treason. The fact that she had children was regarded as an aggravation of the offence, for it was held that she was raising up children to the enemy. These cases show an emphasis on the needs of the State, and on its power to over-ride the claims of the individual. Appeal was made to the ancient Romans who put love of country above love of family, and in this can be seen an idea of solidarity within the nation.[8]

The stress laid on the concept of nationality did not always have such drastic results, but it reappeared in other matters and at later dates. In 1465 Louis XI wrote to the Archbishop of Auch concerning a disputed election to the see of Comminges, in favour of one of his councillors, who had been chosen by one faction in the chapter. The rival candidate was described as not being *natif de nostre royaume*, and the king declared that it was not lawful for anyone to obtain benefices within the realm unless he were a native of it. There was no absolute veto on the appointment of foreigners, because the king might waive the objection, a measure incidentally of the way in which the royal will

could affect the administration of the law. In 1479 a grant of a prebend
at Tournai was contested on the ground that the recipient, Jean Royer,
was a native of the county of Burgundy, which was outside the kingdom of France, and was therefore incapable of obtaining a benefice
within it. The king ordered Parlement to disregard the objection, but it
is not clear if this was on the ground that Royer was not a native of the
county, or because Louis was attempting at this time to extend his
authority into the county (as well as into the undoubtedly French lands
of the Duchy of Burgundy) in the struggle following the death of
Charles the Bold, and was exploiting this case as a means of asserting
his claim. But irrespective of the king's motives, one should note that
Royer's opponents were prepared to justify their opposition to him on
the plea that he was a foreigner. This would hardly have been a likely
plea unless they considered that some regard would be paid to the
claims of nationality, and that this would give them an opportunity to
win their case. In the following year a similar problem arose concerning a Savoyard, who had obtained a prebend at Lyons, and the king
commanded the chapter to receive him, because he did not wish the
inhabitants of Savoy to be regarded as enemies or foreigners. In 1491,
French ambassadors to the pope were instructed to tell him that it was
better that subjects of the realm should be preferred to foreigners,
while a year later Charles VIII informed the pope that he had
banished from Tournai Jean Flamang (or Flamand), who had claimed
a provision to the abbey of St Martin, because *ledict Flamang est
estrangier et natif du pays de Haynau a nous contraire*. In his place the
king put in possession *frere Jehan le Bouchier, lequel est natif de ladicte
ville et a nous seur et feal*. None of these cases would be particularly
noteworthy if considered individually, but if taken collectively, they
illustrate an attitude which presupposes the existence of a territorial
national state.

Similar pressures can be seen elsewhere. In 1474, Louis XI annulled
the election of the Dutchman, Oudendijk, as rector of the University
of Paris, because he was a subject of the Duke of Burgundy, and
certainly the university became more national in character than it had
been at an earlier date, partly, no doubt, because of the appearance of
other universities which kept students in their native countries. On the
other hand, it did not become purely French, but preserved some
internationalism of outlook into the sixteenth century, as when it
sought and obtained from the king the deliverance of students from
Spain and Flanders, who had been imprisoned as subjects of the king's
enemy, Charles V. One must also beware of reading too much into
apparent 'national feeling', which could well have geographical limits
narrower than one might expect. In a settlement in 1453 of certain
issues between the papacy and the Duchy of Brittany, provision was

made for the exclusion of foreigners from Breton benefices, because they could not speak Breton. Clearly these 'foreigners' were Frenchmen.

Despite such reservations it is, however, reasonable to speak of the existence of a national state, and within this, the position of the monarch was increasingly reinforced by religious sanctions. Jean de Terre-Rouge, writing around 1420, was prepared to assert that the king was God on earth, and that resistance to him was sacrilegious as well as unnatural, for he was also head of the body politic. In 1490 a declaration in Parlement took the same line, that for a man to resist the king was to fall into the offence of sacrilege as well as *lèse-majesté*. Clearly the idea persisted throughout the century, perhaps gaining strength as it progressed. The career of Jeanne de'Arc bears witness to her belief in the monarchy's religious character – her letter to the King of England and the Duke of Bedford, ordering them to surrender the keys of the towns which they had taken, and declaring that she had come to vindicate the blood royal, had a haughtiness which a king could not have exceeded, and her aim of having the dauphin crowned shows a popular emphasis on consecration as a sign of God's approval. Words put into Jeanne's mouth in the *Mistere du siege d'Orleans* stress the idea that Charles was king by divine right.

The French king had long laid claim to a special dignity among the monarchs of Christendom – the title *Christianissimus* dated back to the twelfth century. The rhetorical preamble to the Pragmatic Sanction of Bourges in 1438 was a virtual manifesto for the belief that royal rule depended on the support of Providence.[9] Not only did the kings claim divine support, but they also attempted to assert the idea, the origins of which probably went back before the Christianisation of Europe, that they were something more than mere laymen. Probably the conciliar period saw some development of ideas of a sacral monarchy, particularly during the periods in which obedience was withdrawn from the pope, as this could help to strengthen royal authority in its dealings with the Church. After the schism, one can see more explicit statements of the priestly character of the king – in an address to Charles VII, Jean Jouvenel des Ursins said, *vous n'estes pas simplement personne laye, mais prelat ecclesiastique*. This was not merely an attempt at flattery, because he was also prepared to accept the practical consequences of his granting such a status to Charles, by asking that he should call together an assembly of the Church *comme chef et la première personne ecclésiastique* of the land. An outside observer, Aeneas Sylvius Piccolomini, noticed the importance attributed to the religious service of anointing, and said that the French did not recognise anyone as lawful king until this had taken place. That he was correct in this belief is borne out both by Jeanne d'Arc's attitude to Charles VII, whom she continued to call dauphin until his coronation, although he had assumed the royal title nine days after his father's death, and by the action of the estates in 1484, when they petitioned for the consecration and coronation of Charles VIII as soon as possible. Various texts from the fifteenth century, including those of pleadings before the Parlement, assumed that a consecrated king was something more than a mere layman, and it is noteworthy that the kings do not appear to have touched for scrofula before their coronations.

If the king had a religious dignity, he also claimed it as something unique, particularly in relation to the great quasi-independent feudatories. In 1443 the king forbade the Comte de Foix to use the title 'by the grace of God' and he had already laid a similar prohibition on other magnates, including the house of Armagnac. In 1446 the claim of the Duke of Burgundy to rule 'by the grace of God' was also challenged, but the dispute was not settled until 1449, when the king had to accept the use of the phrase, after the duke's specific denial that he claimed any greater right in France than formerly. The dukes of Brittany also used this title, despite royal protests. Louis XI may have been less rigid in his attitude than his father, perhaps because his concern was more with the realities of power than with its trappings, because in 1475 he gave permission to Guillaume de Chalons, Prince of Orange, and his successors to entitle themselves *Prince par la grace de Dieu*, saving always the fealty owed to the king. Even here, however, the implication of the grant is that only the king could permit the prince to use such a title. Connected with this stress on the religious character of kingship was the belief that a tyrannical ruler should be left to God, and writers throughout the fifteenth century tended increasingly to take this point of view, rather than justifying resistance or tyrannicide.

The lawyers were among the strongest of the kings' supporters, and the general tendency of legal theory was to emphasise royal authority, in assertions that it was greater than advocates could express, and was not subject to the opinions of doctors. The king seems in return to have looked favourably on the jurisdiction exercised by the Parlement of Paris, provided that it was clear that such jurisdiction was subordinate to the royal power. The king might as a gesture of good will associate the Parlement's authority with his own, but when royal interests were concerned there was no question of compromise.[10]

Not all legal writing was necessarily monarchical in character, and even in the early sixteenth century Claude de Seyssel, in *La Grande Monarchie de France* written in 1515 and published in 1519, could regard judicial machinery as a possible check on royal power. But Seyssel's views must be seen as anachronistic, for although he had a concept of nationality, he had little real notion of sovereignty. His concern was with the kingdom of France, and a nationalist spirit imbued both his political and his economic attitudes. The fact that his work was in the vernacular suggests his tendency to take a national rather than a cosmopolitan point of view. His outlook may also have been coloured by the fact that he wrote the book after leaving the royal service on the accession of Francis I, a king whose outlook was perhaps more absolutist than that of his old master, Louis XII. It certainly is noteworthy that *La Grande Monarchie* is more critical of the Crown than some of his earlier writings. One should remember also that Seyssel's views were personal and that among his contemporaries there were men with a more authoritarian outlook. Guillaume Budé's *L'Institution du Prince*, written in 1518, was almost exactly contemporary with Seyssel's *La Grande Monarchie* but Budé was prepared to claim that royal authority was vested in the king alone. The later humanist jurists tended to think similarly to Budé: Alciati adapted the Roman law principle of *merum imperium* to the state power existing in his time, declaring that the right to it resided in the prince, and that the use of it by magistrates was only delegated. Dumoulin, writing in 1539, affirmed that all powers of jurisdiction pertained to the king, thereby exalting royal power over all other powers in the land, and he in turn influenced the thought of Bodin.

In France, then, ideas of nationality and of sovereignty had both developed during the fifteenth century in a way which emphasised royal power. When one turns to Germany it is clear that the different political structure led to developments there following another course. In the local territorial states there was often a growth of princely authority, aided in places by particularist loyalty, but besides this one can see traces of a concept of the German nation, as something greater than any local state. One must discount the use of the term 'nation' at the Council of Constance, for there it was essentially an administrative division, adopted to meet an immediate problem, and the German nation included prelates from Hungary, Poland, Denmark, Sweden and Norway, as well as from the German-speaking lands. A quarter of a century later, however, it is possible to see something which looks like a recognisable sentiment of nationhood. In the *Acceptatio* of Mainz of 1439, two references were made to 'our German nation'.[12] In these references the *natio Germanica* seems to have comprised the king, the electors and the archbishops, if the last were princes, so it therefore represented an identification of the nation with the ruling powers in it. At the same time, one can see an external body being prepared to acknowledge the existence of the German nation as something comparable to the French. The chapter general of the Cistercians, meeting in 1439, felt it necessary to take precautions against the danger of a schism, which might lead to different members of the order *tam de natione Germanica quam Gallicana* having to live in different obediences. If such a schism arose, two abbots were named who were given plenary powers to convoke a chapter of the German nation.

In the following decade, during the period of German neutrality between Eugenius IV and the Council of Basel, a similar, perhaps even stronger, sense of national awareness can be seen when the Reichstag, meeting at Frankfurt in June 1445, called for a national church council. In the concordat between the pope and the German princes in 1447, the former refers to the German nation having been relieved of certain grievances by accepting the relevant decrees of the Council of Basel, and in the concordat of Vienna of the following year, the formal agreement was made between the Holy See and the German nation, represented respectively by the pope and the king. In the preamble to the concordat the latter confirmed that he had entered the agreement with the assent of the majority of the electors and of the other temporal and spiritual princes.

During the fifteenth century, the nation and the empire came to be identified, in the term 'the Holy Roman Empire of the German Nation'. The assumption of identity can be seen both in official documents and in the writings of the chroniclers. But as early as the Diet of Rense in 1338 practical considerations had led to the assertion of the idea that imperial power derived from princely election rather than from papal coronation, and this was stressed again by the early sixteenth-century humanists. These suggested that Maximilian should codify German law, thereby emphasising the German character of the empire.[13] At a more popular level than that of the humanists, in the prophetic literature produced throughout the century, there was an increasing degree of national consciousness, though this was usually incidental to the main body of the writing, which was primarily concerned with the Church and its reform rather than with the nation. This is most evident in the proposals contained in the tract called the *Reformation Kaiser Sigmunds* and in the hopes for the coming of the 'third Frederick', the godly emperor who would purify the Church, hopes which were sadly disappointed in the historical Frederick III.

At times this consciousness of nationhood developed stridently aggressive tones, which aspired to the growth of German overlordship outside German lands, or manifested itself in the idea that Mainz would replace Rome as the centre of the Church. This tendency reached its peak in the so-called 'Upper Rhine Revolutionary' or 'Alsatian Anonymous' at the beginning of the sixteenth century, who combined a national fervour amounting to mania with an apocalyptic millenarianism. He claimed that Adam and his descendants down to Japhet were Germans, speaking German, and that the Germans and not the Jews were the chosen people. It is hard to judge how far this writer represented popular feeling, and certainly one should guard against exaggerating his importance, because his work was never published. His work, however, does illustrate how far popular feeling could go, and there is little doubt that the basis of his thought is to be found in the popular beliefs of his time. This nationalism was very different from the ideas which were found in France. There political conditions made it possible for national aspirations to be linked to the Crown and to ideas of sovereignty, whereas in Germany one finds a far vaguer and less practical nationalism of feeling, transcending the political realities of the territorial principalities, but making no contribution to the actual development of political society. It was found in the works of the humanists, who studied Tacitus' *Germania*, and who collected sources for German history. Maximilian offered rewards for old documents, a sign that humanist ideas had penetrated beyond the circles of the scholars, and the scholars themselves, notably Wimpfeling, worked to create a national consciousness.[14] Such patriotic feeling was not incompatible with the particularism of the princely states and of the towns, and it was there, not in the empire as a whole, that one can see a practical growth of sovereignty. By the end of the fifteenth century, the territorial princes had developed *de facto* sovereign power. Even theoretically this was recognised, and it is noteworthy that one of the most important of the German humanist jurists, Ulrich Zasius, was far more prepared to accept ideas of a division of authority than were his French contemporaries – this was a reflection of conditions in German political society.

Indeed, what is most characteristic of Germany is the concurrent development of a double sentiment of nationalism and particularism. This is well exemplified in Luther, who could entitle one of his most important works *To the Christian Nobility of the German Nation*, evidence that he could think of a German nation as something greater than the princely states, but who also looked to the territorial princes for practical action in carrying out changes in the Church. The sense of nationality existed independently of sovereignty, and the development of the latter is perhaps best characterised by the phrase 'Centralisation in Decentralisation'.[15] These princely states developed their own local nationalism, as seen in Werner Rolevinck's book in praise of the Westphalians, published in 1472, and in hostility to foreigners in positions of influence. It is clear that the term 'foreigner' could include other Germans, as in Saxony in 1446, when the estates clamoured for the dismissal of foreign Thuringian advisers, and in 1505, shortly before the reunion of the Bavarian duchies, when the nobility of Bavaria-Landshut complained that their places in the high court were being usurped by *doctores* who were commoners and usually non-Bavarian. Similar territorial nationalism seems to be implicit in the declaration of the Estates in the Rhenish duchies of Jülich and Berg in 1445 that they were acting in the best interests of 'prince and country', in the statement that the counts Palatine were being advised by 'councillors and members of the Palatinate', and in the demand of the Estates of Württemberg at the Diet of Tübingen in 1514 that the foreign councillors of the duke should be dismissed. Such xenophobia, directed against other Germans, found a target also in non-Germans. This can be seen in the hostility of Jakob of Jüterbogk to the *natio Italica*, which resisted the reform of the Church, and in the popular feelings reported to Rome by Aleander in the early years of the Lutheran crisis: 'The whole of Germany is in full revolt: nine-tenths raise the war cry "Luther!", while the watchword of the other tenth who are indifferent to Luther is "Death to the Roman Curia!".'

In fifteenth-century Germany, attempts were made to consolidate power at both imperial and princely levels, but at neither can one see a development comparable in effect to that in France. Attempts were made to introduce more centralised justice, and although they were unsuccessful, the important point is that they were made at all. The most notable figure in this effort to mobilise the forces of the empire was, from 1486, Berthold von Henneberg, the Archbishop Elector of Mainz, whose political activities in opposition to Maximilian I were, none the less, intended to exalt the empire against the instability of territorial particularism, and the results of imperial *Hausmacht* policy. But as Berthold saw the estates rather than the emperor as the basis of the empire, his reform policy would have excluded any kind of sovereignty comparable to that being developed by the French kings.

Equally, princely attempts at the consolidation of authority fell short of the French degree of sovereignty. Territorial lordship *(Landesherrschaft)* was not sovereign in character, but represented a complex of rights enjoyed by both the ruler and his subjects, and even although the juridical power of a prince such as the elector palatine was increased during the fifteenth century, he was still unable to secure exclusive jurisdiction over his subjects. One factor limiting princely influence was pressure from the estates, which had varying success in attempting to secure a share of power. In the Palatinate they achieved little, but elsewhere, as in Württemberg and Hesse, they made considerable gains, notably in the field of finance.

If one looks at the Spanish lands, there is again evidence for national feeling, both positive and negative, and, as in Germany, there were traces of a nationalism wider than the individual states of the peninsula. The main emphasis, however, was on the local kingdom. The most obvious kind of negative nationalism, hostility to foreigners, existed in the fourteenth century, when in 1335 a sharp complaint was made to Avignon about the provision of foreigners to Aragonese benefices, and in 1351, when the Cortes of Catalonia, meeting at Perpignan, resolved to send a delegation to the pope and the cardinals to deplore the conferment of Catalan benefices on foreigners. This opposition persisted into the fifteenth century, and in 1423 Alfonso V of Aragon again took action to exclude foreigners, whom he banned from holding benefices in the kingdom in future, while those who were already in possession were given two years to surrender or exchange them. In Castile also there were traces of national feeling among some fifteenth century writers, such as Fernán Pérez de Guzmán and Rodrigo Sánchez de Arévalo, who criticised earlier Castilian kings who had divided their realm, and who rejoiced when the separated territories were reunited. Arévalo certainly had strong feelings about the rights and claims of Spain, and he apparently referred to Spain as a whole, not merely to Castile. He claimed that it was exempt from imperial overlordship, an overlordship which was so academic that his claim could be relevant only at the level of sentiment. He also suggested that because the Spaniards had shown themselves free of passions in the struggles over the councils (a curious opinion, when one considers men such as John of Segovia or Torquemada!) their claims might be honoured if and when another council were convoked.

It is hard to know how far a genuine Spanish nationalism emerged, distinct from that of Castile and Aragon. Alfonso V of Aragon employed the title *Rex Hispanicus*, but as his power in the Iberian peninsula extended to Aragon alone, one cannot read too much into this. By the late fifteenth century, sailors from different parts of the peninsula would talk about 'returning to Spain', and at the intellectual rather than the popular level there were signs of a more positive nationalism in humanist circles, particularly in the group which gathered round Cardinal Margarit of Gerona, the chancellor of John II of Aragon. With the union of the two kingdoms, a further incentive was given to the growth of national feeling, even although the union was a personal one only, and it is noteworthy that a letter of Charles VIII of France, written in 1494, refers to Ferdinand by the title, King of Spain. Some attempt may have been made to cultivate nationalist feeling in the ecclesiastical field, with the institution of the Feast of the Triumph of the Holy Cross as a thanksgiving for the completion of the Reconquista. The introit for the mass was possibly aimed at an assimilation of Spain and paradise.[16] There is evidence for nationalist feeling, too, when Charles I of Spain succeeded to the empire as Charles V: in September 1519 a promise was extracted from him that the placing of his imperial title before his Spanish ones would not prejudice the liberties of those kingdoms. But even at this stage, when Charles was hereditary ruler of both realms, the union remained personal, and the assertion of Spanishness must be seen as sentimental rather than as a reflection of political developments in the peninsula.

Nowhere is the division of the Spanish lands before the union more apparent than in the different extent of royal power in the two kingdoms, with rights of sovereignty being far more developed in Castile. This seems to have grown in the fifteenth century, for in the earlier part of it the Castilian Cortes made at least sporadic efforts to resist royal encroachments. In 1440 it secured royal assent to a request that briefs issued in the king's name, which were contrary to the laws, should be disregarded. Two years later there were complaints that royal briefs contained such phrases as 'of his certain knowledge and absolute royal power', and the king replied that this wording was not to be employed in future. The same principle was reaffirmed in 1451. In view of this, it is surprising that in 1445 the Cortes had affirmed royal authority in the strongest terms, saying that divine law forbade men to touch the king, who was the Lord's Anointed, to speak evil of him, who was the Vicar of God, or to resist him, for to resist the king was to resist the ordinance of God. This indeed was a declaration of extreme royal claims, and far more characteristic of later developments in Castile than the earlier opposition to them. One may suggest that the different views expressed at this period reflect a struggle for power within the kingdom. The eventual ability of the monarchs to assert their claims depended partly on the fact that the whole structure of the Cortes was weaker in Castile than in Aragon, because the crown was not obliged to call it at fixed regular intervals, and no one had an automatic right to attend meetings. The fiscal exemption of the nobility and clergy meant that only the towns were concerned with resisting royal financial encroachments, and even more important, the Cortes failed to secure any share of legislative power. The Crown seems to have won over the greatest nobles, the grandees, by judicious consultation, and they came to be associated with the royal regime, instead of acting as a focus of opposition to it. Despite moments of crisis in the early sixteenth century, the Crown was able to maintain its position.

The growth of monarchical power in Castile contrasted markedly with the situation in Aragon, where the power of the Crown remained, in theory at any rate, strictly limited. The Aragonese oath of allegiance to the king made this clear; 'We who are as good as you swear to you who are no better than we, to accept you as our king and sovereign lord, provided you observe all our liberties and laws; but if not, not.' Admittedly Alfonso V was autocratic in outlook and high-flown in his ambitions, as can be seen from the wording of his title on his triumphal arch at Castelnuovo, *Alfonso Rex Hispanicus Siculus Italicus Pius Clemens Invictus*, but one may note that this monument was erected in his Italian rather than in his Aragonese lands. In Catalonia he was not strong enough to assert his power against the nobility and the urban patriciate. Under his successor, John II, there was a prolonged period of civil war, but though the king was victorious, he granted an amnesty to his enemies, and took an oath to preserve intact Catalonia's laws and liberties. After the union of the two kingdoms, the differences in character between them were not resolved for many years, although the increasing dominance which Castile exercised in the new Spain greatly strengthened monarchical power. This, however, was by no means complete by the early sixteenth century.

In England also one can see the emergence of both national feeling and, to a limited extent, of growing ideas of royal power. This is reflected in the fact that at the end of Edward III's reign English had come to be used as the language of convocation, replacing Latin for the main proceedings and French for the *gravamina* which it presented to Parliament. The popular term by which Henry Beaufort was known, Cardinal of England, indicates some measure of national sentiment, and it is interesting that the term was employed not only in England but also in a reference to Beaufort as papal legate in Germany in a fifteenth-century *Gesta* of the archbishops of Trier. The writings of two archbishops of Canterbury in this century, Henry Chichele and Thomas Bourgchier, show not only a sense of Englishness, but also a feeling of national pride. Some limitations were recognised on the unity of the nation, notably by William Lyndwood, whose gloss on the phrase *Consuetudinem Patriae* specifically distinguished *patria* from *regnum*, and instead equated it with *regio*, which in practical terms he applied to the province of Canterbury.

In secular writings, too, one can see the appearance of patriotic feeling: Sir John Fortescue waxed lyrical over England, its prosperity, and the quality of its law, comparing it with France, where royal rule was arbitrary and the people were poor, while in the early sixteenth century Edmund Dudley used the phrase 'all true englishmen', which has strong implications of national feeling. Such attitudes could easily develop into xenophobia, as was observed by two Italian writers around 1500. Polydore Vergil, in his *Anglica Historia*, said: 'that it cannot be brought to passe by any meane that a Frenche man borne will much love an Englishe man, or, contrary, that an English will love a French man; such is the hatred that hath spronge of contention for honor and empire;'[17] and the Venetian author of the *Relation of the Island of England* wrote:

the English are great lovers of themselves and of everything belonging to them; they think that there are no other men than themselves, and no other world but England ... They have an antipathy to foreigners, and imagine that they never come into their island, but to make themselves masters of it, and to usurp their goods.[18]

It is harder to see emphasis being placed on the power of the
monarch than in other countries, perhaps because the fate of Richard
II, a king whose policies were undoubtedly autocratic, served to deter
English writers with absolutist sympathies. Although Lyndwood
seems to have accepted the ideas that power descended to man from
God, and that an anointed king was not a mere layman in status, but a
blend of layman and priest, he did not allow the king to have any
special powers in relation to the Church as a result. Churchmen close
to the court, such as royal officials who preached sermons at the
opening of Parliament, could stress the obligations due to a king, and it
is noteworthy that both Bishop Langley of Durham in 1423 and
Bishop Stafford of Bath and Wells in 1432 took as their text *Deum
timete, Regem honorificate*, clearly one which could be adapted to
royalist propaganda. In 1425 Cardinal Beaufort, preaching on the
same occasion, made it clear that the duty of subjects was to obey,
irrespective of whether or not the ruler's conduct had been good in
relation to them. The Parliament Rolls from the middle of the century
are less illuminating – in some not even the text is recorded, and even
when it is no details are preserved of the sermon – but when, in the last
quarter of it, they again become informative, the old emphasis on the
obligation of subjects to obey the king reappears in the sermons of
1478, 1484, 1485 and 1487. An alternative point of view that royal
power was restricted was, however, put forward in the writings of Sir
John Fortescue. Here one sees empirical observation of English governmental practice being combined with theoretical ideas developed
from St Thomas Aquinas. In the earliest of his important treatises, *De
natura legis naturae*, he employed the term *dominium regale et
politicum* to indicate a form of government containing elements of
both royal and political rule, in which kings could not make laws
without the consent of the Three Estates, nor could subjects do so
without royal authority. In his later work, however, the term seems to
imply simply a limited monarchy. Fortescue combined nationalist
feeling with anti-autocratic views when he denied strongly that the civil
law maxim *Quod principi placuit vigorem legis habuit* had any force in
England. Some of his views were affected by his political bias to the
Lancastrians, as in his assertion that the sick would benefit from the
blessing of Henry VI and his denial that Edward IV had any right to
touch for the king's evil (scrofula). It is interesting that a writer could
combine a belief in restricted royal power politically with an acceptance of thaumaturgic powers which allegedly pertained to the
monarch.

The idea of limitations on the king persisted until the early Tudor
period, and in the legal collections of the early years of the Reformation, those of Fitzherbert, Standford, Brooke and St German, there

was no concept of a royal prerogative outside the law. The king was allowed powers of a national sovereign beyond those of a feudal overlord, but these were given strict legal definition, and were not wide, indefinite rights, such as would be implied by a doctrine of non-resistance. The only strong advocacy of monarchical power at this time is found in the tedious allegory by Edmund Dudley, *The Tree of Commonwealth*, where the author says that the whole authority of justice is given to the prince by God, and that subjects are bound to serve and obey him, or else be punished by him. One should probably regard the book as atypical of its period, and explain its sycophantic attitude by recalling the circumstances in which it was written, when Dudley was hoping that it might secure his pardon for suspected treason from the newly ascended Henry VIII. By contrast Sir Thomas More's reaction to Henry VIII's accession was to welcome it, because he hoped that it would lead to the fresh observance of laws which had lost their force. But there is no doubt that the aspirations of the kings to greater power were increasing, and even before the outbreak of the Lutheran crisis Henry VIII was seeking a title from the pope to reinforce the authority which he exercised with some spiritual sanction, comparable with the titles of 'most Christian King' and 'Catholic King' held by the rulers of France and Spain. A letter from Wolsey in 1516 to the Italian Bishop of Worcester, Silvestro de Gigli, said that the king was annoyed at not yet having received the title 'Defender of the Faith', apparently because the pope was afraid that this would offend the French.

Dudley's sycophancy may reflect the actual power exercised by the Crown under the Yorkists and the early Tudors more accurately than the traditional views of other writers. Edward IV and Henry VII were stronger rulers than the former's Lancastrian predecessors, and under Henry VIII one can see such growing royal power being linked with nationalist sentiment. This is obvious in the Act in Restraint of Appeals of 1533, of which the preamble began by declaring:

Where by dyvers sundrie old autentike histories and cronicles it is manifestly declared and expressed that this Realme of Englond is an Impire, and so hath ben accepted in the worlde, governed by oon supreme heede and King having the Dignitie and Roiall Estate of the Imperiall Crowne of the same . . .

The text continued by affirming that the whole body politic, spiritual and temporal, owed obedience to this head. This concept was at variance with older views of the extent of royal power, for in 1506 Justice Kingsmill had denied the absolute powers of the king in spiritual matters, because these belonged to the supreme head of the

Church. Practice, however, had long outrun theory on the question of jurisdiction in spiritual matters, as in the English refusal to accept canon law doctrines on legitimation, and the Reformation crisis saw the development of such ideas of princely power in all fields.

Elsewhere in the British Isles one can see a similar growth of nationalist sentiment. In Scotland there was not only a negative nationalism, based on hostility to the English, but also a more positive development of feelings of Scottishness. The clearest expression of this was in the ecclesiastical field, where increasing interest was taken in the cults of various national saints. This liturgical and devotional nationalism reached its peak in the Aberdeen Breviary of 1509–10, and was probably encouraged by the Crown, because there appears to have been an increase in the number of pilgrimages to the shrines of these saints by kings from James III to James V. But such a growth of nationalism in conjunction with royal power can only be inferred, because one has no analysis of attitudes to sovereignty in pre-Reformation Scotland. The kings appear to have tried to develop their power against the unruly nobility, but recurrent minorities made this hard to achieve. This was done at the practical levels of resuming alienated royal estates, improving methods of taxation, and clarifying methods of jurisdiction, without theorising on the nature of sovereignty.

In Wales, too, there was a sense of nationalism in the late Middle Ages, fostered particularly by the bards and their patrons, who shaped a Welsh consciousness of nationhood. But here political circumstances meant that national feeling was virtually sterile: the failure of the Glyn Dŵr rising meant that Wales was subjected to the political fluctuations of the English dynastic struggles, and only a sentimental attachment to Henry Tudor, as a descendant of the Welsh royal line, was ever able to harness nationalism to any political institution. Even here, once Henry had secured the English throne, it was not necessary for him to draw on the loyalty of the Welsh, and no attempt was made to exploit these feelings.

If Wales was a country where nationalism existed in the absence of political activity and of a national leader, Italy saw the emergence of a sense of nationality in the presence of many contending political forces. This went back at least to the fourteenth century, where it can be seen both in some of Petrarch's writings and in the political career of Cola di Rienzo. In the late fourteenth century, Salutati and Vergerio contrasted Italy with the barbarian world outside, a theme taken up in the historical writings of Flavio Biondo in the middle of the fifteenth. About the same time, in the Italian League, which followed the Peace of Lodi of 1454, the member states refer to themselves by the term *potentiae Italiae*. The term perhaps stresses the division of Italy rather than its unity, in that it recognises the existence of separate states in the peninsula, but it also acknowledges the way in which they could share common interests. By 1500, there seems to have been an increase of emphasis on Italy as such, a greater consciousness of the country as a whole, in comparison with loyalty to the old independent city state, although the appeal of the latter still competed with the attraction of 'Italy'. The tension between the two loyalties can be seen in Guicciar-dini, who declared that there were three things which he most wished to see in his life; of these one was that the republic should be well organised in Florence and another that Italy should be freed from the barbarians. Probably the invasions of Italy by the French and the Spanish, together with the ravages of German and Swiss mercenaries during the wars, played an important part in developing feelings of *Italianità*, much of which tended to be negative in character. More positive was the glorification of Italian achievement, and this can also be found, notably in Ariosto's *Orlando Furioso*.

In practical matters, however, inter-state rivalries normally counted for far more than the attempt to exclude the barbarians. Julius II may have genuinely wished to drive out the French, and Giles of Viterbo, who was closely associated with him, spoke of Italy in biblical terms as a Promised Land. But in practice the 'Holy League', brought together by papal diplomacy to expel the French from the peninsula, served no other purpose than to increase papal power. The unstable fluctuations in the politics of the various Italian states, the precarious nature of the balance of power between them and, above all, their strong mutual hostility make it clear that nationality played little real part in Italian politics. Machiavelli might write in the final chapter of *The Prince* that there was never a period more appropriate for the establishment of a new form of government in Italy, and he might look for a deliverer of Italy from its oppressors, but this was only a sentimental aspiration, which he himself would reject as ludicrous at another time. In the *Discorsi* his view of Italian unity seems to have been based on the aggrandisement of a prince or a republic, nor does he appear to have envisaged the creation of a state embracing the whole peninsula. His political career, as well as his writings, testify to his local patriotism, directed to Florence first and only secondly to Italy, In many ways Machiavelli is best understood if one thinks of him attempting to combine Florentine and Italian patriotism by regarding the latter as an extension of the former.

Nor within Italy can one see the growth of sovereign states as effective as those elsewhere in Europe. Although some individual rulers were able to build up power which was territorially based and authoritarian, and others might aspire to do the same, the extent of their actual authority was far less than that of the French or English kings. In Naples, Alfonso V was able to dominate the royal council and its various offshoots, because he himself could determine both their composition and their authority, and his successor, Ferrante, was faced with baronial discontent at his autocractic policies, notably in the crisis of the Barons' War in the 1480s. But there were too many disruptive forces at work in the kingdom, foreign intervention, papal intrigue, and the rivalry of the great families, for the kings to achieve much beyond survival.

Of all the Italian states, the one which developed most effectively towards a despotism was Milan under the successive rule of the Visconti and Sforza dukes. The duchy was a true autocracy, in the sense that the dukes were free from legal constraints, and that their *voluntas* could set aside *lex*. The dropping of the term 'citizens' and its replacement by 'subjects' took place early in the Visconti period, and illustrates how ducal authority had supplanted communal traditions. As well as the enhancement of princely dignity, the fifteenth century saw an increase in the machinery of government, which served to make it more effective. This development took place largely under Filippo Maria Visconti and provided the basis for the rule of his Sforza successors. But the rulers of Milan could not rely on any real popular support, and the brief return to republican rule after the death of Filippo Maria Visconti indicates how anti-princely feeling could persist under the surface of ducal rule, even if political circumstances made it impossible for the republic to survive. At the end of the century, when the French invasions overturned the political balance in Italy, the towns which had been brought under Sforza rule could take a detached, fatalistic attitude in awaiting the fortunes of war. Piacenza in 1500 and Vicenza a decade later were willing to surrender to the victor in battle, irrespective of who he was. Despotism therefore was unable to provide more than a temporary form of government, and even the dukes of Milan, the strongest of the Quattrocento Italian princes, were not powerful enough to build up a state secure enough to survive in any effective form against external pressures.

In the smaller cities of northern Italy other princes exercised some measure of authoritarian power, but their inclinations towards tyranny were probably greater than their practical control. Little attempt was made to produce theoretical justification for princely rule, and one may suspect that the reason for this was that none of the princely families could claim the sanction of longstanding power. Even where a family had been dominant in its area for a century or more, it frequently exercised its control in a more or less unofficial capacity, without formally supplanting the older organs of government. For a century and a half before 1500 the Malatesta dominated Rimini and the surrounding towns and villages, with effective control over office-holding, finance and legislation, but they left the existing councils apparently untouched – their concern was with actual power rather than with its trappings. The power of these Romagnol despots was too local for them to resist any major political force – indeed by the late fifteenth century they had been forced into a position of dependence on one of the greater Italian powers, from whom they received *condotte*. In consequence they were politically tied to their paymasters, and were liable to fall with them. A further factor affecting the despotic power of local princes was that in many towns, in both north and central Italy, the papacy had claims of overlordship, and although this might be of little practical value to the popes it limited the power exercised by the dominant family in its particular area.[19]

Even when no outside force could challenge a dominant group in a city, it might still have to tread cautiously in order to retain power. Nowhere is this more obvious than in Florence, where the dominance of the Medici and their allies was not transformed into a formal principate until the sixteenth century. No doubt they were *de facto* the greatest family in the city from the return of Cosimo in 1434 to the exile of the younger Piero in 1494, but it is indicative of their position that their power remained *de facto* and not *de jure*. When Lorenzo succeeded his father Piero as head of the family in 1469, he was still only 20, although he had played a part in public affairs as early as 1465. According to the constitution he was too young to take any effective part in government, and it is significant that the assembly which met on Piero's death made no reference to the precise legal position but spoke in vague terms of preserving the Medici *in reputatione e grandeza*. Equally, on Lorenzo's death, special legislation was passed to allow his son to succeed to his father's offices, because he, too, was under age.

Besides the fact that Medici rule was exercised informally, there was also definite resistance to the growth of despotic power, both in practical measures and in theoretical writings. In the time of Cosimo, between 1453 and 1455, an attempt to institutionalise control over the electoral system failed, and in 1458 a law was passed to restrict the creation and powers of the *balie*, the special councils with full powers, used by the Medici and their supporters to gain political dominance. In the time of Lorenzo, Alamanno Rinuccini denounced him as a tyrant, both in his private diary and in his dialogue *De Libertate*. He praised the Pazzi conspirators, and incidentally extended his praise to those who had a year or two earlier assassinated Galeazzo Maria Sforza. Though his views were extreme compared with those of most Florentines, they represent an anti-authoritarian attitude among the intelligentsia.

Perhaps the most striking evidence of how little the growth of strong monarchial, or quasi-monarchical, power affected Italy can be found in

Venice. Here the power of the patrician oligarchy made the city the most stable of the north Italian states, and its success in doing so even drew approval from the Florentine, Guicciardini, who declared that it had 'the best government of any city not only in our own time but also in the classical world'. However great the formal grandeur enjoyed by the doge, he could be compelled to abdicate, or be refused the right to do so and, though he probably exercised very considerable powers of decision, the complex electoral system prevented the rise of any one family to a position of permanent power.

In Italy then the two streams of emergent nationalism, and the growth of autocratic power did not merge, as they had tended to do elsewhere in Christendom. Guicciardini indeed was hostile to ideas of unity, because he considered that this would involve the oppression of one city-state by another, and felt that this would be too high a price to pay. The reason for this difference between Italy and elsewhere must be seen in the existence of a republican consciousness, which could persist even in the face of increasing despotism, and in the political balance between the leading states of the peninsula, whereby the expansion of one beyond reasonable limits could draw the others together in alliance against it. The fragmentation of political power, the result in part of papal policies in earlier centuries, had left the papacy as an important factor in secular affairs of the peninsula as well as in ecclesiastical matters. From its headship of the Church, however, it could draw strength, for despite its inherent weakness as an elective monarchy and despite the internal disorder in its lands, these could not be occupied and dismembered by a hostile power without this creating a sense of outrage throughout much of Christendom.

If one examines the nature of the authority claimed by these strong territorial princes, whose claims to power over their subjects brooked little in the way of limitations, one can see that it included the claim of authority over the clergy in their lands. While there might be no explicit claim that the Church existed on a national rather than a supra-national basis, the *de facto* implications of princely power went far to establishing the foundations of a territorial Church. The circumstances of the fifteenth century reopened the problems of where the demarcation line should be drawn between the spiritual and the secular power, problems which had apparently been settled in favour of the pope in the thirteenth century. It was a far cry from the papalist zenith of *Unam Sanctam* when on 29 November 1432 a proposition made to the Council of Basel by the vicar of the Archbishop of Mainz, in the name of the imperial electors, claimed that the princes possessed the powers of both swords, the spiritual and the temporal. Nor was this view confined to churchmen whose prince was an ecclesiastic, and who might therefore more willingly accept the princely exercise of spiritual power. The Franciscan, Matthias Döring, looking gloomily on the world and seeing in it ignorance, cowardice and moral corruption, exempted from his strictures Frederick II of Brandenburg, whom he saw as the protector of his lands and of the Church. The provincial of the Augustinian hermits of Saxony said, in 1458, that it was less possible to fulfil his aims with the help of the superiors of his order than with the aid of the secular princes. Jakob of Jüterbogk declared that the hope of reform in the Chruch came largely from the princes, while the Mecklenburger Dessin affirmed that the prince was responsible to God for his subjects. These views were not confined to the clergy, for at the end of the century the humanist, Wimpfeling, declared that the prince must govern in the knowledge that he must render account for his rule at the Day of Judgement. Against this background it is hardly surprising that, during the Council of Constance, Thomas Prischuh of Augsburg declared it was the emperor's duty to call a council to heal the breach in the Church or that Cornelius Zantfliet's account of the aims of the Council of Basel should mention Sigismund's efforts for their fulfilment, as though it were natural that this should be the responsibility of a secular prince, although Prischuh's comparison of the emperor with the Good Shepherd was excessive. Such opinions make the description of the Duke of Cleves, *Dux Cliviae est papa in terris suis*, more comprehensible.

The traditional resistance of the papacy to such claims by the secular power was undermined by the conciliar crisis, because the primary concern of the popes was to resist the threat from within the Church rather than that from outside, and they saw in the prince a potential ally against conciliarist claims. Ambrose of Camaldoli, a strong papalist, urged that Christian princes should be stirred up to resist the efforts of the conciliar party. Even the pope himself could emphasise royal responsibilities, as can be seen in a letter from Nicholas V to Charles VII of France: 'For what deed or what plan can be more agreeable to God, more holy or more honourable, than by one's care and diligence to seek for the unity of the Church, and for the saving of souls who stray, that they may be led back to the fold of Christ? This is work fit for a king.'[20] The last sentence, stressing the king's duty to the Church, should be specially noted, but the whole passage presupposes the effective exercise of authority over the Church and over churchmen within the king's lands.

Kings were by no means reluctant to see themselves as protectors of the Church. When Charles VII decided to send an embassy to the Council of Basel, he informed his ecclesiastical subjects bluntly of their duty to obey his commands, and notified the council of what he had done. The preamble to the Pragmatic Sanction of Bourges affirmed, among other things, the king's duty to protect the Church and churchmen, while the letters patent ordering the registration of Nicholas V's bulls concerning the end of the Basel Schism declared that Christian kings were bound, by their dignity, to protect the peace of the Church. The implications of such claims had indeed been emphasised in 1418, when the king's advocate had declared before the Parlement of Paris that to appeal against the ordinances made by the king for the Church was to commit the crime of *lèse-majesté*. The term 'protector of the Church' as a description of the French King recurs regularly during the fifteenth and early sixteenth centuries. Examples may be seen from 1430, when the Parlement affirmed that he was protector of the Church of France and from 1493, when the abbot of Citeaux described the king as *protecteur et deffenseur de l'eglise*. In 1506 the chronicler, Jean d'Auton, wrote of Louis XII as *conservateur des droitz de l'Eglise, deffenseur de sa franchize*.

Under the king, the concept of a national Church could grow in men's minds even before the break-up of western Christendom in the sixteenth century. The spiritual supremacy of the pope was separated from royal control in practical matters, and men could talk of the Church of France or the Church of England as separate entities within the wider Church. The separateness of such Churches was in some measure proportional to the strength of the monarchs who ruled over them, and the effectiveness of the unity established within their realms. In England, William Lyndwood included in his *Provinciale*, or systematic collection of the constitutions of the province of Canterbury, the writ *circumspecte agatis* of Edward I, which had come to be taken as a guideline on the respective competence of royal and ecclesiastical courts. He also recognised that in England royal courts had by custom cognisance of cases of patronage, despite the normal canon law ruling that these pertained to the courts of the Church.[21] At two points, moreover, his gloss on the constitutions stated that the archbishop had the right to supplement papal decrees, and to add penalties, provided that the substance of Church law was not affected. Such a view of the relationship between canon law generally and the law governing a particular province of the Church goes far towards recognising a national Church independent of Rome.

Various actions taken during the century reflect the existence of national Churches, at least *de facto*. This can be seen notably in the breakdown of unity in the international monastic orders, as secular rulers asserted their authority over the houses in their realms. The breaking of the links between Cluny and its English dependencies, which had taken place during the schism, was not followed by an effective restoration of the older ties. During the crisis between the pope and the Council of Basel, the orders themselves were clearly aware of the problems posed by national rivalries, and their effect on the Church. In 1439 the chapter general of the Cistercians foresaw the danger of schism, which would mean that houses of the German nation would live in a different obedience from those of the French, and anticipated the trouble by naming three abbots of the German nation to have plenary powers to convoke a national chapter of the order.[22] Admittedly this was in a crisis, but even after the end of the Basel Schism the popes acquiesced in the increasing independence of national houses. Nicholas V granted independence to the English house of Burton Lazars of the order of St Lazarus of Jerusalem from its mother house of Boigni in France, and this was confirmed by Sixtus IV. In 1480 the same pope granted to Lewes, the most important Cluniac house in England, a bull which placed it immediately under the jurisdiction of the Holy See, thereby freeing it completely from Cluny, and ten years later Innocent VIII, at Henry VII's request, gave the Archbishop of Canterbury visitatorial powers over all the Cluniac houses in the realm. Here the mother houses which lost control of their subjects were in France, but the French, too, might have obligations to attend general chapters outside their own country, and this could displease the king. In 1476 Louis XI issued an ordinance forbidding regular clergy from leaving the realm under pain of banishment, even for this purpose, because those who had gone and returned had been found to have letters in their possession contrary to the good of the king and the kingdom. Such a veto on access to a general chapter could hardly be surpassed as an indication of the authority of a national king against the international orders.

By the end of the fifteenth century, the territorial Church was accepted as a political fact, although it was still regarded as existing within the broader organisation of the Church Universal. The growing consciousness of national individuality and the increasing authority of the prince made the latter the dominant influence in it. All this was to contribute to the situation in which the links holding the Church together proved weaker than the forces pulling it apart.

PART TWO

The Administrative and Political Problems of the Papacy

CHAPTER 3

The College of Cardinals

Within the governing structure of the Church, the College of Cardinals had been acquiring ever increasing importance since the eleventh century. In the government of the Church it could embarrass the papacy by claiming authority in its own right and by attempting to limit the *plenitudo potestatis*. The position of the cardinals was also ambiguous in the context of tensions between popes and princes, because they remained subjects of their former secular lords as well as being closely bound to the pope and to papal service, and as they were drawn from many parts of Christendom, this could affect relations between the pope and a wide range of secular rulers. During the fifteenth century, too, there was a major change in the normal conduct of men who had been promoted. Before the Great Schism, the usual practice was that when a man became a cardinal he would demit his benefice and go to the Curia: this is well illustrated by the departure to Rome of Archbishop Langham of Canterbury, appointed a cardinal in 1368, and by the reaction of the Londoners to the possibility that their respected bishop, William Courtenay, might be promoted in 1378. Probably when Henry Beaufort was named as a cardinal by Martin V, Henry V's idea was that he should be an English representative at the Curia rather than a papal representative at the English court, and when the bishop was named as a legate *a latere* for England, this provoked a complaint to the king from Archbishop Chichele, and a threat from Henry to impound all Beaufort's worldly goods. Later kings do not generally appear to have taken this attitude, although Archbishop Bainbridge of York, when appointed a cardinal, served as such in Italy rather than in England.[1] There never seems to have been any question of Archbishop Morton of Canterbury leaving England, and it is clear that Henry VII wished to have a cardinal resident in his realm. He repeatedly sought Morton's promotion before it was granted in 1493, and the earliest of his requests, in 1488, makes his wishes plain. Speaking of the desired promotion of Morton, he wrote: 'His Holiness would thus do a thing most gratifying to the king and the realm, seeing that they have been so long without such primary light of ecclesiastical dignity, as much to inconvenience the commonwealth.'[2] One suspects that the king may have regarded having a resident cardinal as a matter of prestige as well as of practical advantage. Nor when Thomas Wolsey was promoted in 1515 does there appear to have been any question of his settling in Rome, as Bainbridge had done.[3]

Requests, both successful and unsuccessful, from the English kings to the papacy were fairly typical of all secular rulers. The Aragonese had indeed attempted to secure appointments early in the fourteenth century, and the Castilians were not slow to follow. As a gesture of diplomatic support, a prince might seek promotion for the subject of an allied ruler, as in the request in 1495 by Ferdinand and Isabella for the promotion of Archbishop Blacader of Glasgow, desired by James IV of Scotland. This appeal was unsuccessful, as had been the request of Matthias of Hungary in 1475 for the promotion of the Bishop of Alsofeher. On this latter occasion Sixtus IV sheltered somewhat speciously behind the statement that he was accustomed to consult with the other cardinals on such matters.

On other occasions, royal requests might have to be reiterated over a long time before the pope complied, as can be seen from the case of Charles of Bourbon, Archbishop of Lyons and a cousin of Louis XI. From 1465, the king had attempted to secure his appointment as legate of Avignon, where he could assist in extending French political influence, and from 1469 attempts were made to have him promoted to the cardinalate. Not until 1476 was the red hat eventually granted, and the intervening years had seen some sharp exchanges between the pope and the king, notably after a promotion in 1473, when Charles's name was not included among the new appointments, while those of the Burgundian, Philibert Hugonet, and the Milanese, Nardini, who had fallen foul of Louis in 1468 for intriguing with his enemies, were. Louis complained that simony had played a part in the promotions, but the pope's reply can have given him little satisfaction. Sixtus's defence of his actions is, however, illuminating about the factors considered when men were being selected for the cardinalate. He justified the appointments on the grounds that the men had been chosen for merit, in their learning or piety, their skill in affairs, or their illustrious birth. He had also considered national interests and the wishes of sovereigns: the Bishop of Novara, Arcimboldi, had been named at the request of the Duke of Milan, and two Spanish bishops because Spain had no cardinals.[4] The tone of this reply must have annoyed the king, as his wishes had very definitely not been met, when those of other princes were.

On other occasions, however, the papacy was more co-operative.

Jean Balue, promoted cardinal in 1464 after earlier papal resistance, was then a close adviser of Louis, and Thomas Basin stated bluntly that he owed his promotion to the king.[5] During the Italian wars the French were able to secure a number of promotions when their political influence was strong. Philippe de Commynes wrote of the agreement between Charles VIII and Alexander VI in 1495 that the pope would nominate two cardinals for the king, the bishops of St Malo and Le Mans. Indeed it seems to have been assumed that the secular power would intervene in such appointments; one notes the remark of Jean Barrillon in his journal in 1517, that at this time the pope created two cardinals, the Archbishop of Bourges at the request of the French king and queen, and the Bishop of Cambrai at the request of the Catholic king. It was almost certainly a request from Ferdinand and Isabella that led to the promotion of the younger Carvajal in 1493, while in 1499 the Milanese ambassador in Rome, writing to Duke Ludovico il Moro, mentioned a request from Spain for the appointment of a cardinal. This seems to have been granted, for in March 1500 the Archbishop of Seville, Diego Hurtado de Mendoza, was one of three men raised to the purple.

Rulers of less than royal dignity, even if vassals of a more powerful prince, could also request promotion of their subjects: the number of Breton cardinals testifies to efforts of the dukes in petitioning Rome, or in one case, when Eugenius IV had failed to comply with a request, the conciliar antipope, Felix V. Sixtus IV promoted the duke's brother-in-law, Pierre de Foix, against the wishes of Louis XI, and Queen Anne of France, who was Duchess of Brittany in her own right, secured the promotion of Robert Guibé in 1505. Even a ruler whose power was *de facto* rather than *de jure* could receive papal favour, as in 1489 when Innocent VIII appointed Giovanni de' Medici as a cardinal at the age of 14, though admittedly reserving him *in petto*, in accordance with the wishes of his father, Lorenzo. This was abnormally young, although clearly youth was no bar to promotion if family or political interests were at stake. In 1461 Pius II appointed to the college the 20-year-old Francesco Gonzaga, whose interests were literary and artistic rather than ecclesiastical, while Sixtus IV had promoted a 17-year-old great nephew, Raffaelo Sansoni-Riario in 1477 and the 23-year-old Bishop of Parma, Giovanni Giacomo Sclafenati, in 1483.[6]

The pressures brought to bear on the papacy by secular rulers played an important part in determining the composition of the college, and certainly in some cases unsuitable men were chosen for political reasons. Pius II makes it clear in his *Commentaries* that Louis XI's withdrawal of the pragmatic sanction, which was much desired by the papacy, was accompanied by the request for the cardinalate for Jean

Jouffroy, Bishop of Arras. The pope's action in acceding to the king's wishes was clearly regarded as a *quid pro quo* for Louis' earlier concession, although it may also have been an attempt to deflect the French king from ambitions in Naples. The appointment in 1500 of Amanieu d'Albret, brother of the King of Navarre, illustrates even more clearly how political considerations could affect promotions, particularly under an unscrupulous pope. His name was first mentioned in connection with a cardinalate in the previous year, when his sister Charlotte married Cesare Borgia, and he also had support from Louis XII, who was seeking the favour of the powerful Albret family for his marriage with Anne of Brittany. In 1501 Albret was able to secure a consistorial provision to the long disputed see of Pamiers, although he was unable to gain possession until 1515.[7] A man of unclerical morals, and a not inappropriate protégé of Alexander VI, he is known to have had at least three children and to have accumulated considerable numbers of benefices.

Not only secular rulers, however, were at fault in the appointment of cardinals. The case of Albret shows the connection of papal family concerns with membership of the college, and it is easy to trace examples of papal nepotism throughout the century. Admittedly extenuating circumstances may be pleaded in favour of such actions: when a new pope was elected he was faced in the Curia and the college with a coalition of vested interests, and his own relations were obvious allies to whom he could look. Packing the college was one way of influencing it to support papal policies. Such nepotism had already existed during the Avignon period, and the succession of Pierre Roger, the nephew of Clement VI, to the papacy as Gregory XI foreshadowed the later series of papal nephews, raised to the cardinalate by their uncles, who eventually became popes themselves: Pietro Barbo, nephew of Eugenius IV and pope as Paul II; Rodrigo Borgia, nephew of Calixtus III and pope as Alexander VI; Francesco Piccolomini, nephew of Pius II and pope as Pius III, and Giuliano della Rovere, nephew of Sixtus IV and pope as Julius II. Furthermore this is far from exhausting the list of papal promotions of near kindred, as can be seen from the table of such appointments (see Table 1). Such creations established power blocs within the College, which were all the more serious because many of the nephews obtained influential positions within the Curia, which gave them power on their own account after the death of the uncle to whom they owed their position. Rodrigo Borgia's tenure of the post of vice-chancellor of the Church and Giuliano della Rovere's of that of grand penitentiary made them men to whom others could look for support, and they were the leaders of the rival factions in the conclaves of 1484 and 1492.[8] Nepotism in the college was merely the highest level of the abuse, for other relatives of

the popes received favours in other spheres of ecclesiastical administration, both spiritual and temporal. When a pope died, there tended
to be a reaction against his family, and frequently the absence of any
candidate who could command a two-thirds majority led to the choice
of some compromise figure, who would then seek to advance his own
relations, perhaps in alliance with one of the major figures from an
earlier pontificate.

The figures of promotions illustrate the growth of nepotism within
the college, which became more serious after the succession of Sixtus
IV in 1471. The contrast is stressed by Jedin, who suggested that while
the relatives of Paul II were in fact all worthy men, Sixtus IV's promotions included 'six nephews, and what nephews!'[9] However, not all
cardinals were unsuitable choices, even after 1471, as is shown by such
men as the incorruptible Portuguese, Costa, in 1476; the learned
canonist, Sangiorgio, in 1493, and the austere reforming Observant
Franciscan Archbishop of Toledo and patron of learning, Francesco
Ximenes de Cisneros, in 1507. But though these bear comparison with
those men who had added some lustre to the learning and piety of the
college earlier,[10] their numbers became fewer at the time when the
college itself was increasing in size. The change in the character of the
cardinalate is made plain by Lorenzo de' Medici's advice to his son to
steer a moderate course between the 'Scylla of sanctimoniousness and
the Charybdis of profanity'. Such a course involved the possession of a
good stable, valuable antiques and handsome books. The cardinals, as
princes of the Church, were expected to resemble other princes. The
last creation of cardinals before the outbreak of the Reformation,
while unique in the number of men appointed, an unprecedented
thirty-one, may be taken to represent the kinds of men selected and the
mixture of motives lying behind the appointments throughout the
period. Some would have been worthy holders of the dignity at any
time: the future pope, Adrian of Utrecht; the learned generals of the
Dominican and Augustinian friars, Cajetan and Giles of Viterbo, and
the humble general of the Franciscan Observants, Cristoforo Numai.
Others owed their elevation to political considerations; the Portuguese Infant, Alfonso; the Spaniard, Raymond de Vich, and Louis
de Bourbon, brother of the French Constable. Some were close adherents and servants of the reigning papal family – in this case the Medici –
such as Francesco Armellini and Silvio Passerini, or kindred to it,
Giovanni Salviati and Niccolò Ridolfi. Leo X may have been wise in
nominating to the purple various members of noble Roman families, in
an attempt to avoid bias and party feeling in his selection, but neither
the Orsini nor the Colonna representative was a suitable candidate for
the cardinalate, being totally secular in outlook.[11]

A further characteristic of the fifteenth-century cardinalate was its

Table I   *Papal relatives promoted cardinal, 1417–1517*

Pope	Cardinal	Relationship	Date	Notes
Martìn V	Prospero Colonna	nephew	1426	died 1463
Eugenius IV	Francesco Condulmiere	nephew	1431	died 1453
	Pietro Barbo	nephew	1440	pope (Paul II) 1464
Nicholas V	Filippo Calandrini	half-brother	1448	died 1476
Calixtus III	Juan-Luis Mila	nephew	1456	died 1510
	Rodrigo Borgia	nephew	1456	pope (Alexander VI) 1492
Pius II	Francesco Piccolomini	nephew	1460	pope (Pius III) 1503
	Niccolo Fortiguerra	uncertain	1460	died 1473 (His kinship with Pius noted in *199* III, 295)
Paul II	Marco Barbo[1]	cousin	1464	died 1491
	Giovanni Battista Zeno	nephew	1468	died 1501
	Giovanni Michiel	nephew	1468	died 1503
Sixtus IV	Pietro Riario	nephew	1471	died 1474
	Giuliano della Rovere	nephew	1471	pope (Julius II) 1503
	Cristoforo della Rovere[2]	nephew (?)	1477	died 1478
	Girolamo Basso della Rovere	nephew	1477	died 1507
	Raffaelle Riario Sansoni	great-nephew	1477	died 1521
	Domenico della Rovere[2]	nephew (?)	1478	died 1501
Innocent VIII	Lorenzo Cibò	nephew	1489	died 1503
	Pantaleone Cibò[3]	nephew	—	see note 3
	Niccolo Cibò[3]	brother	—	see note 3
Alexander VI	Juan Borgia	nephew	1492	died 1503
	Cesare Borgia	son	1493	released from clerical status and cardinalate 1498 – died 1507
	Juan Borgia	great-nephew	1496	died 1500
	Pedro Luis Borgia	great-nephew	1500	died 1511

	Francesco Borgia	cousin	1500	died 1511
	Francesco Loriz	great-nephew	1503	died 1506
Julius II	Clemente della Rovere	cousin	1503	died 1504
	Galeotto Franciotto della Rovere	nephew	1503	died 1507
	Leonardo della Rovere	cousin	1505	died 1520
	Sisto Gara della Rovere	nephew	1507	died 1517
Leo X	Giulio de' Medici	cousin	1513	pope (Clement VII) 1523
	Innocenzo Cibò	nephew	1513	died 1550
	Luigi de' Rossi	nephew	1517	died 1519
	Giovanni Salviati	nephew	1517	died 1553
	Niccolo Ridolfi	cousin	1517	died 1550

1 Generally regarded as a nephew of the pope, but see 24, 1.
2 Indicated as nephews in the genealogy in 92, III, 100. Mallett, 180, 302, thinks that they were probably cousins.
3 Not mentioned in 251, but noted in 253, 1210. Moroni, 254, XIII, 126–7, suggests that there were some doubts about the promotion of Niccolo, whom his brother had provided to the archbishopric of Arles, but says that Pantaleone was named as a cardinal at the same consistory as the other cardinals appointed in 1489. I am indebted to Monsignor Charles Burns for this last reference.

The dates of promotion and death have been taken from 251, I–III. The relationships are as indicated in 199, 92, 180, and (for relatives of Paul II) 24.

increasing domination by Italians. No pope until Calixtus III created an absolute majority of Italians, although normally these were the largest single national group represented, and indeed Nicholas V's six appointments of French cardinals exceeded his promotion of Italians, of whom he chose only four. But from Pius II onwards, Italians were an absolute majority among appointments by all popes until the Reformation, with the exception of Alexander VI, under whom Spaniards were more numerous.[12] This increase in the proportion of Italians may well indicate the increasingly dominant part which affairs of the peninsula were playing in the political considerations of the papacy. This is supported by the emergence of representatives of Italian princely families in the college in the last quarter of the fifteenth century. It is also noteworthy that, after Italy, the countries most represented in the college were France and Spain, the two lands outside the peninsula most deeply involved in its political affairs.[13]

This Italian domination becomes even more marked among those cardinals who were active at the Curia and participated in papal

elections. After the death of Nicholas V, fifteen of the twenty existing
cardinals were present at the conclave, of whom seven were Italian. By
contrast all the absentees were non-Italian.[14] In 1471 eighteen cardinals took part in the conclave, of whom fifteen were Italian; the
remaining three were the Greek, Bessarion, who had long resided in
Italy, the Spaniard, Borgia and the Frenchman, d'Estouteville, all
more closely connected with the Curia than with their countries of
origin. In 1484, only four non-Italians were present in a conclave of
twenty-five. It is hardly surprising, when one considers these figures,
that the whole outlook of the papacy became increasingly centred on
Italian affairs.

During the century, the distinction between curial and non-curial
cardinals became more important, and as far as the latter were concerned a problem about their status was resolved by Eugenius IV in a
dispute between the cardinal Archbishop of York, John Kemp, and
Archbishop Chichele of Canterbury. The latter attempted to curb the
claim to precedence made by the cardinal, on the grounds that a
cardinal separated from the pope was an anomaly, and that one who
took part in royal assemblies did so as a benefice holder within the
kingdom, and not in any right of his cardinalate. During the dispute,
the pope had to define the character of the cardinalate, and declared
that it was a jurisdictional office, unrelated to the clerical *ordo* of the
holder. The powers of the cardinals were concerned with the whole
Church, but those of an archbishop were limited to one church only,
and in consequence a cardinal, even if not ordained, had higher rank
than a bishop and precedence over him. No distinction between curial
and non-curial cardinals was recognised. But though in law all cardinals were ranked equally, in practice many of them remained in their
own lands and were not particularly involved with the papacy and its
immediate concerns. For them, the cardinalate was an honour rather
than a position of influence.

When Eugenius IV defined the status of the cardinals in this dispute,
he had to tread very delicately. The college had played a crucial part at
the Council of Constance in securing the depositions of the schismatic
popes, and this had given additional force to claims which had been
developing in the fourteenth century that the cardinals could limit
papal power. This oligarchic concept of the cardinalate does not
appear to have originated before 1350, and the canonists before
Joannes Andreae (d. 1348) did not go further than accepting the idea
that the pope, although he is *legibus solutus*, should consult his bre-
thren on important matters. Papal sovereignty should be exercised
with *decentia* but the *consilium* of the cardinals was not the same as
consensus. The claims of the cardinals were most evident in the revolt
against Urban VI which started the Great Schism, but they can also be

seen in the pacts by which participants in a papal election attempted to bind the future pontiff, the earliest of which dated from 1352. Such claims were as serious a threat to papal authority as those of the conciliarists, and the popes contested them as fiercely. Indeed, the threat was perhaps more serious, and certainly more persistent, because there were always cardinals, whereas councils were only intermittent. On the other hand, the pope had a weapon against the college in the creation of new cardinals from his own adherents, and also if he declined to fulfil the pledges made before the election, little could be done to enforce them.[15] After the schism it was not until the pontificate of Julius II that some of the cardinals were willing to revolt and call a council to act against him. Even then it is unlikely that they would have done so if it had not been for the political pressures on the pope, which gave them an ally in Louis XII of France.

The pope's ability to create cardinals and thereby build up a faction within the college may well have been a major reason for various attempts which were made to limit the numbers so appointed. Furthermore, the existing cardinals had a vested interest in keeping numbers low, because their rights (when resident) to certain parts of the papal revenues meant that the fewer there were of them, the greater the share for each. The concordats between the papacy and various secular powers at the end of the Council of Constance contain a number of provisions relating to the college, some of which reveal the interests of the cardinals and others the desires of the more radical reformers or of the secular rulers. In three of the four concordats it was laid down that the number of cardinals was not normally to exceed twenty-four, though in special circumstances two more might be appointed, and it was also stipulated that they should be men of learning in theology or law. An exception was made here, obviously to gratify kings and princes, that for a few of especially noble birth only 'reasonable literacy' would be required. They were not to be brothers or nephews of any existing cardinal, nor should there be more than one from each of the mendicant orders. New cardinals were to be elected with the collegiate assent of those already appointed. Less precisely, the concordats declared that the dignity should be distributed through the various parts of Christendom, so that countries would be held in equal honour in ecclesiastical dignity. Attempts were also made to limit the holding of monasteries *in commendam* by prelates, and it was specifically noted that such limitations applied to the cardinals.

These concessions were not observed. Under Martin V the number of cardinals rose to twenty-nine, though by his death it had fallen again to only nineteen. Nor did the pope seek their views before issuing bulls, despite the employment by the chancery of the formula *de fratrum nostrum consilio*. This neglect of their claims probably explains the

attempt to extract an election capitulation in 1431, when the participants tried *inter alia* to enforce the obligations laid down at Constance.
At Basel, too, the cardinalate was discussed in 1433, when the council
stated that the cardinals should represent various parts of the world,
and in 1436 when it reiterated the stipulations of the concordats
limiting membership of the college to twenty-four, laid down the
standards of learning (including the relaxation for the relations of the
powerful), and excluded the nephews of living cardinals and of the
pope. The emphasis on representation was made more explicit by a
declaration that no nation should have more than a third of the
membership of the college. The majority of the college should assent
to new promotions, and a form was laid down for cautioning the pope if
he failed to observe the decree, with an eventual appeal to a council.
Many of these ideas persisted long after the failure of the council, as
can be seen from the proposed reform bull of Pius II, in which one
recognises the old stipulations for educational attainment, for the
limitation of numbers (though this is now couched in more general
terms) and division among the nations, and for consultation with and
consent of the existing cardinals.

If these measures had been implemented, they would have given the
cardinals considerable powers to limit the pope, but this was not done.
The proposals in Pius II's pontificate show little more than the persistence of ideas, because the collapse of the conciliar movement as an
effective political force had strengthened the authority of the papal
monarchy. The cardinals themselves were now the only group with the
opportunuty of challenging the growth of papal absolutism. This they
did by reviving the practice of election capitulations, in which some of
the reform proposals reappear. In the end the papacy could disregard
these pacts, basing its action on the claim that its *plenitudo potestatis*
could not be abridged by human action. But even in this one can see
that the events of the Great Schism had affected canonist opinion. In
formal terms the pacts were rejected on the ground of two decrees of
the thirteenth and fourteenth centuries which had dealt with the claims
of the cardinalate, Gregory X's *Ubi periculum* and Clement V's *Ne
Romani*.[16] At the time of the Council of Constance, however, Benedict
XIII was condemned as *perjurus* for failing to observe the oath which
he had taken before his election, this condemnation having the support
of distinguished theologians and canonists. Clearly the special conditions existing at the time had modified traditional views, and they may
well have affected the discussions of the cardinalate by fifteenth-
century writers. For example, Roselli, whose sympathies were strongly
papalist, was prepared to admit that while the cardinals derived their
power of election from the preceding pope, at other times they had
their power from the universal church. He examines, but rejects, the

claim that the other apostles had power equal to that of Peter, asserting that their equality lay only in their priestly order, and did not include jurisdictional power. The supreme duty of the cardinals, the election of a pope, and the rights of the college during a vacancy are also discussed at length. Roselli held that a pope might, *de absoluta potestate*, deprive the cardinals of their sole right of election, but expressed doubts as to whether a council could do this, except when a schism had arisen through the action of the college. In this statement one may see him casting a backward glance at the method of election chosen at Constance. A more crucial problem was whether the cardinals had a right to revolt against the pope. Roselli admitted they had in a case of heresy, and under certain circumstances when the papal see was being contested by rivals, though clearly he would prefer such cases to be judged by a general council. But he was also willing to accept that if the pope were insane or incapable, the cardinals should provide him with a co-adjutor.

Nor was Roselli the only pro-papal canonist writer who had doubts as to whether or not the cardinalate had a divine origin. Torquemada accepted that it had, but Andrea de Barbatia, when consulted by Paul II, declared that its origin was to be found in positive human law.[17] Barbatia also took a strong line on pacts made during elections, declaring that for a pope to adhere to the oath taken before election would be tantamount to a breach of trust and desertion of duty. Even in France, where hostility to papal claims was probably greatest, there is evidence, in an anonymous work of the first half of the fifteenth century, that there was some support for the pope's denial of the cardinals' claim to set limits to papal power. Naturally the apologists for the cardinals, who revolted against Julius II in the early sixteenth century, were at pains to justify their action in summoning a council against the will of the pope, but it is noteworthy that even these allowed the college only limited powers. Filippo Decio admitted that normally the pope possessed the right of summons, and that only in particular circumstances could the cardinals act as they had done.[18] In general then, the college had only limited support in its attempts to restrain papal power, and in the last resort, although its aims were oligarchic rather than popular, it had to look to a general council as the only practicable means of setting limits to the power of the pope.

The aims of the college, as set forth in the election capitulations, suggest that it was self-centred rather than disinterested. The main series of pacts began with the 1458 conclave,[19] and was probably provoked by the nepotism of the deceased pope. The promise to pursue the war against the Turks, the only oath taken by Calixtus III in 1455, was renewed, but many new stipulations were added. The future pope promised to reform the Curia and to consult the cardinals, both in making appointments there and in conferring major benefices outside it. The decree of the Council of Constance limiting the number of cardinals was to be observed, and existing cardinals were to assent to new nominations, as well as to give approval before grants of nomination to princes, both secular and ecclesiastical. At the same time the rights of the cardinals to their benefices and commendams were to be upheld, and any cardinal whose annual income was under 4,000 florins was to receive 100 florins a month from the papal treasury. Reform might seem desirable to the college, provided only that its own rights were not infringed. Six years later, after the death of Pius II, the conclave subscribed a very similar pact. Not more than one of the college should be a relative of the pope, and papal kinsmen should be excluded from control of the more important fortresses in the Patrimony and from the post of commander-in-chief of the papal army. But after Paul II was elected, he not only ignored that pact but even brought pressure to bear on the cardinals to accept a revised form of the document, containing his own programme of government. After this tension persisted for a long time between Paul and the cardinals, although the pope did concede a number of privileges to them, and granted pensions to the less wealthy members of the college.

In 1471 there was a drastic recasting of the chapters of the election capitulation, and the form which was then adopted was the basis of all subsequent pacts until the sixteenth century. A division was established between the *capitula privata*, concerned with the privileges of the college, and the *capitula publica*, dealing with the reform of the Church. It reflects the basic interests of the cardinals that they showed far more interest in the former, having them confirmed by notarial instrument, than they did in the latter, the observance of which would have been far more beneficial for the Church. The topics covered in the capitulation were not new: there was a promise to wage war on the Turks, and a pledge to devote the revenue from the newly discovered alum mines to this end. The Curia was to be reformed, with the counsel of the majority of the cardinals, and it was not to be transferred from place to place within Italy without the consent of the majority. If the pope wished to take it outside Italy, all the cardinals would have to agree. For the creation of new cardinals, the consent of two-thirds of the college was required and the provisions on age and intellectual requirements laid down in the concordats of Constance (including the concession to near relations of kings) were reasserted. Only one papal relative could be appointed, but no such restriction was now mentioned on the relatives of cardinals, a significant shift of emphasis from the reforming ideals of Constance to the self-interest of the college. Throughout the articles, stress is laid on the need to secure the consent of the cardinals or at least of a majority of them. Their interests and those of their friends and servants were to be maintained, and they were to have freedom to advise the pope. The most striking demonstration of how the cardinals protected their own interests occurs in clause 6, whereby the pope was bound to make no provision of benefices taxed at the Curia, except in consistory with the consent of the majority of the college; one exception was made to the rule, that it was not to apply to benefices which he might confer on the cardinals themselves. Another important clause is number 3, in which the participants promised to call a general council within three years to work for the defence of the faith against the infidel and for the reform of the Church. Such a stipulation suggests that the cardinals may have been hoping to use the conciliar weapon as a means of asserting themselves against the danger of papal absolutism.

On the death of Sixtus IV, who had not observed his promises, the conclave of 1484 attempted to set even severer limits to the pope's freedom of action, and the pact agreed went even further in its display of blatant self-interest by the cardinals. The first article renewed the demand of 1458 for a monthly pension of 100 florins to each cardinal whose annual income did not attain to 4,000 florins, and members of the college were to hold all their benefices, even if these were incompatible. Furthermore, they were to be exempt from the payment of certain taxes, and any debts to the Camera for them were to be annulled. If, however, they were creditors of the previous pope or the Camera, they were to receive payment for the debt. If a secular prince prevented a cardinal from drawing the fruits of his benefices, because he was displeased at his vote in an election – a measure, incidentally, of the pressures to which cardinals might be subjected – the pope was to compensate him from Church revenues. Help was also pledged to those cardinals who had failed to get possession of goods lawfully assigned to them. The cardinals were concerned not only with revenues, but also with the exercise of temporal power, because another article provided that each cardinal should have land or a castle near Rome, with full jurisdictional powers over it. There were various stipulations for safeguarding the rights of the cardinals to give private counsel to the pope and for protecting them against the threat of any arbitrary proceedings. Privileges granted by previous popes were to be confirmed, as was the holding of the offices of chamberlain, vice-chancellor and grand penitentiary, all of whom were to be maintained in their previous privileges. Cardinals were not to be sent on embassies unless they consented to go, presumably to prevent a pope dispatching them from the centre of power under cover of honourable employment.

All these clauses were contained in the first half of the pact, and it was only the second part which contained pledges concerned with the interests of the Church as well as with collegiate privileges. The first of these dealt with the need for a crusade against the Turks and the second with measures for curial reform; the demand in the 1471 capitulation that the Curia should not be transferred from place to place within Italy without the consent of two-thirds of the college was reiterated.[20] The demand, for the calling of a general council to meet the Turkish threat and to work for Church reform was also taken over from the *capitula* of 1471 without, however, any time being set for its meeting.[21] As in 1471, the general tone of the pact was that the pope should be bound by the consent of the cardinals in all important actions, including the appointment of new members of the college. The attempt to limit the number of cardinals to twenty-four was renewed and the old demands for the maintenance of certain academic standards and for the limitation to one of the number of papal relatives to be promoted were repeated. No new appointments were to be made until existing numbers had been reduced.

These provisions made the aims of the cardinals clear, less the reform of the Church than the maintenance of their own privileges, and there was no change as the fifteenth century gave way to the sixteenth. Indeed, the authoritarian conduct of Alexander VI, who defied the college in the large number of his promotions, merely provoked the cardinals to new attempts at curbing his successors. In 1503, after Alexander's death, the cardinals considered the 1484 capitulation, and were given a day to amend it before they finally settled their terms. It was probably the same document which they subscribed again a few weeks later after the death of the newly elected Pius III.[22] Julius II, however, found a canonist in Cardinal Sangiorgio who assured him that he was not bound by the electoral pact. In 1513 another unsuccessful attempt was made to impose a capitulation, with similar terms to those in earlier pacts, although the cardinals now demanded a higher minimum income, 6,000 florins annually instead of 4,000, and higher supplementary payments, 200 florins a month instead of 100, for those whose annual income did not reach the stipulated figure.

These failures to limit papal power were due partly to disinclination and partly to lack of means. In the last resort, many cardinals may not have been particularly enthusiastic about setting bounds to the pope's authority, because they themselves may have been aspiring to the tiara at a future election and have been reluctant to diminish the power which they might then wield. Also, once a pope had been elected, there was no method of controlling him, and the failure of the rebel cardinals in their struggle with Julius II merely underlined the ultimate weakness of the college as a whole. The council which they summoned could exist only by courtesy of the secular powers whose political opposition to the pope made them temporary allies. This could hardly lead to the cardinals being a strong force for ecclesiastical reform, and they themselves had too many interests in the preservation of existing conditions for reform to have had much appeal to them. Indeed their fear of it was remarked on in a letter of the Emperor Maximilian in 1510.

Yet although in the last resort the pope could always remain master, it would be wrong to underestimate the influence which the college could and did exercise, influence, moreover, which the secular princes of Christendom recognised. It might be unable to turn the papacy into a limited monarchy, but it still gave counsel to its master. The major offices in the central administration of the Church were filled by cardinals, often those related to the pope who appointed them. They were entrusted with duties which might take them away from Rome, such as the preaching of an indulgence or the attempted mediation of peace between warring princes. Regularly too, major judicial cases were referred to cardinals for decision. Martin V appointed two of them to investigate charges of irregularity against John Cameron, Bishop of Glasgow, and when one was absent from the Curia another was named to replace him, while a single cardinal heard the petition of the Abbot of Arbroath for exemption from the jurisdiction of the bishop of St Andrews.[23] Their duties might extend into less likely fields, as in time of war when they might be responsible for the leadership of papal armies or navies. Giuliano della Rovere, the future Julius II, showed his military skill during the pontificate of his uncle, Sixtus IV, in a campaign in 1474 against Spoleto and in the upper Tiber valley, while two years before, Cardinal Carafa was admiral of the Christian fleet which captured Smyrna during the war against the Turks.[24]

These were powers which cardinals might hold formally in virtue of their office, but probably their greatest influence was less formal, and lay in their constant attendance on the pope and regular access to him in the daily routine of the Curia and in their participation in consistories. Such contact could count for more than any theoretical claims. No pope, however autocratic, could dispense entirely with all the powerful men to whom, at first, he owed his election, or who, later, owed their offices to him. The existence of factions in the college, or changing political circumstances, could mean that a pope might be inconsistent in those to whom he turned for counsel, and this in turn explains why individual cardinals would establish connections with other powers as a way of safeguarding their private interests. Even the relatives of the pope had to look forward to the situation which would arise at the end of the pontificate, when the other cardinals might well turn against them. Such reasons made them willing to render services to a secular prince, who might offer rewards for the present and

security for the future. Alternatively, they might exploit papal favour
to advance the interests of their lay relatives, perhaps in the hope that
they could afford protection later if need arose.[25]

At one particular time the college exercised additional power,
namely during a papal vacancy, when it also possessed the political
influence and responsibilities normally pertaining to the pope in person. On 1 September 1503, a fortnight after the death of Alexander
VI, the orators of the French king petitioned the college to deliver to
them the castle of Viterbo where the French army was then encamped.
Admittedly such periods when the cardinals could immediately affect
political decisions were intermittent in occurrence and brief in duration, but clearly secular princes might appreciate the advantages of
having a friendly cardinal at these times. Even more, the primary duty
of the college, that of electing the pope, had political implications as
the papacy became increasingly involved in the power struggles of the
Italian wars. If princes were to obtain influence in Rome in times of
crisis, it was necessary for them to establish their connections in
periods of normality.

Even in routine ecclesiastical administration the secular power
could benefit from a friend at the Curia, and during the last years of the
fifteenth century and the early years of the sixteenth, there emerged
the office of cardinal protector of individual nations, a position which
reflects the practical support which its holder could give to the interests
of the country which he served. It did not come into existence without
opposition, and in the first half of the fifteenth century both Martin V
and the Council of Basel attempted to safeguard the impartiality of the
college from national bias, and later Pius II also opposed any kind of
territorial protectorship.[26] Such resistance to the practice was ineffective and eventually the position became institutionalised. An informal
French protectorship existed in the person of Cardinal Balue as early
as 1485, though the appearance of the formal title with reference to a
particular state did not come until Cardinal Francesco Piccolomini was
designated as Protector of England in 1492, a post which he held until
his elevation to the Papacy shortly before his death in 1503. He is
known to have had connections with England before this date, and also
had associations with Germany, so his nomination probably reflects
the political alignments of Tudor and Habsburg against France at this
time. By 1499 he was also Cardinal Protector of Germany, and may
have been so as early as 1493. The critical period in the development of
the office was the pontificate of Julius II, when one finds references in
papal documents to cardinals as national protectors. The number of
countries, and even lesser states, which had protectors also increased
at this time.[27] The formalisation of the post made it possible for a
cardinal protector who was absent from the Curia to depute one of his

fellows to undertake any business which might arise concerning the country for which he was responsible.

Obviously by this date the papacy was modifying its attitude to the office, although there was still some opposition to it. The reform proposals of 1497 were still concerned with preserving the impartiality of the cardinalate, although it seems to have been accepted that the pope could permit an individual cardinal to serve a secular ruler *tanquam consiliarius, vel secretarius, aut protector, vel procurator*. Even as late as the Fifth Lateran Council, when the protectorship was a well established institution, certain reform proposals follow closely on those put forward at Basel, though modifications in the text may indicate that there was now some acquiescence in the idea of the office. Within the following decade, however, there must have been a drastic change of opinion, for an anonymous reform draft, from Adrian VI's pontificate, suggested that the office of protector should be incorporated into the organisation of the Church, and recognised its duties and the need to fulfil them by proposing the appointment of a vice-protector. These developments reflect the relationship between the secular rulers and the central organisation of the Church, because it involved the recognition of the reality of the nation as a factor within Christendom, while the role which the cardinals played in it shows how they were involved in the relations between the papacy and the secular princes.

The cardinal protector, however, was not usually a national of the country which he served – Piccolomini's career illustrates this. One can see that various European princes, even before the office was in any way formalised, were active in securing the cardinals' goodwill, which could have considerable political value. When major diplomatic issues were at stake there were often disagreements between different cardinals, as in the crisis of the Barons' War in Naples, when Balue was principal advocate of the Angevin party and Rodrigo Borgia of the Aragonese. Nor, as indeed at earlier dates, was it only in great matters of state that princes might seek for support, as can be seen from a register of the Neapolitan chancery in the middle of the fifteenth century. Here one can see a record of systematic lobbying of the cardinals to seek support for requests which had been made to the pope, and it is clear that the king felt that they possessed genuine influence, which might be exerted on his behalf.[28]

Similar communications with the college can be found from other rulers. In 1478, when Louis XI was urging Sixtus IV to abandon his hostility towards Lorenzo de' Medici, he wrote not only to the pope, but also to the college collectively, asking the cardinals to persuade Sixtus to moderate his policy. From early in the reign of his successor there are considerable numbers of letters preserved, mostly to the college collectively, and many seeking support in connection with provisions to benefices. In the 1490s, too, there were royal requests to the cardinals for intervention in similar cases. In 1506, James IV of Scotland sought the assistance of the cardinal of St Mark for the promotion of his treasurer to the see of Dunkeld when it should fall vacant. Such ties as developed between individual cardinals and the secular rulers of Europe, and the factions which developed in the college during the political struggles of the late fifteenth and early sixteenth centuries, served to make the position of the cardinals difficult, and at times there were some who pursued their own policies independent of the pope. In 1502 a group of cardinals, headed by Giuliano della Rovere and Raffaello Riario, came to Louis XII at Milan and offered to give him their support in Rome. Such support could well be transitory, and when, a few years later, Rovere as pope quarrelled with the French king, another group of cardinals sought his alliance in an attempt to call a council against their master.

Cardinals who served at the Curia rather than in their native lands might find themselves in a position of ambiguity in relation to their temporal lords. The most difficult situation which might arise was when one was sent as a papal legate to his country of origin, particularly if at the time of the mission relations between the pope and the prince were in any way strained. This was the case in 1451, when Cardinal d'Estouteville went to France, at a time when the pope was believed to be favourable to the Duke of Burgundy. The cardinal made firm assertions of his loyalty to the king,[29] but the latter remained suspicious, sought further information from the legate before the cardinal was allowed to enter the realm, and forbade him to employ the title until the king assented to him doing so. The result of this was that he again protested his loyalty to France over the previous twenty years. Admittedly the letter was concerned with presenting its author in a way acceptable to the king, but the latter's acceptance of the assurances would suggest that there was some element of truth in it. The episode illustrates how a member of the college might be torn between his two masters, although the fact that the mission was entrusted to a French cardinal does suggest that the pope in some way regarded him as a natural intermediary between himself and the king.

Nor was it only to France, nor in situations of particular political difficulty, that a native born cardinal might be sent as legate. Nicholas of Cusa, created a cardinal in 1448, was sent to Germany to preach the jubilee indulgence of 1450, and was given authority to hold provincial councils to carry out reform. In one sense, however, the nationality of such men was irrelevant, for both d'Estouteville and Cusa were primarily curial cardinals, who had been sent on particular missions, and their position was in no essential way different from that of any other high ranking envoy, sent out to act on behalf of the pope. Such men were the elder Carvajal, who served with high distinction on no fewer than twenty-two legations, and Bessarion, who was not only legate in Germany in 1460–1 but was also appointed to the same rank to preach the crusade in Venice in 1463. By the start of the sixteenth century, however, one can see the emergence of the resident cardinal legate *a latere*, often a man of major importance in political affairs as well as in the Church. Georges of Amboise was the closest adviser of Louis XII of France, obtained the red hat from Alexander VI at the time of the annulment of the king's first marriage in 1498, and was created legate in 1501, the title being renewed in the following year. Pius III renewed the legatine powers, and Julius II increased their territorial scope to include Avignon and Brittany. From 1504 until his death in 1510, despite Gallican distrust, his authority was unchallenged in the French Church. His power rested on the twin pillars of royal support and papal authorisation, and illustrates how the Church could be subordinated to its two masters if they were prepared to co-operate. In such cases, it is likely that the dominant influence was that of the temporal ruler, who was closer to his subjects than was the distant pope.

In 1510 Maximilian attempted to secure a similar situation in Germany, by proposing the appointment of a permanent legate, who should be a native German, but at this stage nothing more was done. In 1514 his representative, Cardinal Lang, attempted to secure for himself a permanent legateship in Germany, with the emperor's support, but Leo X was able to avoid making such a grant, and urged the other cardinals to reject even a compromise solution which he had put forward for diplomatic reasons. But in 1518 Lang was able to block the entry to Germany of another cardinal legate, Cajetan, who had been sent to preach the crusade, until he had been granted equivalent status. His powers were not comparable to those of Amboise, but the wish of the emperor that he should be granted them indicates how a secular ruler could hope to extend his influence over the Church. A similar situation was that of Wolsey in England. His creation as a cardinal in 1515 was prompted largely by the pope's desire to obtain the goodwill of Henry VIII, and in 1518 he, like Lang, was able to exclude a foreign cardinal, Campeggio, from exercising his legatine powers, which he had to share.

Clearly by the early sixteenth century, the position of the cardinals was deeply affected by the growth in the power of the secular ruler, and many of them had come to terms with this by open acknowledgment of their loyalty to him. As the papacy became increasingly important in political struggles, especially after the outbreak of the Italian wars, the strains on the individual's loyalty increased, the more so as the popes

did not follow any consistent alliance with a particular power. As each
alliance might be followed by the nomination to the college of some
leading ecclesiastical subject of the pope's latest ally, it is easy to see
how rival factions could emerge within it, politically aligned to the rival
powers of Europe. For example, the creation of three French cardinals, including a nephew of Georges d'Amboise, in 1507 was one of
the concessions which Julius II had to make in return for assistance in
his Bolognese campaign of the previous year. Indeed, it is surprising
that these alignments in the college were not more serious than they
actually were. Possibly the very absence of many cardinals from Rome
meant that their secular loyalty was seldom forced into open collision
with their obedience to the pope, while the latter had to accept the
existence of their loyalty to the prince. A cardinal who became
involved in full-scale revolt might be deprived of his title, as was the
fate of those who took part in the second Council of Pisa, though these
were subsequently restored, and others again might be arrested if their
opposition to papal policy was too extreme.[30] The execution of Cardinal Petrucci by Leo X in 1517, and the arrest of two others, Sauli and
Riario, who had been involved in a conspiracy against the pope's life,
falls into a different category, because it was prompted by the need to
punish a criminal rather than by political considerations.

The willingness of the cardinals to support their temporal lords in a
conflict with the pope, clearly reveals the political character of the
Renaissance papacy. The spiritual headship was impugned only by
assertions of conciliar authority, and no secular ruler had as yet laid
claim to total authority over the Church in his lands. Men such as
Amboise or Wolsey could intrigue politically for the advantage of their
secular lord, without any apparent feeling of treachery to their spiritual
master, perhaps because they regarded the pope primarily as another
politician and possibly because they could expect that the fortunes of
politics would in time bring about a reconciliation between them.
Herein lay the difference between such men and those of the next
generation: when it was the spiritual authority of the pope which had
been questioned, the choice which lay before all churchmen was
graver, and a nomination to the cardinalate might be construed by a
prince as a hostile political act. John Fisher's death on the scaffold and
the twenty years of exile suffered by Reginald Pole show a change, not
merely in the relations between the secular and the spiritual powers,
but also in the attitude of men to the pope, whose role as the spiritual
leader of Christendom had been re-emphasised by the very challenge
which had been made to it. As long as the political activities of the pope
were more conspicuous than the spiritual, men were more disposed to
treat him simply as a politician, and the importance of political consid-

erations in the appointment of cardinals made it natural that they, too, should share this point of view.

CHAPTER 4

The Financial Problems
of the Papacy

The Great Schism had a serious effect on the financial position of the papacy, and this was aggravated by the continued struggle between the popes and the conciliar movement. While rival popes contended for the support of the princes of Christendom, the financial control established during the Avignon period broke down. This led not only to a decline in spiritual revenues from the provinces of the Church, but also to a weakening of temporal resources, as the papal lands in Italy fell into the hands of contesting *condottieri*. This loss of financial power was to be a major influence on the policies followed by the fifteenth-century popes. On the one hand attempts were made to negotiate with the secular rulers of Christendom for the payment of ecclesiastical taxes, on the other action was taken to try to recover control of the Italian lands and their resources. The latter course, although incurring greater expenses for the pope, probably held out greater hopes of success in the long run.

Secular encroachments on ecclesiastical revenues were not new: even before the outbreak of the Great Schism rulers throughout Christendom, with far more power than the Italian territorial *signori*, had been able to extract a large share of Church revenues from their lands, and the years of crisis from 1378 had strengthened their position. By comparison, the popes had lost less seriously in Italy, where Boniface IX had been an effective and powerful ruler. Admittedly the temporal power was weakened under his successors, who were threatened by the expanding power of Ladislas of Naples. By 1414 the latter was the dominant political force in central Italy, but his death in that year created a power vacuum, which others hastened to fill. His career typifies the authority which such men could exercise, extensive but impermanent, and liable to melt when they departed from the scene.

Against this the institutional permanence of the papacy gave it a capacity for recovery which none of its rivals could match. With the decline in revenues from elsewhere in Christendom, the need to draw on the resources of the papal state increased correspondingly, and financial requirements explain much of the concern of the fifteenth-century popes with questions of Italian politics.

One cannot make a satisfactory general assessment of the financial problems of the papacy over the whole period, because these varied with the levels of revenue and expenditure under different popes, and these in turn were affected by the exigencies of politics. It is pointless to consider papal revenues in terms only of the resources available, because these have to be related to the charges which had to be met. At the beginning of the period, however, the resources of the papacy were certainly strained. When Martin V was elected pope, the cost of the coronation festivities had to be met by a loan from Florentine bankers, though this was merely a short-term debt and not a case of serious penury, because the loan was repaid in the following February. There were other debts too, which the pope had to settle before he left Constance. Such payments were, however, less critical to the papal finances than the problems which Martin inherited from the period of the Schism. Administrative machinery existed, but it needed considerable attention if it was to work effectively. In the early years of Martin's pontificate various measures were taken to improve fiscal efficiency and to eliminate problems remaining from the years of the schism, but despite these, the pope ran into financial difficulties at times. When he returned to Rome in 1420 he had to pledge a mitre with a Florentine merchant to obtain a loan of 2,000 florins from the College of Cardinals in order to raise immediate cash to bring the necessary supplies of corn into the city.[1] In the long run this was not particularly serious, because the pope does not appear to have had difficulty in obtaining credit, but military expenditure in the following winter raised graver problems, for castles had to be pledged to creditors and revenues from land were anticipated.[2] However, by the end of the pontificate the position improved. Between 1423 and Martin's death, no mercenaries had to be paid by assignment to them of a tallage on a particular area, a system liable to abuse. Instead they were paid either directly from the papal Camera, or by assignment on a provincial treatury. This represents the extent of Martin's achievement in restoring financial stability.

Martin's earliest attempts to meet financial problems were concerned with ecclesiastical revenues due from the countries of Christendom. Here the most serious problems were caused by the failure of the papal collectors to fulful their duties. In some cases there had been improprieties in administration, and even where it was in order, it was inefficient and arrears of payment were due. At Liège and Trier the collector had failed to account for a period of seven years under Alexander V and John XXIII; at Bremen a new collector, named by Martin, had to employ excommunication and interdict to bring his predecessor to order, and in Scandinavia the collector's books had to be revised in 1418 by two canons of Lübeck.[3] In some cases debts were regarded as irrecoverable, and in the concordat concluded between the pope and the French nation at the end of the Council of Constance there was a provision that half the debts due on annate payments should be remitted if the other half were paid within six months. As well as overhauling the administration in the collectories, the papacy attempted to reorganise them throughout Christendom. Generally their boundaries were determined by the lines of the old ecclesiastical provinces, but in some cases attention was paid to political divisions. In Hungary the collector's competence was limited to the lands under the jurisdiction of the Emperor Sigismund, and in Savoy the collectory did not even correspond to existing diocesan divisions.

Church reunion also created problems in the central administration, where the Curia had to bring together the Camerae of Gregory XII and John XXIII, secure the balances in them for the new pope, and amalgamate the staffs from each. The treasurers whom Martin inherited were regranted their dignities, but the functions of the office were filled by Antonio Casini, Bishop of Siena, who had held the post under John XXIII, and the others presumably kept their dignities as sinecures. Among the tasks facing the new adminsitration was that of resources held by the former popes. Gregory XII had died on 18 October 1417, shortly before Martin's election, as governor of the March of Ancona, a post to which the Council of Constance had appointed him at his abdication. The financial authorities were interested both in his private property and in the official revenue in his Camera, including the payments due from it for debts and salaries. In some cases they had to take proceedings for the recovery of the property which had passed into unauthorised hands. Problems also arose with John XXIII's cameral revenues.

Although these reforms may have improved administrative efficiency, both at the centre and in the provinces, they did not necessarily increase actual revenues. At the local level, the collectories themselves had to be maintained, and at Strasburg the accounts for 1418–30 show that expenses absorbed a third of receipts. Even more serious was the resistance of the secular rulers to papal taxation and their encroachment on the proceeds. This can be seen notably in France and in Spain, where the cardinal legate Alemanno Adimari raised a subsidy of 60,000 florins, of which 50,000 went into the royal coffers. The Spanish situation was particularly difficult for Martin, because a number of the clergy still adhered to Benedict XIII, and the young Alfonso V of

Aragon, though quite prepared to abandon the antipope, wished some recompense for adhering to the Roman pope. In the negotiations between the king and the legate, the question of money remained in the foreground. Of course, diversion of clerical revenue to kings was not new, but it was still serious in view of the political problems with which Martin was faced and the costs involved in meeting them.

Alongside the traditional administration of the Church's revenues, one also sees the development of the papal privy purse. This went back at least to the Avignon period, and by the end of the fourteenth century could obtain its money from virtually any source of papal income. During the schism taxes on the sealing and registration of papal letters became one of the main sources of this fund, but one also finds direct transfers of cash from the Camera. The only common factor in its expenditure seems to have been the personal interest of the pope in the particular matter, and the secrecy of the account was due to its employment in financing matters of high policy which the pope did not wish to have publicised. The system was flexible – in the later years of Martin V, the pope ceased to take money from the passage of bulls into this account, and it went instead into the Camera. But by the early years of Eugenius IV, income from bulls was again being paid into the secret fund, together with money from annates and compositions for dispensations, which had been separately accounted under his predecessor. In general, finance was less centralised than under the Avignon popes, with taxes being imposed through the curial bureaucracy, instead of being paid direct to the pope.

Yet another contrast with the Avignon period was the marked increase in the proportion of the revenue obtained from the temporal resources of the Holy See. Although Martin V's income in 1426–7 was smaller than the average annual income of Gregory XI, immediately before the Great Schism, the actual amount drawn from the papal states had risen and, as a proportion of the whole, it had increased from not more than a quarter to almost a half. This shows both the problem and the achievement of Martin V, faced with a sharp decline in the revenues from ecclesiastical sources, but making substantial gains in temporal resources. Such dependence on the States of the Church, however, brought problems in its train, because it meant that financial support depended on the pope's capacity to exercise political control over his subjects. In most cases Martin V appears to have been sufficiently strong to maintain such authority, but with the political weakness of Eugenius IV there was a corresponding decline in his finances. Even Martin had difficulties in some regions, and it has been suggested that even when the papacy was at its strongest it did not manage to collect more than about half the debts owed to it.[4]

The Church's lands were not merely a source of revenue, but also served to guarantee loans made to the papacy. This might create problems, because when the popes were under financial pressure, they might be compelled to abandon political control, either temporarily or permanently. Eugenius IV gave Borgo San Sepolcro in pledge to Florence for a loan of 25,000 florins, but the lands reverted to the pope when the debt was paid and for the rest of the century remained subject to the Church. Such pledging of lands could lead to permanent alienation, if the pope failed to meet the debt for which they were security. This can be seen in the career of Ranuccio Farnese, who had been favoured by Martin V and, unlike most of this pope's allies, succeeded in retaining papal favour under Eugenius IV, whom he served as a *condottiere*. By not enforcing the payment of debts owed to him, he secured substantial territorial gains. In September 1431 Eugenius acknowledged indebtedness for 4,000 florins, half of which had been lent to Martin and half to himself in the first six months of his pontificate. By 1433 the debt had risen to 11,900 florins, despite the payments in cash which he had received,[5] and in compensation he acquired grants of land. Already in 1431 he was given in perpetuity lands which his family had held since the previous century on a theoretically temporary basis; in 1432 he obtained the fortress of Marta for five years, with definite ownership if papal debts had not been repaid by that date, as in the event they were not, and he received further concessions in 1434 and 1436. These acquisitions formed the nucleus of later Farnese power in the Patrimony of St Peter. There was a parallel situation in the March of Ancona, where papal indebtedness gave an opportunity to the Montefeltre family to gain possession of Urbino.

Despite these problems, however, the papacy continued to exploit the financial resources of the temporal power, and in some of the medium sized communes within its territories was able to derive considerable revenues from this source. For example, over half the communal income of Ancona was paid to the Church as tribute. It seems likely that by the time of Pius II, the temporal power was making a profitable return to the papacy, and certainly in the middle of the century the proportion of the papal revenues drawn from it seems to have increased continuously. It has been estimated that under Sixtus IV it yielded about 63 per cent of the total, though this may have been the peak of its contribution, as the popes developed other sources of funds later in the century. In absolute terms, the resources of the temporal power continued to increase, although they provided a smaller proportion of the whole. One of the most notable gains for the papacy came in Julius II's recovery of the papal lands in north Italy, after which the contribution of Bologna to the Church's revenues became important. A commune might still secure a remission of taxes, as in 1513, when Perugia was freed from paying its annual subsidy of 8,000 florins. During the sixteenth century, the pendulum swung back, with the revenues from the States of the Church again increasing more rapidly than those from its spiritual resources, presumably because of the loss of revenue from large areas of Christendom in the Reformation period.

The resources from the Italian lands were not systematically organised, but represented an assortment of taxation rights, with a tangle of immunities and exemptions. Though known by different names in the various provinces, and levied by different means, these were basically the same. There were the fiscal rights which the popes had as feudal lords, there was a hearth tax, and there was a monopoly of salt, although under Martin V it is hard to say how far this prevailed against the interests of the local *signori*. These revenues were secured from the Patrimony of St Peter, Campagna, Marittima and the March of Ancona, and remained important until the mid-sixteenth century, but the records are inadequate to indicate the actual sums secured. One estimate for the pontificate of Martin V is about 20,000 florins annually, and another for later in the century is 34,500 florins, but such figures can be no more than approximations. During the fifteenth century there was an increase in the revenues from some of the communes within the Papal States, Rome itself, Perugia, Orvieto and Viterbo. In Rome there were tolls, the *dogane di Roma*, paid on the goods brought into the city by both land and water, and these made an important contribution to papal revenues. Of the major cities in the Papal States, Bologna was exceptional in retaining virtual financial autonomy, except for meeting the costs of the papal legates there, and paying a *census* to the Camera from its wine tax. Finally, of the resources available to the popes in the early fifteenth century, there were transhumance dues *(dogana dei pascoli)*, which enabled them to exploit the pastoral resources of their states and of Naples.

During the pontificate of Pius II, an important new source of revenue was acquired, when rich deposits of alum were discovered at Tolfa, near Civitavecchia. Previously much of this mineral, which was used in textile manufacturing, had come from the Levant, but one of the main sources, Phocea, near Smyrna in Asia Minor, had fallen into the hands of the Turks in 1455, and the payment of tribute to the Sultan had led to a rapid increase in prices.[6] The popes hoped to exploit the alum revenues for financing a crusade, and in order to do so tried to use spiritual sanctions to ban imports of the mineral from Turkish lands. Pius II forbade Christian merchants to import alum from the East, Paul II excommunicated those who did. Such sanctions could not, however, be employed against the purchase of alum from Christian lands, and attempts were made to eliminate competition there by establishing restrictive agreements between the papacy and other suppliers. In 1470 a cartel was established with the alum producers of Naples, but the agreement seems to have been abandoned within a year or two. Elsewhere in Christendom one find negotiations with the secular rulers to obtain a papal monopoly and concessions to the prince to secure his acquiescence. Charles of Burgundy was granted a commission of $5^5/_9$ per cent on the sales made in his lands in 1468, while Henry VII of England laid down in 1506 or 1507 that papal alum was to be imported in an English ship, hired at 1,000 marks a year, and that if the ship were captured by pirates, the merchants would have to reimburse the king. Furthermore, the importers could use the money obtained from this trade only for the purchase of English goods. Protectionist policies which were not specifically directed at the papacy could also affect alum revenues as for example, the tariff imposed by Louis XII of France in 1512. This was aimed at protecting the French alum mines against imports from Spain and Naples as well as from the States of the Church, but as Tolfa was the principal source of the mineral it is likely that the papacy would be more seriously affected than the other powers.

Generally the popes failed to enforce any lasting monopoly, and alum from Tolfa had to compete in a free market with supplies from other sources. Economic forces proved stronger than attempts to maintain the monopoly through the use of spiritual sanctions, which were directed not only at alum imported from Moslem lands, but also at the export of the mineral except from ports which were acceptable to the popes. But the use of such measures was still found against Turkish alum as late as 1506, when Julius II renewed Paul II's excommunication of those who imported it, and also granted a plenary indulgence to those who destroyed such imports.

Originally, it was hoped that the revenues from the alum mines would provide finance for a crusade, but the failure of the papacy to carry out any scheme for a full-scale expedition to the East meant that the profits from them were either taken into the general pool of papal resources or employed to subsidise princes who were engaged in battles against the Turks on their own account. The sums so dispensed were considerable, but varied from year to year. In 1465, 57,000 ducats were paid out to this end but only 10,000 in 1466, while in 1469 and 1471 the sums were 15,000 and 18,000 respectively. It is hard to calculate the net profits made by the papacy from the enterprise, particularly during the fifteenth century, when there were complicated contracts between the Camera and the entrepreneurs who managed the mines. These fixed the minimum selling price for the alum, with the producers paying a royalty to the pope, this being on a sliding scale if the selling price rose above the minimum. From 1500 this system was replaced by the simpler method of the farmers paying a fixed annual rent for the mines and being free to sell the alum to their best advantage. In the earlier period, however, revenues were linked to the scale of production which was itself variable. After an initial high level between 1462 and 1466, there was a decline in production between 1467 and 1470, and an even more marked fall between 1470 and 1478, probably because the quantities mined in the earlier period had created a surplus in the European market. At the same time a decline in the selling price meant that the papacy had to accept a reduction in the royalties. It may well be that the fixed rates paid to the pope after 1500 led to a smaller decline in actual revenue than has sometimes been thought.[7]

If one turns from the temporal revenues of the church to those derived from its spiritual authority, one can again see changes during the fifteenth century. During the schism there had probably been some decline in the payments which the clergy traditionally made on appointment, namely services and annates, and sometimes the Camera had to order an inquisition to find the value of a benefice, of which it had no record in its books. In the concordat between the papacy and France at the end of the Council of Constance, reference was made to the wars which had devastated the realm, and it was stipulated that bishoprics and abbacies which fell vacant in France and Dauphiné in the next five years should pay only half the services due. Resistance to these taxes was encouraged by the attempt of the Council of Basel to abolish them, and the secular rulers of Christendom discouraged their payment. After the promulgation of the Pragmatic Sanction of Bourges, there was a sharp decline in the payments made for minor benefices conferred by the pope in Charles VII's lands. In the last quarter of 1438 these had amounted to 879 florins, but by the second half of 1439 the figure fell to 477 florins, dropping even further in the following year, when the sum for twelve months amounted to only 632 florins.[8] After this struggle, the French clergy were able to secure a permanent reduction in the amounts payable in services.[9] Such an alleviation of payments was not, however, universal and it is noteworthy that immediately after the schism there was a sharp increase in the assessments of several major sees. On 5 January 1420 Martin V raised the service tax on the archbishopric of Mainz from 5,000 to 10,000 florins and that on Trier to the same amount from 7,000. John XXIII had provided a precedent for this in reassessing the archbishopric of Gniezno in Poland from 200 florins to 5,000, a sum which was actually relaxed to 2,000 in 1423, although it was demanded from 1436 onwards, and elsewhere in eastern Europe one can see a comparable increase at Esztergom in Hungary, where the assessment was doubled in 1423 from 2,000 to 4,000 florins. About the same time there were increases for the English sees of Chichester and Exeter and for the Irish see of Armagh. In England, there was a change in the form of paying services about 1431, with the papacy demanding cash for the delivery of the bulls of appointment, instead of the older form of payment by instalments, which had been employed by over half the English prelates under Martin V. Later in the fifteenth century and early in the sixteenth a number of English houses ceased to pay services, but instead paid an annual *census*, which by no means provided an equivalent amount to the papacy, and even the greater regularity of payment could have been little compensation.[10]

Changes in the rates of services were, however, comparatively rare earlier in the century, although according to Göller they became more frequent during the reign of Sixtus IV, possibly because this pope had difficulties in balancing his budget. Certainly payments from England increased considerably between the third and fourth quarters of the century, and annate payments were also increased then. About the same period, similar increases in payment can be seen from prelates in the Mark of Brandenburg.[11] As with other aspects of fifteenth-century papal finance, one cannot find any precise figures of the payments made, the more so as not all benefice holders were able to meet the obligations which they had undertaken and had to be released from some part of them, often several years after payment should have been made.[12] Even where the actual sums can be ascertained, they do not always help the historian who is trying to assess the basic resources of the papacy. An indirect piece of evidence for this is a register of the division of *servitia communia* among the cardinals in the decade 1460–70 which presumably gives figures applicable also to the papal share of the taxes, but the main impression left by these is their wide fluctuations: of the sums divided among the cardinals the annual average was 21,716 florins, but the figures for individual years ranged from only 9,836 florins in 1462 to 31,569 florins in 1465. If the papal share of these taxes ranged as widely, as one may reasonably assume, it must have raised considerable governmental problems, because of the difficulties in estimating available revenue.

In view of the encroachments of secular rulers on the revenue from annates and services during the schism, the papacy had to devise new forms of taxation to compensate for its losses. Among these were increased payments made for the passage of bulls, and those for the issue of papal graces such as dispensations. In this connection one sees the rise of an entirely new financial office under the official called the datary, whose principal characteristic was his close association with the pope. Originally, his duties were in the passage of supplications for graces, but to these tasks financial responsibilities were added. These were specially concerned with the collection of fees for dispensations and compositions, as well as from the sale of offices. The office had its own depository for money, closely linked with the papal privy purse. It certainly existed as early as 1462, but came into greater prominence during the pontificate of Sixtus IV, continuing to increase in importance subsequently. By the start of Alexander VI's reign, the datary appears to have had absolute control of the money obtained from compositions.

Yet another new source of revenue was found in exploiting the system of indulgences, which must be considered as part of the whole system of papal finances. It is not accidental that the development of plenary indulgences for holy years (jubilees) was contemporary with the drawing off of annates by the secular rulers in the time of Boniface IX, the pope who, above all, was responsible for the transformation of indulgences, which represented a voluntary offering of the faithful, into a major source of funds. After the Council of Constance there was decline in the number of indulgences granted – quite irrespective of the theological disputes over their validity, there was financial resistance to the practice. Under Eugenius IV, however, the number increased again, and further increases followed under Pius II and Sixtus IV, despite continuing criticism of the system in the middle of the century, and despite the views of men preaching indulgences who did not regard them primarily as a means of collecting money. This last is exemplified in the preaching of the jubilee indulgence of 1450 in Germany, when Cardinal Nicholas of Cusa stressed the spiritual aspect of the grant and the need for the individual recipient to perform good works and be sincerely penitent in order to obtain its benefits. He opposed the idea that the main aim of the indulgence was alms, and more particularly alms for Rome. Despite this, the popes certainly derived considerable advantages from the system, and it is noteworthy that a volume of collector's accounts for Burgundy for 1476–80 was largely concerned with the levy of indulgence money. By the early sixteenth century, udner Julius II and Leo X, the sums paid for indulgences had risen again to immoderate amounts. In the development of the system the pontificate of Sixtus IV marks a turning point, both because it was he who first declared that indulgences could be extended to the dead, and because of a change in the administration of indulgence money in Rome, where the profits were transferred from the Camera to the Datary.

The financial advantages which the papacy derived from indulgances were soon curbed by secular encroachment on the revenue produced. This is all the more explicable when it is remembered that most indulgences granted in Rome followed requests to the pope, and did not originate in any papal initiative. The lay powers had many opportunities for demanding a share, and they were not backward in taking it. A king could demand payment to allow the export of money from his realm, or he could insist on sharing in the profits. On some occasions this might be comparatively small, as in England in 1476 and 1478, when the royal proportion was limited to a quarter of any sum above 10,000 florins, but often it was markedly greater. A theoretical system was developed by which one-third of the profits from an indulgence should go to the fabric of the church to which it had been granted, one-third to the Camera and one-third to the prince, but a tendency seems to have developed for the papal third to be disposed of without the pope's consent, and the prince's share was often nearer a half.[13] There might be some excuse given granting a share to the prince, as in the payment to the Duke of Burgundy of a third of the jubilee indulgence of 1475, for the expenses to be incurred in the defence of Christendom, but there were no guarantees that the money would be spent on this.[14] Perhaps the grant to Ladislas of Bohemia in 1509 of two-thirds of the alms from an indulgence, for the protection of the faith, may have been justified because his lands, which included Hungary, were on the frontier between Christendom and Islam, and the defence of the faith against the Moslem advance was a continuing factor in papal policy throughout the century. Comparable to this was the grant of indulgences for fighting against the Moors in Spain, which not only attracted men in search of spiritual benefits but also was a major source of revenue to the Spanish Crown.[15]

Of the money which passed out of papal hands, not all was diverted to secular uses. It might be employed for such pious purposes as church building. It could also be diverted to social purposes, as in the Netherlands where much of the money used for building dykes came from this source. One may presume that charitable acts towards other men were regarded as a form of piety, but it was extending the bounds of pious action excessively when funds from indulgences were used for war taxation, as in Hungary, Poland, and the lands of the Teutonic Order. Only in the case of a crusade could this be justified, and in the last case an attempt was made to claim that a war against the Russians fell into this category.

There are many examples of secular rulers obtaining a share of the profits, with or without papal consent. In 1458 Frederick II of Saxony secured not less than half of the 'Turkish indulgence' issued by Calixtus III after the fall of Constantinople, and Pius II confirmed the arrangement in 1459: in 1472 Christian I of Denmark obtained papal consent to a half share, after various misappropriations of indulgence profits in 1455, 1461 and 1465. These opportunities for the princes gave them a somewhat ambivalent attitude to the whole system. As with other forms of papal taxation, they were prepared to acquiesce, provided that they themselves could benefit, as can be seen from their attempts to limit the territorial scope of a particular indulgence in order to secure advantages for their own lands. When there was secular opposition to the indulgences, it was less against the principle than against the fact that the papacy was not conceding a sufficient amount of the money. This had important implications for papal revenues, because it meant that indulgences were too vulnerable to the pressure of secular powers to be a dependable source of income. Also any odium incurred by the popes through the abuses of the system was out of proportion to the gains which they made from it.

The papal dispensing power, and the payment of compositions by those who sought to obtain dispensations also gave scope for increased fiscal activity. In the early fifteenth century there was only one kind of matrimonial dispensation, but by its end there were five. Besides these there were dispensations to conduct visitations on behalf of bishops or archdeacons, for the legitimation of bastards, or for trading with the infidel. Not only was there an increase in the number of separate dispensations which might be obtained, but the cost of them also rose, although some attempt was made to compile a scale of payments according to the rank and resources of the payer. In origin the composition was a voluntary payment in return for a grace, but as the numbers seeking favours increased and dispensations proliferated, some order clearly had to be introduced into the system. These practices, which could incur suspicion of simony, provoked criticism, and there was a proposal for suppressing such compositions in the first draft of the scheme put forward by a reform commission of cardinals in 1497, but by the final draft they were accepted with only formal restrictions – clearly they were too valuable to be lost – and in the end the whole scheme of reform was dropped.[16] In the early sixteenth century there were two lists of the tariffs due for different types of composition, the earlier from the pontificate of Julius II or from the very end of Alexander VI's reign, the later from 1519. These show both the extent of the dispensations obtainable, and the payments to be made, which not infrequently exceeded 100 ducats and might rise as high as 600.

Despite all these methods used to raise revenue, the papacy still failed to prevent the accumulation of a long-term debt, although it was not until 1526 that this was formally funded by Clement VII, when he established the *Monte della Fede*, secured on toll resources, with interest at 10 per cent. In practice, however, a system of obtaining loans, repayable virtually in the form of annuities, was established in the fifteenth century through the sale of curial offices. This appears to have begun during the schism, when it was practised by Boniface IX, but at this stage still on a limited scale. In the middle of the century, under Calixtus III, it became a major source of papal income, and it was systematically consolidated under Pius II, who both increased the

number of curial employees and organised them into colleges, each of
which received certain fees which were divided among its members.
Under Paul II there was a reaction, in which the pope abolished the
college of abbreviators and ordered the repayment of the money which
had passed in return for offices. This, however, was only temporary,
and in the years which followed, until the early sixteenth century, the
number of 'venal' offices proliferated. Pius II's foundation of the
college of seventy abbreviators in 1463 had been worth about 30,000
ducats, the establishment of the college of twenty-four secretaries in
1486 brought in over twice that amount (62,400 ducats). In the same
year, when the papacy was faced with the costs of a war in Naples, a
college of seventy-one collectors of the seal provided another substantial sum. Criticisms of the system continued, notably at the time of the
1497 reform commission, although there were divergences on the
subject between different members of it. Cardinal Carafa attacked the
sale of offices and benefices as a scandal to the Church, while his
colleague, Cardinal Piccolomini, was more modest in his proposal that
offices which had not been venal before the time of Sixtus IV should
not be sold.

The range of prices for these offices varied considerably. A list of
1514 shows that the seven clerkships of the Camera and the auditor-
ship of the Camera each cost 10,000 ducats. There were three masters
of the seal, who each had to pay 6,000 ducats, while there were also a
substantial number of posts costing only a little over 1,000 ducats (a
hundred and one solicitorships at 1,100 ducats, and ninety-one archiv-
ist posts at 1,200 ducats – there were also ten more costly posts with
this title at 1,800 ducats). Under Leo X the sale of offices provided
about one-sixth of ordinary papal income, and at the end of his pontificate over two thousand offices were venal. The system even prompted
the suspicion that cardinalates were being granted for money. It has
been estimated that these offices represented capital of about 2.5
million florins, and the salaries paid to their holders an annual interest
charge around 300,000 florins, which would absorb a substantial part
of the papal revenues. Throughout the sixteenth century the cost of
servicing the debt remained high, and indeed increased. Under Clement VII, before the sack of Rome, it required some 30 per cent of
ordinary revenue, while under Pius IV (1559–65) the figure rose to
over 50 per cent. A further problem connected with the sale of offices
was that the income from it, as from many other sources, could be
irregular. In December 1505 the value of offices sold was 20,250
ducats, while in the following April, it was little over half that sum, at
11,850 ducats.

The development of the system of venal offices was the most conspicuous change in the character of papal revenues in the late fifteenth

century, as can be seen by comparing two documents, of 1480 and 1525 respectively. Besides this there was an increase in the amounts coming in from spiritual revenues, notably in money paid through the Datary for compositions and dispensations. There were increases also in revenue from the papacy's temporal resources, although these were not evenly distributed over the whole area of the Papal States. There was, for example, little change in the payments from the Patrimony, Umbria or the March of Ancona, but a marked rise in those from the city of Rome. In the Romagna there was an increase in the taxes paid directly to the pope, as the campaigns there under Alexander VI and Julius II meant a virtual extinction of the independent *signori*. Their disappearance meant a decline in the sums owed by feudal vassals for the payment of their *census*, but on balance the popes gained from the change, because *census* payments had at best been irregular.[17] Even so, it is hard to estimate the precise income of the papacy at any particular date, or how far it would suffice to meet its requirements.

If the income of the papacy is hard to estimate, it is even more difficult to judge the scale of its expenditure. Obviously the routine costs of the curial bureaucracy were considerable, and there is little doubt that this saw expansion during the century as the machinery of government became increasingly elaborate. This bureaucracy was concerned not only with ruling the Church, but also had to deal with the government of the lands over which the pope ruled as a temporal prince. In the latter field, the papacy inevitably was drawn into the same kind of expenditure as any secular ruler, the maintenance of military forces to defend its lands or to recover territories which had temporarily escaped from its control, and the support of diplomatic missions to meet the requirements of its international political interests. These became increasingly important after the outbreak of the Italian wars in 1494, because these drew the popes more seriously into the wider politics of western Europe, whereas previously their concerns had been mainly with the affairs of the Italian peninsula. Besides administrative and political expenses, the popes were also patrons of learning and the arts, mainly in Rome but not exclusively so. Nicholas V was an enthusiastic book collector, and a generous patron of humanist scholars, whom he supported with greater zeal than discrimination. Pius II supported building at Siena and Pienza, where he founded a cathedral, and under Sixtus IV a major programme of rebuilding was started in Rome, one which began the process which changed the medieval city into its later Renaissance form. By the early sixteenth century, Rome became the most important centre of the arts in Italy, drawing to it the greatest figures of the age, who came to serve successive popes and benefit from their patronage. Money was not always forthcoming, if the papacy had other commitments – this is well

illustrated by the stormy relationship between Julius II and
Michelangelo, where financial difficulties were probably complicated
by the self-will of both parties involved.

If one attempts to assess how effectively papal resources met
requirements, some points are clear. The papacy certainly existed on a
basis of long term credit, but as this was not hard to secure, it is likely
that in general contemporaries regarded its financial standing as
reasonably good. Generalisations are, however, dangerous because
some popes were better at maintaining a favourable balance than
others. For much of the fifteenth century the manager of the Rome
branch of the Medici bank acted as depositary general for the pope,
and one can trace some variations in papal finances from the bank
records, which supplement the information from the cameral *Introitus*
and *Exitus* books, which are not always complete.[18] The Camera seems
to have managed its accounts better under Martin V and Eugenius IV
than later, although Calixtus III worked to reduce debts incurred
under Nicholas V. The major part of this saving came from reducing
expenditure on the Vatican palace, and there was also a cut of some 40
per cent in monthly household expenses. For the next two pontificates
the Medici did not hold the office of depositary, and although cameral
records throw some light on the reign of Pius II, and show, where
complete, larger deficits than surpluses, they are inadequate for that of
Paul II, for which only two monthly totals survive, one showing a small
deficit and the other a small surplus. Under Sixtus IV the Medici
resumed office, though with certain misgivings, expressed by Giovanni
Tornabuoni, the manager of the Rome branch, who wrote to Lorenzo
de' Medici that the office involved more trouble than profit, because
the pope was living beyond his means, and expected the depositary to
advance sums to fill the deficit between income and expenditure. By
June 1472, this loan had soared to 107,000 florins (and that was far
below the massive deficit of 807,382 florins recorded in the *Introitus*
and *Exitus* books for the twelve months from August 1471 to July
1472), although pressure on the bank was reduced when Tornabuoni
secured assignments of revenue from the customs and on salt pits in the
Marches. The political clash between the papacy and the Medici after
the Pazzi conspiracy in 1478 complicated the question of repaying
debts, because at first the pope repudiated them, although the matter
was reopened in 1481. Innocent VIII also incurred criticism from
Tornabuoni: 'His Holiness is more prone to ask favours than to fulfil
obligations'. Later the tone of the letters to Florence altered, when in
1487 the pope tried to make economies by disbanding mercenaries
and curtailing court expenses. Tornabuoni commented, overoptimisti-
cally as it turned out: 'If the Pope is well off, we are too'.[19] Not the least

interesting point about this comment is that it indicates the financial standing of the papacy, for it was the willingness of the bankers to regard it as credit-worthy which enabled it to depend on borrowing to level out the unevenness in its possible income.

Even so, by 1491 papal funds were at a low ebb, and Innocent VIII advanced this as a plea when he attempted to secure a tenth on English clerical incomes. The plea may well have been genuine, because the papacy was considerably in debt at the accession of Alexander VI. The new pope was able to improve his finances, despite his generosity to his family, and by 1496 succeeded in balancing the budget and even producing occasional surpluses. In this achievement, a considerable part was played by the pope's personal frugality and economies in household expenditure. It is not certain how effectively the finances were run between 1498 and Alexander's death, and increases in both expenditure and extraordinary income, paid into the privy purse, make the routine cameral records of less value to the historian. Since Cesare was able to seize considerable cash sums from this on his father's death, the balance between income and expenditure was probably favourable. Julius II also took care to maintain his finances at an adequate level to meet the costs of his wars, so for much of his pontificate the papacy probably remained unencumbered by serious financial difficulties.[20]

Much of the cost of servicing long-term debts, in the form of salaries paid to the holders of venal offices, was met by the payment of taxes by those doing business with the Curia. This led to a cash flow to Rome, the scale of which is hard to estimate compared with that from the direct tax payments made by the provinces of the Church. In some ways these payments were even more likely to rouse resentment outside Rome than the taxes levied in the various nations of Christendom. Those who paid them would see the money going to support a curial bureaucracy inflated in numbers far beyond what was strictly necessary, while the secular rulers saw a form of taxation in which they could not share, because the taxes were paid at the Curia instead of being levied locally, in the manner of direct clerical taxation or indulgence payments.

The two principal sources of papal revenue, the temporal resources of its Italian lands and the spiritual payments from Christendom, both influenced papal policy. The need to strengthen the former was a crucial factor in determining papal actions in the peninsula, while in order to secure the revenues from the wider Church, the popes had to negotiate with the secular rulers of Christendom, the second masters of the clergy. When, however, the secular princes had political interests in Italy, which might be incompatible with those of the pope, the latter had then to walk a political tightrope between his different material interests, quite irrespective of any role which he had to fulfil as spiritual head of Christendom.

CHAPTER 5

The Administration of the Church

The developments in the financial system show one way in which the government of the Church adapted itself to meet papal needs in the post-conciliar period, but they were only one aspect of the changes. The century after the end of the Great Schism saw a number of important developments in governmental machinery, which reflected real changes in the concerns of the papacy and in its relationship to contemporary secular society. This is most clearly seen in changes within the Secretariat and in the establishment of forms of permanent diplomatic representation at the various European courts: fields in which the changes not only present similarities to those in government elsewhere but also indicate how far the papacy was involved in the political problems of western Europe. At the same time, there were aspects of administration in which the Curia had a unique role, as in the judicial activity, where it was the fountain of justice in all matters of ecclesiastical law. Here one sees continuity with the Avignon and schism periods rather than major innovations. Within the papal Chancery, too, one can see a strong element of continuity, and even a cursory examination of the regulations issued by the post-schism popes shows that these were highly eclectic in character, deriving from both the rules which had been laid down before 1378 and the newer ordinances issued during the schism by the popes of all factions.[1] The growth of the practice of venality in curial offices, which had occurred during the schism, was revived under the financial pressures of the middle and late years of the fifteenth century, and created a large number of posts which lacked any real function. This contributed to the criticisms of papal government, which can be seen in the continuity from the period of the schism of talk of reform, talk which was not, however, translated into action. While reformers were generally anxious to reduce the scale of government, in practice the Curia continued to grow, as it was far easier to create new offices, for whatever reason, than to eliminate old ones, and as each new office was established, it created a further vested interest against reform.

The details of administrative change do not always have any bearing on the problem of papal relations with princes, but many of them were connected with the basic question of how far the pope could exercise authority in face of the competing claims of the secular power. Indeed, immediately after the Council of Constance the pope was faced with the practical difficulty of re-establishing a single Curia from the groups of officials who had adhered to the contending popes of the schism. The process was gradual, and was carried out in different ways. Frequently the numbers of officials in a group had been laid down in the fourteenth century, and the first priority was to reduce the actual number to the stipulated figure. Sometimes those who were surplus to the figure were given the reversion of the offices as they fell vacant. Numbers were not, however, always reduced, as in the case of the cameral clerks, of whom there were nine in 1425, despite the suggestion of a reform commission in 1423 that four would have sufficed as they had formerly. There was a similar problem after the Basel Schism, which was solved by uniting the antipope's scriptors to those of the Roman Curia and forbidding new appointments until numbers were reduced. From this period onwards a united papacy had a single Curia, and changes in it were prompted by other considerations than the existence of rival powers within the Church.

The judicial activity of the Curia arose, as in earlier centuries, as much from the attitude of its subjects throughout Chirstendom as from any deliberate attempt to extend the sphere of papal influence. During the Avignon period the increase in the number of cases brought to the papacy for decision had necessitated a reorganisation of judicial procedures, and the emergence of the tribunal which came to be known as the Rota, or, more formally, as the Audience of Causes of the Apostolic Palace. During the schism, Boniface IX issued a regulation limiting the powers of the auditors of the Rota in cases where they were personally involved and committed such powers to the cardinals. Martin V renewed this rule, and also a constitution of Gregory XI, which safeguarded the auditors from interdict or excommunication at the hands of any judge except the papal chamberlain, thereby protecting them against external pressures which might affect their judicial impartiality. One problem which gave rise to concern was the length of some litigation, because various of Martin's constitutions were related to appeals. One, of April 1422, tried to set limits to them, and another, of the following January, reinforced this by imposing a financial penalty on an unsuccessful appellant. In 1426 yet another measure dealt with the problem of frivolous appeals. But in practice these decrees were not particularly effective, and certainly it was a great deal easier to issue regulations than to ensure their enforcement. Litigation could hardly be other than protracted when the parties to the suit came from a distant part of Christendom and each in turn had to present its case in Rome. Even before judgement had been given, an appeal could be made by a party who took exception to the action of the auditor hearing it, and even after a definitive sentence the defeated party could appeal if he felt that the court had not been properly informed.

Even when Martin V was trying to limit the protraction of suits, applications to him show how ineffective his efforts were. One case, relating to the deanery of Aberdeen, was heard at different times before no fewer than four auditors over a period of at least four years as the rival parties made successive attempts to have earlier decisions set aside, and in the end the suit lapsed with the death of one claimant, with an appeal still pending.[2] In the middle years of the century the law's delays were no less, as can be seen in the dispute over the payments between the parish clergy of London and the city Common Council, which supported an individual who had resisted the demand for certain payments and sent envoys to the Curia to argue the case.[3] In origin the Rota had been concerned purely with ecclesiastical matters, but it seems to have extended its competence to hearing appeals in civil cases from the Papal States.

It was impossible for judicial proceedings to be both thorough and speedy, and it is clear, particularly from the willingness to reopen proceedings, that thoroughness was regarded as more important than speed. The system allowed for the full hearing of both (or in some cases all) sides of a case, and it was the litigiousness of suitors rather than the dilatoriness of judges which was largely responsible for delays. Indeed, the very willingness to pursue a suit in Rome, with all the expenses involved, shows the respect of both clergy and laity towards papal justice. The papacy, too, made attempts to ensure that cases were heard by suitably qualified men. Martin V tried to ensure that the qualifications of notaries of the court of audience should be examined by the vice-chancellor or his representative, and to enforce residence on the scriptors of the Penitentiary, and attempts were made to limit membership of the latter court, with its cognisance of spiritual matters, to the priesthood.[4] By the last quarter of the century, however, the post of scriptor of the Penitentiary had become venal, and under Innocent VIII such a post seems to have been held by a minor. A check may still have been kept on the qualifications of those actually working in the courts, as was carried out when Domenico Jacobazzi was appointed an auditor of the Rota in 1492.

If one turns from justice to other kinds of administration, it become clear that the late medieval Church was a much governed body. By the end of the fifteenth century the Chancery was issuing some 10,000 letters a year, and the size of the Curia more than quadrupled between the Avignon period and 1514. It is not easy to estimate how the activity of the departments of government changed, but some indication of this may be given by the quantity of documents emanating from them. This can be only approximate, because one cannot tell what proportion of the whole is represented by the extant material. If one examines the series of Vatican registers, containing copies of Chancery letters, the evidence is inconclusive for the period between Martin V and Leo X. The small number of surviving registers from the pontificates of Martin V and Eugenius IV, under one a year for the former and approximately 1·5 a year for the latter, seems suspiciously low, compared with a figure of slightly over 6 a year for Nicholas V, and those of between 9 and 12 a year for his successors down to Julius II, with the solitary exception of Paul II, from whose pontificate of nearly seven years only 22 registers survive. Why there was this decline in Paul II's time is uncertain, but it probably reflects either a loss of registers or a decline in the regularity of registration of letters. The lower figure for the two first pontificates may reflect losses during the movement of some curial archives from Rome to north Italy in the reign of Eugenius IV, when the pope was away from his capital. Clearly the simple enumeration of registers is a very rough guide to administrative activity, but the greater preservation of them later in the century suggests perhaps increased concern with governmental procedure, irrespective of the quantities of bulls issued.

If one turns to the Lateran registers, containing copies of letters issued by the Datary, there is the immediate problem of extensive losses, the greatest of which occurred during the Napoleonic period, when many of the archives were removed for a time to Paris. It is, however, possible to supplement figures for extant registers by an eighteenth-century index, compiled by Giuseppe Garampi, though this should be treated with caution, partly because the arrangement by pontifical years seems excessively regular and partly because of inaccuracy in the number of years assigned to two popes, Nicholas V and Calixtus III. The average annual number of registers was around 13 until the time of Pius II, under whom it rose to 17 to 18. The rise was maintained in subsequent pontificates, 21 to 22 for Paul II, 16 to 17 for Sixtus IV and 18 to 19 for Innocent VIII, while under Alexander VI there was another increase, to 29 volumes a year, a figure sustained under Julius II.[5] These figures suggest that the Datary at any rate increased its activity from mid-century, at first gradually, but more steeply in the two decades on either side of 1500. As the principal concern of the datary, apart from his financial role, was with supplications, these figures suggest that there was an increase in the number of graces being sought from the Curia.

Another important development in papal government during the century occurred in the secretariat. Originally correspondence had been handled in the Chancery, from which the Secretariat emerged during the Avignon period, when, under John XXII, the political letters of the popes were entrusted to officials who were not members of the older body. One factor in this change may have been the fact that the vice-chancellor, the head of the Chancery, was by this time a cardinal, holding office for life, who might therefore not be politically sympathetic to the reigning pope. By the early period of the restoration papacy, under Martin V and Eugenius IV, the duties of the secretaries were clarified in such matters as the passage of graces through the administration. By Martin's time too, some of the pope's political correspondence was preserved in the formulary books of the Secretariat, a fact which suggests that the office was already becoming the centre of papal diplomacy, though the formularies may have been compiled elsewhere. Some writs from the Secretariat survive from the fifteenth century, but the main series does not begin until the sixteenth, and most surviving registers are not originals but copies.

Originally the secretaries, who at the outbreak of the schism were six in number, and whose numbers were kept low by Martin V and Eugenius IV, had equal status, but in Eugenius's later years Bartolomeo Roverella, Bishop of Adria, began to acquire a position of primacy among them, Nicholas V increased the numbers, making appointments with less regard to the needs of the office, and also named Pietro de Noceto as *secretarius domesticus* or *secretarius secretus*, giving him a more formally defined higher status, which may be seen as the first stage towards the later office of papal secretary of state. Noceto was an important figure in diplomacy, a man to whom missions and negotiations were entrusted, both under Nicholas and early in Calixtus III's pontificate. This latter pope also tried to limit the numbers of secretaries, by allowing only six to participate in the fees paid to the office, although he exempted his two personal secretaries from this limitation. Among the secretaries one finds various distinguished humanists, including Poggio, who had been a secretary since the time of John XXIII, Flavio Biondo and George Trapezuntius, both of whom had sons who also were appointed to the same posts. Besides this lay element, one also finds bishops playing a more important part in the Secretariat from the time of Pius II.

The increasing dignity of the *secretarius domesticus* becomes apparent under Sixtus IV, whose principal secretary throughout his pontificate was Leonardo Griffo, appointed first to the bishopric of Gubbio in 1472 and raised to archiepiscopal status ten years later as Archbishop of Benevento. Griffo remained principal secretary for a year under Innocent VIII, under whom the Secretariat was reorganised. The motive for this reorganisation was largly financial, for the number of secretaries was increased to thirty when they were granted collegiate status, and the sale of these posts brought in 62,400 ducats, which were a major addition to papal revenues during the Neapolitan war. Many of the men subsequently appointed clearly regarded the office as a sinecure, and the *rentier* character of Secretariat posts is shown clearly by a grant in 1502 to the Hospital of St John Lateran of an office in it, with a share in its emoluments, in return for a payment of 600 ducats.

The bull officially constituting the Secretariat as part of the governmental machine was *Non debet reprehensibile* of 1487, and one important feature of the new regulations was the clarification of the role of the *secretarius domesticus*, who was to reside in the papal palace and always be available for the pope's summons. Later he became an intermediary between the pope and the other secretaries, though as the amount of confidential business increased he obtained assistance from his colleagues. Above all his concern was diplomacy, relations with the princes of Christendom and their resident ambassadors at the Curia, and with papal agents abroad. This in itself reflects the growth of papal diplomatic activity, and one result of this was the increasing dignity of the principal secretarial post, a dignity evident from the importance of the men appointed to it. One of these under Alexander VI was his doctor, Alvisi Podocataro, who became a cardinal in 1500, although admittedly by that time he had probably ceased to be secretary. When another, Bartolomeo Floridi, Archbishop of Cosenza, was imprisoned in the Castel S. Angelo for forging bulls, he was replaced by Adriano Castellesi, who was sole domestic secretary from 1500, and was himself promoted to the sacred college of 1503. The latter was very dependent on the pope and on Cesare Borgia, falling from influence at the end of the pontificate, and a similar dependence on the reigning pontiff can be seen in Julius II's secretary, Sigismondo de Conti, who was not only much experienced in the workings of the Secretariat, of which he was a member for twenty-seven years, but also was closely associated with the Rovere family. Such appointments illustrate the personal interest of individual popes in foreign policy, and their wish to have men personally connected with them in the key position, which always remained a working office. Indeed the growth of the domestic secretary's influence may have been affected by the practice of venality in the Secretariat and the appearance there of men who were not working officials.

At the same time, one cannot dismiss the remainder of the Secretariat as inactive, for it is at precisely this period that one sees the emergence in a more clearly defined form of the various classes of papal writ preserved in the series of *Brevia Lateranensia*, the earliest volume of which dates from 1490, though the volumes in Armarium XXXIX in the Vatican Archives contain earlier material of a similar nature.[6] These writs, documents less solemn than bulls, developed a wide range of forms, which show increasing activity by the Secretariat, despite the separation of diplomatic duties to the domestic secretary. Furthermore, this expansion of the Secretariat's work can hardly have been at the expense of the Chancery, as the latter body's production of documents shows no signs of decline.

The next period of major developments in the Secretariat was the pontificate of Leo X, when one noteworthy change is the appearance of Italian instead of Latin as the language of correspondence between the papacy and its agents. In this, the popes were conforming to the practice followed in the chanceries of the Italian princes, and their action indicates the extent to which the papacy was regarding itself as an Italian state rather than as a universal monarchy. It is also significant that at precisely this time the Curia was more homogeneously Italian than it had been at an earlier date. Here one sees a change from the immediate post-Schism period, when the union of the administrations of the contending popes had given the Curia an international charac- ter. The demands of the reform councils that nations should be propor- tionally represented in it were impracticable, but until the middle of the century the non-Italian element remained of some importance. From then on the Italians gained the upper hand, and the remaining foreigners were generally in minor positions. The only other nation which retained some importance was the Spanish, largely through the influence of Alexander VI, and significantly after his death there was a marked reaction against it. In an age of increasing national selfaware- ness, Italian dominance of the central administration of the Church was a potential source of friction with ultramontane rulers. Also, however much theory might assert the pope's supranational claims, his practice was increasingly that of an Italian prince.

Some gesture towards the universal claims of the Holy See is reflected in the division of the secretariat into two under Leo. The public correspondence of the Curia was the responsibility of the *sec- retarius domesticus*, now more of a curial official than the pope's private servant, and was in the hands of two very distinguished Latin- ists, Pietro Bembo and Jacopo Sadoleto, while Bernardo Devizi di Bibbiena acted as personal secretary to the pope, whom he had served in that capacity before his elevation to the papacy, handling his private corrrespondence in Italian with diplomatic agents, princes, and foreign notables. The older college of secretaries declined in practical im- portance, and many posts in the vernacular Secretariat were held by men who had no title which attached them to the curial hierarchy. Under Leo X Florentines filled many of these posts, evidence of the pope's personal concern with the membership of this office and the matters for which it was responsible. This new Secretariat survived for several pontificates, during which its relations with the older body were not always clearly defined, although certainly it encroached steadily on its functions.

The concern of the secretariat with diplomacy is a reminder of the Church's importance in the international relations of the West, and the changes in it during the Italian wars indicate the extent of papal involvement in the manoeuvres of European power politics and the needs of the popes to maintain a network of connections with their own agents and with the secular powers. Even before 1494, however, the papal court was a centre of diplomatic activity, for it was at Rome in the mid-fifteenth century that one first sees the establishment of resident embassies by various Italian powers, whose example was followed some time later by the ultramontane princes. The papacy itself was slower to set up permanent diplomatic representation, remaining content with the traditional system of temporary legates, a sign perhaps that it regarded itself as being above the other powers which could, if they so desired, come to Rome. Originally the popes appear to have mistrusted the idea of a permanent embassy: a constitution of Martin V, of 20 April 1422, laid down that the ambassadorial status of envoys to Rome should lapse when the business of the embassy was completed, and the draft reform bull of Pius II took the same line – obviously an embassy was still regarded essentially as an *ad hoc* body. Nevertheless regular representation at Rome existed at least in the persons of the proctors of secular rulers who were appointed to conduct routine business there. For example, Thomas Polton, who had been constituted as Henry V's proctor at Rome in 1414 still was serving there in 1420, and the terms of his appointment, like those of his predecessor, John Catterick, gave him far-reaching responsiblities. Basically the proctor was concerned with ecclesiastical business, such as obtaining provisions to benefices, but the line between this and diplomatic questions was often narrow and he might well find the range of his duties extended. He ranked lower than an ambassador, but could perform many of the same duties. It is often hard to ascertain precisely when an embassy became permanent, because many special ambassadors, sent to Rome on a particular mission, remained there after its completion. The Italian states, led by Milan, maintained some form of permanent representation from the 1440s or 1450s, while by 1500 the great powers, headed by Spain, had also entered the field.

Embassies to Rome were one side of the machinery of papal diplomatic activity. The other side, papal representation in the various states of Christendom, was likewise a gradual development of which the details are not clear. The older view, that of Richard, was that resident nunciatures arose out of the collectorships, with diplomatic duties being added to earlier financial ones. This was particularly true of the more distant lands of Christendom where the area of a collector's powers tended to coincide with the territorial state, rather than in France and Germany where the activity of an individual collector was often limited to one or two ecclesiastical provinces. Lesage, however, has suggested that the prolongation of a particular mission could lead to the effective establishment of a permanent nunciature, and that diplomatic representation need not necessarily arise out of financial organisation. He comments justifiably on the precise terminology employed by curial officials in designating envoys, and stresses the distinction between *nuntius et collector* and *nuntius et orator*. But although Lesage's work must modify some of Richard's conclusions, it does not appear necessary to dismiss entirely the idea that diplomatic representation could arise out of the financial system. The popes did not follow any systematic policy of developing resident embassies, but rather tended to use various means of communication with their subjects throughout Christendom, employing whatever method seemed most convenient on each occasion. Indeed one can see, as early as the schism, a reverse process taking place, when a man originally named as a nuncio was given permanent status as a collector.[7] The important point to note is that the popes found it desirable to establish some permanent representation at the secular courts of Christendom, irrespective of how this was done.

Under Pius II, papal envoys normally held different titles according to their powers and rank. If the emissary was a cardinal, he would have the title of *legatus de latere*, or would at least exercise the same powers as a legate of this kind, but if he were of a lower rank, the prerogatives of a *legatus de latere* could be granted only as a special favour. When Archbishop Roverella of Ravenna was promoted to the cardinalate in 1461 he used the fuller title thereafter, instead of the lesser dignity of *legatus missus* or simply *legatus*. Those envoys styled *nuntius* were usually of the second rank, and held less full powers: in the majority of cases (over 70 per cent) the dignity was more closely defined by an additional title, such as *orator*, *collector* or *commissarius*. Envoys with the title of *nuntius et orator* were certainly engaged in diplomacy but other *nuntii* also might fulful diplomatic tasks. Originally, papal ambassadors were appointed for a particular purpose and for a limited time, but in the late fifteenth century an embassy might have its life prolonged, and this can be seen as an intermediate stage before the establishment of a permanent legation. Under Sixtus IV one finds letters of credence being issued to reside at a prince's court, until the commission was revoked, and under Julius II this practice became general.

Permanent diplomatic representation developed differently in various parts of Europe. From the 1460s the nunciatures in Germany began to approximate to residential embassies, remaining in being for long enough and dealing with a sufficient range of matters to have a character similar to that of the later permanent nunciatures.[8] In Spain, Naples, Venice and England, the nunciatures developed from the collectorships rather than from other bodies, as political responsibilities were added to financial ones. The hostility of Louis XI of France to Antonio Venieri of Recanati, papal collector in Spain, indicates that his activities were more than merely administrative and financial. These posts might be held by natives of the country or by curialists, although it is sometimes difficult to decide how individuals should be regarded. The Spaniard Bernardino Lopez Carvajal, for example, served for a long time in Rome before his appointment as collector in Spain. Before long, however, he was treated also as resident ambassador and although his stay in Spain was short, from September 1484 to late 1487, he clearly became *persona grata* with Ferdinand and Isabella. He served as their ambassador in Rome, and at their request was named a cardinal in 1493. His career illustrates the informal character of diplomatic organisation, in that he could serve both popes and princes as an ambassador, and shows the problems which might arise when a man had a loyalty to his secular ruler as well as to the papacy.

A parallel to this may be seen in England, where Giovanni Gigli acquired diplomatic influence when he was papal collector, and on his departure from the country in 1496 was entrusted with Henry VII's business with the pope. Polydore Vergil, sub-collector in England in the early sixteenth century, wrote that the collector normally filled a diplomatic role as well as a financial one, and that this explained why the post was filled by a man as distinguished as Adriano Castellesi. The same explanation applies equally to other men who held the office, and one may add that the work of the sub-collector was similarly twofold in character.[9] There was little development in the early sixteenth century. Silvestro Gigli, nephew of the former collector, was promoted *nuncius et orator*, but was later deprived of the title, and thereafter the collectors were the only permanent agents in England. The range of their activity was recognised by the title of one of them, Bonvisi, *collector, nuncius et orator ad regem Anglie*.

Papal diplomatic representation in Italy became best established in Venice, though here, too, the development was gradual, with the collectorship and the nunciature sometimes existing concurrently and at other times being absorbed into one. A resident ambassador, Leonini, was sent to Venice in 1500, with orders to remain there, and in this emphasis on residence one has a clear sign of change in diplomatic organisation. The situation in Naples was complicated by the fact that the pope, as suzerain, had reserved feudal rights of superiority, which meant that the collectors there were faced with special duties.

As elsewhere, their original powers were fiscal, but they were also given responsibility for certain duties of political control. The resistance of the Aragonese dynasty in Naples to these meant that the collectors were replaced by special nuncios, but it was a long time before any permanent nunciature was established.

The piecemeal character of the development of papal diplomatic representation is clear in Portugal and Poland, where there was an alternation between the appointment of nuncios and the employment of collectors as diplomatic agents. The political divisions of Germany and its comparatively slight involvement with papal diplomacy probably explain the limited nature of representation there, though one may note that Cardinal Marco Barbo, who had served as a legate there and in Eastern Europe in 1471, remained interested in the affairs of those lands and maintained contacts with them nearly two decades later. Immediately before the Reformation there was a mission established under Lorenzo Campeggio, which was clearly intended to be permanent because he was replaced when he left. The Swiss cantons also received their first resident *nuncio* at this time, and this can be linked directly with the alliance of March 1510 between them and Julius II.

The major European power with which the popes were most deeply involved politically was France, and here it is easy to trace regular dispatch of envoys from the Curia to the king. For a long time, however, the popes relied on special missions rather than creating any permanent resident nunciature, and although some of these remained in existence for over a year, the financial officials served as the continuing element in papal representation.[10] In the 1470s there were various *ad hoc* embassies, with gaps between them, and this seems to have been the normal practice of papal diplomacy in France until the end of the century, although Sixtus IV may have considered establishing a more permanent form of embassy shortly before his death in 1484. In 1500 Alexander VI sent Bishop Giovanni Ferreri of Melfi to France, where he remained resident at court for three years, working more for Borgia interests than for those of the Church. It was probably on account of this Borgia connection that his embassy was not renewed on Alexander's death. The matter was further complicated by the range of powers exercised by the resident legate, Georges d'Amboise who, though theoretically limited to exercising spiritual jurisdiction, in practice became the intermediary between France and the Curia in political and diplomatic matters also. This, however, did not prevent Julius II from sending envoys to the French court with instructions to reside, and supporting them by the payment of regular sums to meet expenses. Not until the pontificate of Leo X was the continuous representation of the pope at the French court finally established, with the mission of Leone Lodovico of Canossa from 1514.

The crucial period in the development of permanent representation
was the last decade of the fifteenth century and the first two of the
sixteenth. The same years also saw the closer involvement of the
papacy in the major struggles of European diplomacy after the French
invasion of Italy in 1494, so it is likely that the creation of the new form
of papal diplomatic machinery was a response to changed circumstances. At a time when the spiritual claims of the Roman see were still
unchallenged, its political activities were subject to widespread opposition, and in these popes had to adapt their methods to those of
contemporary secular society. The existing machinery of *ad hoc*
embassies had been adequate for the conduct of the Church's spiritual
government and even for occasional political concerns, and it reflects
the increasing secularisation of the popes' interests that they also had
to develop methods of diplomatic organisation better suited to a
greater political involvement with the secular powers. In this process
the individual concerns of particular popes played a significant part,
and it is likely that the absence of any consistent line of development
was due to changes of policy between different pontificates.

This personal influence of the pope on the methods of diplomacy is
only one aspect of the power which he could exercise in administration.
The changes in the Secretariat, outlined earlier, were considerably
influenced by the pope's need for a personal agent who could deal with
his concerns rather than being tied by the routine duties of the office,
and it is clear, too, that the datary was essentially a confidential
minister, who would exercise his discretion on the pope's behalf. It is
noteworthy that tenure of this post changed with each pontificate
rather than continuing under successive popes. Elsewhere in the
administration offices were given to favourites and relatives of the
reigning pope.[11] The list of vice-chancellors particularly shows nepotism; the post was held successively by nephews of Eugenius IV and
Calixtus III between 1437 and 1492, with a vacancy of only three and a
half years between them when no appointment was made. After 1505
the post was held successively by two nephews of Julius II and a cousin
of Leo X.[12]

Such developments in papal government did not go unnoticed by
contemporaries and criticisms were voiced about the worldliness of the
Curia. This was not new even during the schism, and throughout the
following century reform proposals were frequently mooted but as
frequently came to nothing. Demands for *reformatio in capite* were
directed at the curialists as much as at the persons of the popes – indeed
in the Avignon period the private behaviour of the curial officials was
more criticised than that of the popes themselves. In the fifteenth
century there was some justification for such grievances, because there

is no doubt that the curialists received a number of privileges in virtue of their offices. These might include special prerogatives in obtaining benefices, for themselves if they were clerics or for near relations if they themselves were laymen, and the right to have exemption from taxes on the passage of bulls granted to them. Not all officials had such benefits from office, but sufficient numbers of them had for this to contribute to the antagonism felt to Rome, perhaps the more so as the Curia became increasingly Italian in character.

After the Great Schism, the issue of reform, which had been raised at Constance but which had had to take second place to the restoration of Church unity, became inextricably mingled with questions of papal authority, because it was feared that the papacy, acting on its own, would not put reform into practice, although Martin V at least was willing to issue a constitution in 1420 to maintain the decrees of the Council of Constance on the disposition of benefices. Some men might look to a council to reform the Church, but the popes held that if reform was to take place, it must be the responsibility of themselves and their subordinates, rather than of any body which regarded itself as superior. The practical problem of this approach was that it made the achievement of reform dependent on the popes, who seldom were willing, on major issues, to do more than pay lip service to it. Even papal partisans had few illusions about the characters of the men who held the office. Roselli wrote that it was not given to a man of holy life but rather to kindred and relations.[13] Such men were hardly likely to embark on a root and branch reform, and although various schemes were put forward, none passed beyond the proposals stage. In general too, the reform programmes remained conservative, looking back to past practices rather than attempting to meet new problems in new ways. Attempts were made to enforce proper attire and conduct on members of the Curia, penalties were laid down for officials guilty of levying excessive taxes or of negligence, and there were some half-hearted efforts to discourage absenteeism, but these did not amount to very much. The pope appointed a commission of cardinals to draw up a reform programme before the meeting of the Council of Pavia-Siena, and this was revised before the Council of Basel, but on neither occasion did the pope put the proposals into practice. With the renewal of the struggle for dominance between Eugenius IV and the Council of Basel the practical question of fundamental reform was pushed into the background, although the pope did issue various decrees in 1438 and 1439 restricting the numbers of various classes of official. Only after the dissolution of the council was the papacy again able to take up the issue of reform. From the second half of the century three principal sets of reform proposals survive, put forward respectively under Pius

II, Sixtus IV and Alexander VI, and the failure of the popes to make these effective shows clearly the difficulty of obtaining reform from the head.

In Pius's time, the most comprehensive draft proposals were the 206 articles put forward, with papal encouragement, by Domenico de' Domenichi. These were directed primarily at the Curia – three-quarters of the articles were concerned with its officers and with curial matters generally, and a further twenty-two related to the College of Cardinals. One problem which Domenichi, and indeed the authors of other reform proposals, regarded as serious was the size of the papal bureaucracy, for several suggestions were made for a reduction in the number of officials.[14] Another man who submitted suggestions for reform was Nicholas of Cusa, whose ideas included a simplification of curial practices and the reform of moral standards there. However, he laid little stress on altering constitutions and the main emphasis of his proposals was on regular observance in monasteries and honest living among clerks in Christendom as a whole. Twenty years later, under Sixtus IV, a bull was drafted to enforce various reforms but, because of oppostion from the majority of the cardinals, it was never promulgated. It was less broad in outlook than the proposals of Pius II's time, being more concerned with the regulation of details in curial offices than with wider ideas of moral reform. The hostility of the cardinals, which blocked the reform, is perhaps a fair indication of the urgent need for it.

The scheme of reform was renewed in 1497 under Alexander VI. That this most unlikely pope should appear as a reformer is best explained by the immediate circumstances, because his action seems to have been prompted by his distress and perhaps temporary feelings of guilt after the murder of his son, the Duke of Gandia, when he declared that he was renouncing worldly desires and wished to reform the Church. The pope may well have been sincere, at the time, for when he appointed a commission of six cardinals to investigate what should be done and to formulate reform proposals, it is noteworthy that the men chosen included three whose reputation stood high: Carafa, Costa and Piccolomini. Although there were several Borgia adherents, they were by no means dominant, so it seems likely that although the pope wished to maintain some control over the proceedings of the commission, he may have been concerned with more than giving it an appearance of respectability. The members of the commission put forward various suggestions for reform on their own initiative, and received memoranda from outside with further proposals. Many criticisms reflect the state of the papal court under the Borgias, as in the section of Cardinal Carafa's memorandum which said that female relatives of the pope should not have access to the papal palace, or in

Piccolomini's proposal that the pope should live modestly and have suitable persons in his household. The reform proposals were not, however, merely directed at the pope in person, for these cardinals also attacked the system of venal offices; Carafa declaring that it was a scandal to the Church and Piccolomini proposing that offices which had not been venal before the time of Sixtus IV should not be sold. The scheme of reform was developed through several drafts, but the suggestions made, that the reforms should be divided among several bulls, and be printed after issue, were quietly dropped as Alexander's concern for reform diminished and his zeal for Borgia interests revived. In fact the scheme of reforms was comparatively modest and conservative, looking back to the proposals of Nicholas of Cusa, the draft bull of Sixtus IV and the election capitulation of 1484, all of which seem to have been available to the commission. Even during proceedings, the cardinals modified their proposals between successive drafts: the original scheme envisaged a more comprehensive abolition of useless offices than that contained in the final draft, and the payment of compositions through the Datary, which had been suppressed in the first draft, was only restricted in the final scheme.

The chief reason for Julius II's summons of the Fifth Lateran Council may have been political, to undermine the assembly called by his opponents, but it is not surprising that its meetings gave rise to various reform proposals, both in the provinces of the Church and at the centre. In June 1513 a commission was appointed to deal with the reform of the Curia and its officers, and in October it was divided into five sub-commissions dealing with reform respectively among the clerks of the various treasuries, the abbreviators, the Rota, the Secretariat and the Penitentiary. Each sub-commission, however, was assigned as an adviser a representative of the class of officials concerned, and these men seem to have played a large part in blocking effective reform. Though it was impossible to break down vested interests, some measures were effected; a reform bull of 13 December regulated taxes and banned various administrative abuses, and this was followed in May 1514 by a more comprehensive reform bull. This was divided into three sections: the first being concerned with collations, commendams and dispensations, the second with the cardinals, and the third with the faithful in general. The longest section was the second, a fact which can probably be explained by the exercise of papal influence in an attempt to turn the tables on the college, after the revolt of some of its members, who had called the assembly at Pisa. The reform measures proposed in this bull and in another of the following year were comparatively slight, limiting abuses rather than suppressing them, and defending the rights of the Church and of clerics rather than meeting its internal problems.

The proposed measures were inadequate to meet the problems of the Church, above all that of the overgrown curial bureaucracy. When one compares the proposals actually implemented with the most substantial memorandum presented to the pope on reform, that of the Venetians Quirini and Giustiniani, the difference is immense.[15] The measures taken were conservative reforms, tinkering with abuses and reiterating rights and privileges, but not taking any radical steps to change Church organisation in such a way that the critics would have been appeased and the needs of Christendom met in a manner appropriate to the changed conditions of the sixteenth century. By comparison, the memorandum foreshadowed many of the steps taken later in the century, at the Council of Trent and after, and the implementation of the proposals in it would have done much to modify the whole character of papal government. Although these made no concessions to conciliar claims of superiority, they included a call for regular meetings of general councils to assist in enforcing reform. Papal legates were to supervise episcopal administration, and the cardinals were to assist the pope in his responsibility for the whole ecclesiastical hierarchy. The religious orders should be reorganised, canon law revised, and liturgical uniformity introduced. Behind the reform memorandum lay a stress on spiritual renewal which, combined with the centralising tendencies of individual proposals, was intended to transform the Church from the head downwards.

Yet however lofty the aims of the two men were, one may wonder if their ideas were really practical. It was easier to criticise the worldliness of papal policies in Italy and abuses of Church administration than to detach the pope from politics, or to modify administrative machinery which was, after all, meeting the demands made on it by its subjects throughout Christendom in routine matters as appointments to benefices or judicial decisions in spiritual cases. No consideration was given to the interests of the secular rulers, and while Quirini and Giustiniani might have felt that these should not be allowed to influence the Church, any proposals which failed to take into consideration the practical power which these rulers not only already exercised but which they were trying to extend, were fundamentally unrealistic. Indeed, the success of the papacy in defeating its conciliar rival had been due largely to its ability to secure the support of the secular princes in the struggle, but it had done so, as will be shown in later chapters, only by compromising with them over Church government, and giving *de facto* recognition to their influence over the Church in their lands. One may doubt if the princes of Christendom would have welcomed the supervision of their bishops by visiting legates, and in an age when liturgical practices could reflect feelings of nationalism, even proposals for a uniform liturgy might have aroused antagonism.

Although many of these reforms were actually carried out in the post-Tridentine period, one may wonder how far this was made possible by the shocks which the Church sustained during Reformation, and by the continuing acquiescence of the papacy in a measure of effective secular influence over the national Churches.

When such ideas of reform were so frequently advocated, why were none of the measures put into practice? It would be easy to blame the worldliness of the popes, the vested interests of the cardinals and the curial officials and the inertia common to all large institutions, but this would be no more than partly true. The activities of the Church's central administration were the result less of expanding papal claims than of the demands made upon it by its subjects, particularly in the spheres of provisions and jurisdiction. Individuals, both great and obscure, looked to Rome for privileges of many kinds, whether it were a dispensation for marriage despite the restrictions of consanguinity, commutation of a vow of pilgrimage, or a dispensation to a clerk to hold more than one incompatible benefice in plurality.[16] These at least were matters with which the Church could claim a right to be concerned, but other questions which were referred to Rome might have nothing to do with ecclesiastical issues. If a layman brought a secular suit before the Church courts, an aggrieved party could appeal to the pope. Such was the appeal of Andrew de Crumby, who had been assigned certain goods belonging to John Blich in payment of a debt, on a judgement by the town officers of Haddington in East Lothian. After John's death, Thomas de Bening brough a suit before the bishop's official that John had been indebted to him and that Andrew was bound to pay him from the goods assigned to him. Judgement was given in his favour, but according to Andrew's later petition, proper legal procedure was not observed, so he sought to have the case nullified. The noteworthy point is that although all three parties to the case were laymen and the suit had no spiritual content, the action of one of them, by bringing a suit in a local ecclesiastical court, could lead to an appeal to Rome.[17]

A further reason for recourse to Rome might be a request for a ruling on conduct, as in 1426 when the Duke of Bedford, while regent in France for Henry VI of England, sought advice about observing certain fasts, which were a local custom in France but were not generally enjoined by the Church. Equally a monastery might seek permission to vary its liturgy, because it could not obtain books according to the normal rite of its order, after its own buildings and books had been destroyed by fire in the course of war. The great bulk of the grants recorded in the papal registers, however, cover such matters as licences to inviduals to choose their own confessor, to have a grant of plenary remission, to possess a portable altar, or to hear mass before daybreak or in places under interdict.[18] These grants could not have been made on the initiative of Rome, but could only be a response of the papacy to requests from its subjects, so the scale of these favours must indicate how petitioners flooded the Curia with requests. This is borne out by examining the registers of supplications in the archives of the Datary: no fewer than sixty such exist for the period 1418–22 and a further sixty-five for the years 1423–8. Probably in the years immediately after the Great Schism there was a temporary increase in the number of supplications, from men who had received grants from popes whose titles were later regarded as dubious, and who wished to have them confirmed by the new and unchallenged pope. During the period 1428–79 there were on average ten or eleven registers a year, but thereafter the number increased to an average of twenty in the years 1479–95 and to twenty-nine for the period 1495–1534.[19] These figures make it clear that curial business, originating in the petition of individuals, continued to increase until the Reformation, and suggest that, despite all the complaints made about the system, the attempts of the reformers to curb the size of the bureaucracy were doomed to failure from the start by the activity of those who might stand to gain from papal favours. Furthermore, despite the cost of obtaining graces at the Curia and the resulting flow of money from the countries of Christendom to Rome, the secular power seems to have been unable to check this flood of small business.

It was necessary for the recipients of such grants to have them in a legally guaranteed form, and this in turn contributed to the complexity of the system and the proliferation of business. If there were any doubt as to the validity of the letters granted, a further supplication would be made for a *reformatio*, or issue of new letters in the correct form. The occasion for a *reformatio* might be an omission or an error in the original supplication or the failure in the grant to state that it was being made notwithstanding the existence of a contrary rule of the Chancery. The issue of grants was a highly technical business, requiring considerable skill from the appropriate officials, if the system were to work effectively for the petitioners. These were not concerned with reform, except perhaps in desiring a reduction of the fees charged for issuing letters, but they were interested in the system working efficiently. The increasing number of supplications in the early sixteenth century, for which there does not appear to be any very obvious reason, must have posed problems for the curial administration, but one need not believe that it was unable to deal with the flow of business, since the issue of graces seems more or less to have kept pace with the number of supplications received. But if it did avoid congestion of business, it is hard to see how this could have been done with the reduced staffs envisaged by the advocates of reform. The only members of the Curia whose position was totally open to criticism were those holders of venal offices who regarded them as sinecures, and even there the financial difficulties of the papacy safeguarded them from attack, as they provided a source of revenue with which the pope could not easily dispense.

Possibly the pressures for reform have been exaggerated by historians. Certainly they were present, but they came less from the general body of Christendom than from the spiritual reformers within the Church, articulate men who could argue for the desirability of change in the machinery of church government. But for every reformer who looked at the Curia and its abuses, there must have been many petitioners who saw it as a source of possible favours. It was far easier for those opposed to change to resist it than for those who desired it to mobilise an effective force which could bring pressure to bear on a reluctant pope, and in these circumstances it is hardly surprising that attempts at reform proved futile.

CHAPTER 6

The Political Problems
of the Papacy

Besides the problems of the popes in Church affairs, they incurred
other difficulties from their role as Italian princes. In one sense this was
inseparable from their ecclesiastical function, because the temporal
power provided resources to maintain the Church's administration, a
fact acceptable to orthodox reforming opinion at Constance, but in
another it involved them in purely political struggles, both with other
Italian powers and with princes elsewhere who had interests in the
peninsula. Such struggles affected papal attitudes to the princes of
Europe as much as their competing interests in ecclesiastical administration, and often it is hard to say whether political or ecclesiastical
factors bulked more largely in the response of the papacy to a crisis in
relations with some secular ruler. One suspects that the popes had at
times difficulty in distinguishing the differing responsibilities of Italian
princes and universal pontiffs.

Papal politics were concerned above all with Italy and the Mediterranean world, and the history of the fifteenth-century papacy is inextricably bound up with relations between the Italian states. Three main
areas of activity may be distinguished before 1494: the Eastern question, posed by the advance of Islam; the problem of Naples, where
papal rights of suzerainty led to involvement in dynastic struggles, and
the struggles of northern Italy, where attempts to consolidate the Papal
States encountered opposition from other powers. It is not always easy
to see consistency in the policies followed except in broad terms, but
behind the manoeuvres for position in particular crises, behind apparently unscrupulous changing of sides and behind the varying outlooks
of individual popes, there were certain general aims, shared by most
holders of the papal office. In these they were liable to clash with the
secular powers, and after 1494 when the European princes became

more heavily involved than before in attempts to extend their influence in Italy, a greater consistency was imparted to papal policies of resistance.

The aspect of papal policy which aroused least hostility between Church and State was the one where the dual spiritual and temporal roles of the pope were most closely mingled: relations with the Moslem world. The Turkish advance which pushed back the frontiers of Christendom affected the popes as the latter's spiritual head, but it also threatened Italy directly, thereby impinging on the Church's territorial interests. Since the eleventh century the papacy had been involved in the crusading movement, so it was natural that in the fifteenth it should concern itself with the new threat from Islam. Morever, by proclaiming a crusade the pope asserted his position as head of Christendom, a fact which may have given the cause a psyhological appeal in Rome, particularly if political conditions were setting narrower bounds to papal activity elsewhere.

Until 1453 papal reaction to the Turkish threat was bound up with negotiations for the union of the Greek and Latin churches, with the Byzantines seeking military assistance in return for ecclesiastical concessions. The Emperor Manuel II toured the West seeking military aid between 1399 and 1403; contacts were maintained during the period of the councils and under Martin V, and these culminated in the pontificate of Eugenius IV, when a form of union was agreed at the Council of Florence. Comparatively little military help was given, though in 1422 Martin ordered the Knights of St John to use their base in Rhodes against the Turks, appealed to the Venetians for naval assistance, and renewed penalties against those who had commerce with the infidel. Only after the apparent success of the Council of Florence were steps taken to organise a crusade, though one may note that it took place outside Byzantine lands. The Turkish threat was most serious in the Danube valley, where the Serbian despot, George Brankovich, had been reduced to vassalage, and the Hungarians were leading the resistance. King Ladislas welcomed the crusade, but hoped for more troops than the pope could send to him under Cardinal Cesarini. The campaign, however, was a disaster. There were quarrels among the Christian leaders, leading to the withdrawal of the Serbs and the absence of the Albanians when battle was finally joined with the Sultan's army, and in 1444 the crusade was routed at Varna, with both Ladislas and Cesarini among the dead.

Byzantine failure to adhere to the union of Florence and papal determination to maintain the advantages which they secured increased tension. A letter of Nicholas V in 1451 declared, in effect, that there would be no crusade unless the Greeks accepted the union. When in the following year Cardinal Isidore of Kiev was sent as legate to Constantinople, with the aim of enforcing the union, he was however, accompanied by a force of archers. Probably the Sultan's preparations for a siege, including the sinking of a Venetian ship in the Bosphorus and the subsequent execution of its crew, had at last, albeit too late, alerted the West to the danger. The fall of Constantinople rallied feeling more strongly. Cardinal Bessarion, who for years had been the most active propagandist for a crusade, continued to urge a counter attack, and Aeneas Sylvius Piccolomini wrote to the pope urging him to prepare a holy war. Nicholas sent legates to the Italian cities, commanding them to stop their internecine wars, and when he promulgated his crusading bull in September 1453, he provided that the cardinals and curial officials should contribute a tenth of their income to its costs.

In one way the fall of Constantinople was more important as a symbol than as a practical threat, because by 1453 the Moslem expansion had left it as a relatively isolated pocket of resistance, bypassed by the main Turkish lines of advance in the Mediterranean and on the Danube. But for the papacy, 1453 marked a dividing line in its Eastern policy, because it could now advocate a crusade, without the problem of trying to enforce ecclesiastical unity on the Greeks. Initially, the shock of the news drew together the Italian states in face of a common danger, and almost certainly contributed to the Peace of Lodi and the establishment of the Italian League. Promises of help for the crusade were also made in Germany. Soon, however, crusading zeal declined. In Italy the Venetians, with commercial interests in the Levant, preferred accommodation with the Turks to war, and in Germany, as the Speier chronicler sourly commented, the people 'had too many quarrels among themselves on their hands to want another with the Turks'.

In contrast, the papacy remained concerned, and the Turkish question probably influenced the conclave after Nicholas V's death in 1455. As the cardinals sought a compromise between the Colonna and Orsini factions, Bessarion was originally the most favoured, and when he could not command the requisite two-thirds majority, they chose Alonso Borja, a Spaniard with a background of crusading tradition. As pope, he devoted much energy to launching a crusade, and although no full scale force was sent to the East, his measures had some limited success. Above all, Christendom did stem the Turkish advance on the Danube, where the papal legate, Cardinal Carvajal, and the Hungarian leader, John Hunyadi, aided by the preaching of the Franciscan, John Capistrano, defeated the Turkish army besieging Belgrade. But although the pope was represented by his legate, he could give little practical help, as the German clergy resisted Carvajal's attempt to raise a title. In the Mediterranean the pope mobilised more effective forces, building and hiring galleys. The chamberlain, Cardinal

Scarampo, was entrusted with the preparations, and Calixtus gave 200,000 ducats from his secret treasury to help with expenses. Within six months of the pope's election, a first squadron set sail, under the Archbishop of Tarragona. A second squadron was equipped, with Scarampo himself as Admiral, and when his forces moved to the East, he was joined by remnants of the earlier fleet. His force, though never large, was adequate to defend the remaining Christian islands in the Aegean, even to defeat the Turkish fleet at Mitylene in 1457, and in the following year briefly to occupy Corinth and the Acropolis at Athens. But this marked the limit of his success. The European powers failed to provide reinforcements – Alfonso V of Aragon, who had promised the Neapolitan fleet for the crusade, diverted it to attack the Genoese in pursuit of his own aims. When the pope died, the impetus went out of the campaign, Scarampo returned to Rome, and the galleys were allowed to rot.

The cardinal had not been an enthusiast for the crusade, and had undertaken command of the fleet reluctantly at the pope's orders. But the Eastern question was a live issue at the conclave, and the first article in the election capitulation bound the pope to carry on the Turkish war. Pius II, who was elected, spent much effort trying to mobilise support for the crusade, and summoned a congress to Mantua to plan for it. To his bitter disappointment, it revealed no crusading fervour, nor were the secular powers prepared to sink their own interests in a common cause. The chief German spokesman was Gregor Heimburg, an old enemy of the pope, and the French envoys were more concerned with Angevin claims in Naples than with the Turkish danger.[1] After the congress, Pius himself had little opportunity to advance his cause, as he was more concerned with Italian affairs. In 1462 he made a further attempt to rouse Christendom by declaring that he intended to go on crusade himself, and the death of the Venetian Doge, Prospero Malipiero, who had advocated peace with the Turks, increased the possiblity of naval support. The Venetians were further encouraged to support the crusade by the fall of Bosnia to the Turks a year later, and Bessarion was sent to the republic as legate. There he issued detailed instructions to preachers of the crusade, empowering them to grant remission of a hundred days of penance to those hearing their preaching. More important, there was a plenary indulgence for participants in the crusade, and the preachers were allowed to consider lesser indulgences for those making money contributions. Popular support, however, was not enough, as it was not matched by assistance from the princes who could have provided troops. The other Italian powers, particularly Florence, were suspicious of Venice, while the ultramontane princes were unprepared to act. The Duke of Burgundy's envoy promised support, but this came to nothing. Even before Pius' death, the whole enterprise had collapsed through lack of support, and when he died it was abandoned without delay. When Paul II, after his coronation, raised the Turkish question with the envoys of the Italian states, and a scheme was proposed for contributions, no one was willing to pay them, and the larger states tried to impose conditions on the pope. For most of his pontificate Paul could do little apart from subsidising the Hungarians and Albanians, who were bearing the brunt of the Ottoman advance. Only in 1470, with the fall of Negropont and the conquest of Euboea by the Turks, did the discordant Italian powers find it possible to sink their differences in face of common danger. Paul, who had been at loggerheads with both Naples and Venice, came to terms with them, and the Italian powers concluded a general defensive alliance. After Paul's death Sixtus IV took up the task of organising resistance, equipping ships and entering into treaties for Naples and Venice to provide naval support. In 1472 the combined fleets, under Cardinal Carafa, inflicted serious damage on the Turks, capturing Smyrna, which was plundered and burned.

At this period, however, papal policy towards the Turks never developed beyond small-scale campaigns. The reason for this can be seen in Pius II's failure, namely the lack of support from the European powers. The Church's resources, from all revenues, were inadequate to support any larger force than the fleets sent out under Scarampo and Carafa. If, as in Carafa's case, the papal fleets were reinforced by ships from secular powers, there was the danger that rivalries between them, or disagreements on policy between the papal admiral and his secular allies, could lead to a withdrawal of ships. As a result, the strategic initiative in the struggle between Christendom and Islam remained with the latter. Italian powers with commercial interests in the Levant were tempted to reach some agreement with the sultan. It was, in fact, increasingly common for the Western powers to recognise that Turkish power was an established factor in the political scene, better met by diplomacy than by the war.

As long as the Turkish advance continued, however, the Western powers saw it as a danger, and the popes played an important part in rallying Christendom during periodic crises. Reaction from the West to the siege of Rhodes in 1480 may have helped the Knights of St John to beat off a full scale attack and inflict one of the first major set-backs on the Turks. The pope sent ships, prepared others, and granted an indulgence to those concerned with the resistance. Almost immediately, however, the Turkish treat came nearer, when Otranto fell to Islam in August 1480; for the next thirteen months the Turks had a base on Italian soil. The pope appealed to Europe, but in the end the Italian states, drawn together by the danger, played the dominant part in the campaign to recover Otranto, although a Portuguese fleet was on its way to assist. At the same time the sultan's death removed a major force behind the Ottoman advance. With the withdrawal of Turkish pressure on Italy, it was even possible for the Neapolitans to hire them as mercenaries a few years later, evidence of a totally secular and non-crusading attitude to Islam. A similar outlook can be seen in the reaction to the Ottoman succession struggle and the flight to the West of the unsuccessful candidate Prince Djem, whose presence as a hostage till his death in 1495 served to discourage further Turkish attacks. Originally the sultan made an annual payment to the Knights of St John to keep his brother a prisoner, and later he negotiated with Innocent VIII to the same end, when the pope had tried to exploit his possession of the captive to call a crusade. This attempt had failed because the north European powers were too involved in their own quarrels to be interested in it. In practice, the papacy acquiesced in the existing situation, and although there was still some talk of crusade during the Italian wars, it was no longer a serious proposition. The Turkish factor in European politics was increasingly regarded as political rather than religious.

The main effect of papal crusading plans on relations with the secular rulers was financial, although one cannot separate this from political problems, particularly in the cases of the other Italian powers; in Hungary, where Turkish pressure was a real threat, and in Spain, the other notable point of contact between Christendom and Islam, although there it was the former which had the initiative in the fighting. Elsewhere, crusading meant taxation rather than warfare. In France and Germany, the secular rulers opposed papal attempts to arouse support for crusades on the ground that money was being withdrawn from their lands, and the papacy could circumvent this only by granting to the princes a share in taxes and in such voluntary payments as indulgence money. This meant that the papacy could not pursue its desired policy without secular acquiescence, which was obtainable only at a price. For the powers of the West, apart from Spain, crusading was purely defensive: there was no prospect in the fifteenth century, as there had been in the late eleventh, of occupying lands in the Levant. But if the secular powers, despite such lack of interest, could bargain with the papacy over financial terms, it is not surprising that the popes faced even greater problems in spheres of politics where lay rulers had opportunities for aggrandisement.

Nowhere was the rivalry of princes in Italy more marked than in Naples, a realm which had for generations been a papal fief, though the obedience owed had been more theoretical than real. During the schism succession disputes there had been aggravated by the political aims of contending popes, and although the existing dynasty survived the intervention of the ducal house of Anjou, it was clear by Martin V's accession that a major succession crises was imminent. When the powerful King Ladislas died in 1414, the throne passed to his sister, Joanna II, a middle-aged widow with no heirs, but with a succession of lovers, whose influence became a public scandal both personally and politically. In 1420 the pope allied himself with Louis III of Anjou, on the understanding that Louis should become heir to the kingdom and expel the politically most able of the queen's lovers, Giovanni Caracciolo, and the latter called in Alfonso of Aragon, who won effective control. Alfonso in turn became resentful of the favourite and arrested him, so Joanna came to terms with the pope and adopted Louis of Anjou as her heir. Until 1431 Martin and the Angevin party dominated the Kingdom, with the pope exploiting his advantage to secure promotions there for some of his Colonna relatives. Martin's death ended a period of comparative peace, and in the renewed troubles Caracciolo was murdered. Alfonso attempted a further intervention, but failed to secure the queen's support. Louis of Anjou predeceased Joanna, who on her death in 1435 bequeathed the kingdom to his brother, René.

The removal of Joanna's disastrous personal influence clarified the political situation, and left three parties with an interest in the succession: René, on the strength of her will, Alfonso in virtue of his previous adoption as heir, and Eugenius IV, who claimed the kingdom as a lapsed papal fief. The pope lacked power to enforce his claim, having recently been expelled from Rome by a republican revolt and being engaged in his quarrel with the Council of Basel, and René was a prisoner of the Duke of Burgundy, so Alfonso had the initial advantage. When he fell into the hands of the Duke of Milan, Filippo Maria Visconti, his position seemed in danger, but, after persuading the duke that he would be wiser to support the Aragonese than the Angevins, he resumed the struggle. Civil war continued in Naples until Alfonso's victory in 1442. Although the pope lacked means to sustain his own claim, his support was considered of value, and both claimants negotiated with him for recognition. René's claim was complicated by the attempts of the French King to exploit papal difficulties with the council. Eugenius hoped to secure French support against it, by offering the Neapolitan succession to the Angevins, but equally he dared not be too closely identified with René's cause, lest his position as suzerain might be endangered if Alfonso were victorious. The pope also wished to be sure that the French would fulfil the conditions which he was imposing in relation to the council. A document of investiture was drawn up, but was not handed over to René, and the pope expressed a willingness to revoke it, on the pretext that the conditions of investiture had not been met, if Alfonso submitted his claims to the pope as an impartial arbitrator. Alfonso paid little attention to these overtures, and in fact papal intervention meant little, as the fate of the kingdom was determined by war.

Charles VII had a stronger weapon in negotiations with Basel, and in playing off conciliar claims against the pope, than Eugenius had in the offer of Naples. French support for the council and the promulgation of the Pragmatic Sanction of Bourges could reasonably be construed by the pope as hostile acts. On the other hand, the inconsistency of French policy, in not recognising the election of Felix V, the logical conclusion of conciliar action, can almost certainly be explained by the Neapolitan situation. René's brother, Charles of Anjou, who was influential at the French court, remained loyal to Eugenius, so although the council had considerable support in France, it could not secure recognition for its pope, which might have lent some credibility to its claim. But in so elaborate a game of bluff and counter-bluff, this was the limit to the advantage which the papacy could derive from its rights in Naples, because the king continued to exercise effective control over the Church in France, under the terms of the pragmatic sanction.

Although Naples remained under Aragonese rulers for the rest of the century, continuing Angevin claims affected Franco-papal relations. Alfonso came to terms with Eugenius, partly to secure the succession for his legitimised son, Ferrante, and the pope granted this in return for military support in northern Italy and the abandonment of Felix. Papal claims of suzerainty might be reasserted in retaliation for Alfonso's interference in the Papal States; in 1457 Calixtus III possibly considered granting the crown to his nephew, Pedro Luis, and certainly he later ordered an investigation into Angevin rights, perhaps to prepare a reversion to them. He and Alfonso both died in 1458, and Pius II was more friendly to the Aragonese, just when baronial unrest was giving opportunity for intrigues with the Angevins. The pope invested Ferrante with the kingdom, although national divisions in the Curia can be seen in the fact that the French cardinals did not sign the bull of investiture. As twenty years before there was intense bargaining. At the Congress of Mantua Pius attacked the pragmatic sanction when the French envoys tried to reopen the question of Naples, and when Louis XI became king he abolished the pragmatic in an attempt to conciliate the pope. The French envoy in Rome, Bishop Jouffroy of Arras, may have been trying to secure a cardinalate for himself before pressing his master's Neapolitan policy and demanding the withdrawal of papal support from Ferrante in return for abrogating the pragmatic. He also hinted at possible French support for the crusade. Louis also entered into negotiations with the Italian powers, including Pius's enemy, Sigismondo Malatesta, and the Sforza at Milan, who supported the pope's pro-Ferrante policy. A marriage was proposed between

René's son, John, and Ippolita Sforza, who had been pledged in infancy to a son of Ferrante, so papal action would have been needed to dissolve the earlier contract. Tentative moves were also made for a marriage between a papal nephew and a relation of Louis himself, either a sister or a bastard daughter.

Angevin military success in the winter of 1461–2 led to Aragonese concessions to the pope. Ferrante yielded his claims on Terracina and granted the title of Duke of Amalfi and grand justiciar of the kingdom to a papal nephew. Even so, Pius wavered briefly in his support for Ferrante, but in the end stood by him, encouraged perhaps by the French failure to detach Milan from Naples. In August 1462 a victory for Ferrante marked the turning-point of the war, although René's son, John of Calabria, did not leave Italy and abandon the struggle until 1464. The war secured Ferrante's title, and he was never again in danger of being overthrown, despite revolt and unrest. The absence of French intervention, probably because of Louis XI's preoccupation with Burgundy, left him stronger *vis-à-vis* the papacy. Indeed he was more often than not the aggresive party in his relations with the popes, refusing to pay tribute to them, taking military action to seize the duchy of Sora, which had fallen into papal hands during the succession war and supporting Roberto Malatesta in resisting papal attempts to secure control of Rimini. Only common danger, after the fall of Negropont to the Turks, restored peace between the king and Paul II. Sixtus IV was more conciliatory, coming to terms with Ferrante in the interests of his relations. His nephew, Lionardo della Rovere, whom he appointed prefect of Rome, was married to a bastard daughter of the king and endowed with the duchy of Sora, over which the pope renounced his right of sovereignty. He also gave up the right to feudal tribute, and the king promised to take part in the Turkish war, defend the coasts of the Papal States and if need be give military support to the pope. The later years of the ponfiticate saw renewed hostility, temporarily suspended during the Turkish occupation of Otranto, culminating in the defeat of an invading Neapolitan army by Roberto Malatesta at Campo Morto in the Maremna. Only papal hostility to Venetian power in north Italy restored peace between Sixtus and Ferrante, which was maintained till the pope's death.

During Innocent VIII's pontificate continuing tension over the king's failure to pay tribute was exacerbated by the revolt against Ferrante, in which the Neapolitan barons raised the banner of the Church. As the pope could obtain little support in Italy, he turned to France for help, though without success. Under the influence of the Aragonese, who disliked the prospect of a French presence in Italy, a peace settlement was agreed in August 1486.[2] The aftermath of this shows that Ferrante's concessions were purely tactical, for within two days he seized a number of barons to whom an amnesty had been promised. In the next year he formally repudiated the treaty and snubbed the nuncio sent to protest. For two years a state of half-hostility persisted, but in 1489 Innocent held a consistory at which he delcared Ferrante deposed. In September 1489, the pope, whose envoys had been negotiating on various matters with the French for a year and a half appealed more formally for help, proposing that they should come and conquer Naples, which could be used as a base against the Turks. The French were also warned of the danger to them if the kingdom fell into the hands of Maximilian of Habsburg, to whom also the pope might appeal. French action was, however, limited to the dispatch of warning letters to Ferrante, as they had little interest in Italian affairs at this time when indeed there was more concern with the affairs of Brittany. Possibly the French may have feared that, as in the past, they might be left in the lurch if the pope came to terms with Ferrante. The threat implied in these exchanges may, however, still have been a factor in bringing the Neapolitan king to terms in the winter of 1491–2. Peace terms were reached and, despite French opposition, further negotiations dealt with the succession problem to provide for the continuance of Ferrante's line there. The whole crisis, however, renewed French interest in Naples just when Charles VIII was old enough to begin his personal rule. The French kingdom was now more complete territorially than before, with the fall of Burgundy and the incorporation of Brittany. At the same time the fall of Granada to the armies of Ferdinand and Isabella enabled the former to renew Aragonese interests in Italy, using the resources of his wife's kingdom as well as of his own.

On the election of Alexander VI, Ferrante pursued a characteristically opportunist policy. At first conciliatory to the pope, he was soon intriguing with his enemies, but then came to terms with him again, spurred on by the threat of French intervention. The pope's family ambitions gave Ferrante a bargaining counter. Alexander's 12 year-old son, Jofrè, already Archdeacon of Valencia, was to be released from his clerical status and married to an illegitimate daughter of Ferrante's son, Alfonso, receiving the Neapolitan title of Prince of Squillace. Papal negotiations with Spain also displayed an anti-French tone. Alexander's bull dividing the newly discovered lands in the Western hemisphere between Castile and Portugal was promulgated at the instance of the Spanish rulers, and another of the pope's sons, Juan, Duke of Gandia, married a cousin of Ferdinand of Aragon.

Alexander's best policy was to avoid a definite engagement to one side, so that both might hope for favours, and while Ferrante lived this was possible. His death in January 1494 forced the pope's hand although Alexander was able to secure advantages from it. Alfonso,

Duke of Calabria, who needed papal support to secure the throne, paid the tribute which his father had resisted, and put pressure on the troublesome Virginio Orsini to submit to the pope. In return the pope wrote firmly to Charles VIII, warning him against attacking Naples.

The intervention of non-Italian powers in the peninsula after 1494 created new political problems for the papacy, but as this originated in the affairs of northern Italy as well as of Naples, earlier papal involvement there must be considered. The most important development of the period was the emergence of Milan, Florence and Venice at the expense of the smaller states in the area, and their relationship with Rome was primarily spiritual, being unaffected by claims to suzerainty as in Naples. But in the States of the Church, contiguous with these powers, the papacy had the problem of semi-independent feudatories, some of which , such as Bologna, were wealthy enough to resist papal attempts to enforce obedience, and the instability of politics gave scope for threatened, and sometimes actual, intervention by them. The complex relationships of the north Italian states, with each other, with Naples and with the ultramontane powers also affected their attitude to the papacy. The latter's struggles to control its feudatories were not an undersirable concern with secular affairs, for the revenues from the temporal power were an important part of the Church's budget.

The death of Ladislas of Naples in 1414 created a power vacuum in Italy and in the resulting disorder the *condottiere* Braccio established a virtually independent power in Umbria at papal expense. Martin V, financially weakened by the limitations on spiritual taxes imposed by the concordats of Constance and by the loss of temporal revenues in the States of the Church, pursued a policy of gradual recovery through diplomacy. Concessions to other *signori* enabled him to build up a party to balance the power of Braccio, who himself came to terms with the pope in February 1420 on conditions very much to his own advantage. Until Braccio's death in 1424, he wavered in allegiance, sometimes serving the pope and sometimes his Neapolitan enemies. Martin found more trustworthy allies in his Colonna relatives, whom he placed in strongholds throughout the Papal States. This consolidated his power in the short term, but created future trouble for the papacy, because the Colonna, unwilling to relinquish power on Martin's death, rebelled against his successor.[3] Such secular nepotism was a recurrent weapon of the fifteenth-century popes, paralleling the promotion of clerical nephews to the cardinalate. The character of nepotism varied, sometimes the employment of the pope's relations was subordinated to the Church's interests, at other times family advancement was a pope's principal object. As with the cardinalate, there was a marked increase in secular nepotism under Sixtus IV, and under Alexander VI it became even more an end in itself. The policies of popes such as Martin

V, however, seem to have restored some security in the Roman *campagna*, as can be seen from the abandonment around this time of hill-top village sites, strategically powerful but economically unviable.

Martin's policies show both the problems of the temporal power and the methods of meeting them. He exploited rivalries between feudal families, pressed his relatives into the Church's service, and, where there was still communal government, accepted a compromise between the rights of local officials and his own legates. Papal influence could vary with the character of the individual legate.[4] Martin's concern with practical power rather than with legal niceties is shown by his treatment of his vassals more as their employer than their lord. The pope's problems with his immediate subjects were further complicated by external intervention. Early in the papal restoration, Florence was on good terms with the popes – Martin spent some time there before he could return to Rome, and Eugenius IV not only had Florentine military support against the Colonna revolt in 1431 but also found refuge in the city after his expulsion from Rome by the rising of 1434. Behind this Florentine-papal alignment lay a common distrust of Milan, which under Filippo Maria Visconti was becoming increasingly powerful between the Alps and the Apennines in the 1430s. The expansion of Venetian power on the mainland had already brought the republic into conflict with Milan and alliance with Florence in the previous decade. Tension between Milan and the Emperor Sigismund, who needed papal favour to secure imperial coronation, led to an alliance between Filippo Maria Visconti and the Council of Basel, an action which increased papal hostility to the Milanese duke. Here ecclesiastical issues became involved in Italian politics, a fact which shows how papal dealings with princes could not be settled in purely secular terms. This also emphasises the vulnerability of the popes and their foes' opportunites. In 1433 Filippo Maria's forces harried the Papal States and threatened Rome, with the duke claiming that he was acting in the name of the council. Indeed this contributed to Eugenius's forced recognition of Basel's legitimacy in early 1434. In Italy, too, papal military weakness led to concessions, when Eugenius had to appoint Francesco Sforza Vicar of the March of Ancona, of which he was already *de facto* lord. The papal grant, however, served to detach Sforza, for a time, from Visconti service.

The republic set up in Rome in 1434 was short-lived, for the city fell to papal troops later in the year. Eugenius was himself concerned with events in the north, the struggles with Milan and with the council, and the negotiations with the Greeks at Ferrara and Florence. These matters were interrelated: the pope gained prestige from the Greeks negotiating with him rather than with Basel, and the choice of Florence for the transfer of these discussion was probably prompted by it being out of range of the Milanese armies. The council, too, may have tried to exploit Italian political divisions by choosing the Duke of Savoy, Filippo Maria's father-in-law, as its pope, although the Milanese duke did not in fact adhere to Felix V. In the autumn of 1441 Eugenius came to terms with Milan, and by withdrawing support from the Angevins in Naples found a new ally in Alfonso. The pope could now return to Rome, from which he had been absent for nine years, and for the remainder of the pontificate had better fortune. Support for the council crumbled and when Sforza re-entered Milanese service against the Venetians, the lands in the March returned peaceably to the papacy. These gains were balanced by the loss of Bologna, which remained independent after a revolt under Annibale Bentivoglio in 1443.

Visconti's death in August 1447, some six months after Eugenius, was a turning point in north Italian history. After a two-and-a-half-year struggle Sforza secured the duchy, against the claims of the republican party in Milan; Alfonso of Aragon and Naples, who produced a document asserting that the late duke had named him as successor, and Charles of Orleans, Filippo Maria's nephew, who was supported by Charles VII of France. The succession struggle gave scope for Venetian expansion, which led to a diplomatic realignment of the north Italian powers, with Florence switching its alliance from Venice to Milan. The papacy felt threatened by the Venetian advance, particularly in the Po delta and further south.[5] Rivalries became more acute in the second hald of the century, and were of course to contribute to the wars after 1494.

The Milanese succession crisis eased some papal problems in the north. Nicholas V pacified Bologna, where he had been bishop, and the constitutional relations of the city to the papacy were defined in 1447. It was recognised that the pope was suzerain and not despot, with his authority limited by law, and it was laid down that the legate could not determine any matters without the consent of the city magistracy. In theory power rested with the papacy, but in practice the Bentivoglio retained control, and the legate had to secure the goodwill of the citizens. In the Romagna and Umbria the pope came to terms with the *de facto* rulers, granting vicariates to various families of local *signori*. Various republican scares in Rome, notably the Porcari conspiracy of 1452–3, offered little real threat to effective papal power there, and indeed after Eugenius IV's return in 1443 no pope was driven out by a popular revolt, although Pius II, from choice, spent little time there. Although the pope was in a strong position to intervene elsewhere in Italy, Nicholas did not initiate diplomatic action, only adhering to the defensive league of the northern powers in 1454 after it was already concluded. He did, however, send Cardinal Capranica to Naples to secure Alfonso's adherence to the league. The alliance reveals the existence of Italian feeling, for it was directed against external intervention, perhaps Turkish or French, as well as against attempts to foment revolution within Italian states. It also shows that the papacy recognised its interests in the politics of the peninsula as a whole.

During the pontificate of Calixtus III, affairs in northern Italy were generally quiet. His Spanish origins raised a new problem, in that he had no obvious allies, such as the Colonna had provided for Martin V or the Venetians for Eugenius IV, and this may explain his recourse to nepotism, which at least provided some military successes. As legate in the March of Ancona, Cardinal Rodrigo recovered the rebellious city of Ascoli, while a secular nephew, Pedro Luis, was the dominant military figure in the Papal States.

Although Pius II's energies were largely occupied in crusading plans and by Naples, he also attempted to recover authority within the States of the Church, notably against Sigismondo Malatesta of Rimini. Here personal antagonism exacerbated political difficulties, and the pope may have overplayed his hand in 1459, when he secured the surrender to himself of Mondavio and Senigallia, lands held by Malatesta since the reign of Eugenius IV, during negotiations between the lord of Rimini and the allied forces of Ferrante of Naples and the count of Urbino. A year later, with the pope embroiled in Naples, Sigismondo tried to recover the towns, and not until 1463 was a settlement reached. By this Sigismondo had to make substantial concessions, though he retained Rimini and his brother, Cesena, in return for an annual tribute of 1,000 ducats.[6] A major beneficiary of Pius II's favour was the Count of Urbino, who did good service to the pope in return, helping to enforce order in the lands close to Rome.[7] Elsewhere Pius mediated between rival town factions and at Bologna the moderation of the legate, Angelo Capranica, helped to preserve goodwill between the city and its suzerain, without disturbing the realities of Bentivoglio power. The pope's relations gave him military service, the most notable being his nephew, Antonio Piccolomini, whom Ferrante, whose bastard daughter he married, made duke of Amalfi. After the fall of Sigismondo Malatesta Piccolomini secured lands in the March of Ancona, which he retained under Paul II, but had to surrender under Sixtus IV. His most permanent gains, however, resulted from papal negotiations with Ferrante rather than from concessions of Church lands. Papal relations with Venice were often tense, partly because of crusading problems but also through territorial and political disputes, notably the Venetian support for the Malatesta, from whom the republic purchased Cervia, with its valuable salt pans, in 1463. According to the pope's own account, Pius denounced this action to the Venetian envoy in Rome until the latter shook with terror, but this story appears to be fabricated. Moreover, Pius could not risk antagonising Venice completely, as its support would be essential for a crusade.

Although Paul II was a Venetian, his election did not please the republic, which had quarrelled with him in 1459, when he had been provided to the see of Padua but had to relinquish it under pressure from the city rulers, who had an alternative candidate. Tension, however, centred on ecclesiastical rather than territorial issues. The political stability of northern Italy was endangered by the deaths of Cosimo de' Medici in 1464 and Francesco Sforza in 1466, for their sons were less politically skilled, and Paul threw his support behind a league to preserve peace, agreed between the three northern powers in January 1467. He also tried to establish peace in Italy in order to organise forces against the Turks. He had greater success in the States of the Church, extending papal influence in Perugia, overthrowing the troublesome Anguillara family, and increasing his power in the Romagna on the death of Novello Malatesta, though he did conciliate Novello's nephew, Roberto Malatesta, with various fiefs. On Sigismondo's death, Roberto gained control of Rimini and Paul formed an unaccustomed alliance with Venice. Jealousy of Venetian encroachments in the Romagna secured Roberto support from Florence, Naples and Milan.

This crisis shows how the jealousies of the Italian powers affected the relations of the papacy with its vassals. There is little doubt that the Venetians joined with the pope in the hope of securing Rimini for themselves, while the other major Italian states were determined that neither Venice nor the pope should make territorial gains. For the rest of his life, Roberto Malatesta survived largely through the reluctance of each power to see his lands passing to one of their rivals. This problem of the feudatories became more acute under Sixtus IV, who, more than any of his predecessors, turned nepotism from a convenient weapon of papal power into a policy in its own right, and the feudatories, especially in the north, were the main targets of papal aggrandisement. Imola, a papal fief bought back from the Sforza, was conferred on his favourite lay nephew, Girolamo Riario, who was married to an illegitimate daughter of the Milanese duke in 1472. In 1474 Giovanni della Rovere, the younger brother of Cardinal Giuliano, married a daughter of Federigo of Urbino, and was given a territorial base in the Romagna with the grant of the vicariates of Senigallia and Mondavio. In the following year, he also secured the position of Prefect of Rome.

This sudden burgeoning of Rovere power aroused ill-feeling in Florence. The opposition of Lorenzo de' Medici to raising money for the purchase of Imola led the pope to obtain the necessary loan from the rival Pazzi family, to whom he then transferred the Church's banking account. When papal forces under Cardinal Giuliano were attacking the rebel lord of Città di Castello, the Florentines mobilised troops nearby and intervened diplomatically, with Sforza support, to secure more moderate terms for the offender than Sixtus wished. In these circumstances, the pope's nomination of Francesco Salviati to the archbishopric of Pisa was regarded by Lorenzo as a hostile act, and he was not allowed to take possession of his see. Galeazzo Maria Sforza's assassination in 1476 weakened Girolamo Riario's position at Imola and, with Pazzi support, he became the moving spirit in the plot of 1478 to overthrow the Medici. When the plot failed, the conspirators, including Archbishop Salviati, were hanged.[8] These events led to war between the papacy and Florence. The captivity of the pope's great-nephew, Cardinal Riario-Sansoni, whose presence in Florence had been utilised by the plotters, though he himself was not involved, increased the tension, because Lorenzo held him hostage for the safety of the Florentines in Rome, and did not release him for some six weeks. This was the limit of Florentine concessions: a bull excommunicating Lorenzo and an interdict on the city were both disregarded. In the ensuing war, Lorenzo sought support from Venice and Milan, which persuaded the wavering Giovanni Bentivoglio to join against the pope, while the pope secured support from Naples.

More serious was the intervention of Louis XI of France, whose letters show strong support for Florence without making specific accusations against the pope. On 12 May he expressed outrage at the conspiracy, on 10 August he warned Sixtus of the danger of scandals to the Church, and six days later the preamble to an ordinance forbidding the clergy to seek benefices at Rome or to send money there reaffirmed French friendship with Florence, and accused the pope of employing revenues which should have been used to defend the faith against the Turks in attempts to usurp the lordships of Italy. In the following months the king sent numerous letters to the rulers of Naples, Florence, Milan and Ferrara, as well as to the pope, the College of Cardinals, and two of the pope's relations, Cardinal Domenico della Rovere and Girolamo Riario. By 1479 his diplomatic activity extended to the emperor and two German princes, presumably in response to papal action there during the winter.

Louis' aims seem to have been to extend his general influence in Italy and to limit the pope, rather than intervene directly, and his success can be measured by his involvement in all the negotiations, even although no French troops were sent to the peninsula. In November 1479 his agent in Naples reported that Ferrante was willing to agree peace terms. The latter emerged as the key figure in Italian politics, and in view of the danger to himself of French influence south of the Alps, he probably was willing to restore the Italian balance of power to prevent this, and listen to Lorenzo's persuasions to abandon his alliance with the pope. With the loss of Neapolitan military support, Sixtus came to terms with Florence and lifted the interdict in December 1480.

This crisis increased Ferrante's influence in the north, and the pope, and even more Girolamo Riario, were the losers. As Girolamo sought further scope for his territorial ambitions in the Romagna, the uneasy balance was again upset. In 1480, he secured Forlì on the death of Pino Ordelaffi, although he was unsuccessful at Faenza, which remained under the Manfredi family. To secure support in this area, the pope offered Ferrara to Venice, because Ercole d'Este, technically his vassal, had refused to publish certain papal rescripts and had tried to avoid paying his annual tribute. Moreover, as Ferrante's son-in-law he was disliked by both the pope and the republic. The subsequent war was inconclusive: in the first phase Sixtus was allied with the Venetians, who supported him against Naples and were left in the lurch when he came to terms with Ferrante and guaranteed Ercole d'Este possession of his lands, probably because he feared increasing Venetian power. In the second phase the other four great powers allied against Venice, and the pope not only took military measures against the city but also proclaimed an interdict. In the eventual peace settlement the only territorial adjustment was to the benefit of Venice, which obtained the Polesina (between the Po and the Adige) at the expense of Ercole d'Este, while Riario made no gains at all.

Nearer Rome Girolamo's ambitions caused trouble, as his friendliness to the Orsini led to Colonna suspicions and the outbreak of faction fights in 1484. The Colonna castles were attacked and the head of the family was captured and executed, but Riario failed to occupy all their strongholds. Then in August 1484 the pope's death removed the foundation of Girolamo's power. There are considerable similarities between his fate and that of Cesare Borgia some twenty years later. Without papal backing, neither could preserve their dominance. Girolamo seems to have hoped to overawe the conclave into electing a pope of his choice, but before this took place a truce was arranged by which he would surrender the Castel S. Angelo in return for a money payment and withdraw to his own states. He realised his weakness, and went to Forlì, where he ruled tyrannically until the citizens there murdered him in 1488.

By comparison with Sixtus, Innocent VIII was little involved in north Italy, and his conduct was inconsistent. A league between the pope and the Venetians in February 1487 was abandoned within a few weeks in favour of a Florentine alliance, by which Lorenzo de' Medici's daughter, Maddalena, married the pope's son, Franceschetto. The pope's main political concerns were in Naples and this, together with his general ineptitude, meant that he could not exploit the disorders of the Romagna to the advantage of the Church's temporal power. The crisis there in 1488, following the murders of two important *signori*, Girolamo Riario at Forlì and Galeotti Manfredi at Faenza, showed total papal impotence, for the outcome was determined by the rival amibitions of Florence and Milan, with Giovanni Bentivoglio skilfully walking a tightrope between them. Weakness and vacillation characterised much of Innocent's activity – it hardly merits the term policy – further south, in his relations with Colonna and Orsini factions around Rome and in some feeble efforts to strengthen his position in Perugia. His relations shared his indecisiveness, and although he sought and secured good marriages for them, they lacked the ambition to emulate Girolamo Riario's efforts to build up a signory in the Papal States. Franceschetto Cibò, the husband of Maddalena de'Medici, was little more than a hanger-on at the papal court, and failed totally in allaying civic feuds when sent as papal envoy to Perugia, where the pope's brother, Maurizio, was equally unsuccessful. Only when Cardinal Piccolomini was sent there was he able to pacify the Baglioni and maintain some papal influence.

Alexander VI was a far more skilful politician, and he was elected at a critical moment, because three months earlier Lorenzo de' Medici's death had removed Italy's cleverest statesman. His son, Piero, could not hold together the alliance between Naples and Milan, where the increasing power of the regent, Ludovico Sforza, over his nephew, the son-in-law of Alfonso of Naples, was arousing tension. Ludovico was already looking to France, and Ferdinand of Aragon, who did not accept as permanent the division of Naples and his kingdom made in 1458, was also becoming concerned with Italian affairs.[9] The conclave of 1492 was dominated by rival political pressures from Milan and Naples, with the key role being played by Ascanio Sforza, whose primary concern was to avoid the election of Giuliano della Rovere, and who seems to have persuaded his supporters to switch their votes from Carafa to Borgia to prevent this.[10] The election is best understood in political terms, and the choice of Borgia, who had the abilities of a temporal ruler so conspicuously lacking in his predecessor, in preference to the spiritually more worthy Carafa or Costa, was above all a political act, even if the cardinals were also influenced by the prospect of a share in the numerous benefices which he held.

Alexander inherited a difficult political situation, both within the Papal States, where Innocent VIII's ineffectiveness had allowed other Italian powers to extend their influence, and in his relations with Italian and ultramontane princes. These problems were inseparable, because rival families within the lands of the Church looked for support to other Italian powers, whose rivalries in turn gave scope for

French and Aragonese intervention. If papal power was to be restored, it was desirable to maintain a balance between the Italian states and to keep foreign powers out of Italy. The pope's Spanish descent may have enabled him to stand aloof from some of the traditional feuds of his immediate subjects, but it did not put an end to them, although his long residence in Italy had perhaps left him more Italian than Spanish in his international political attitudes. When Alexander distributed his benefices among the cardinals who voted for him, these included representatives of the three great Roman families, the Orsini, the Colonna and the Savelli. But underlying hostilities made any agreement precarious. Within a month of the election Franceschetto Cibò sold his castles of Cerveteri and Anguillara to Virginio Orsini, with support from both Ferrante of Naples and Piero de' Medici. This disposal of papal possessions without permission was not unreasonably seen as a breach of the Church's rights, and the evidence of Florentine-Neapolitan understanding led the pope into negotiations with both Ludovico Sforza and the French. Initially this led to an alliance in April 1493 between Milan, Venice and the pope, the league being sealed by the marriage of Lucrezia Borgia to a cousin of the Milanese regent, Giovanni Sforza of Pesaro, one of the abler soldiers among the Romagnol vicars. This move strengthened the pope militarily, benefited his family, extended his political influence in the Romagna and alarmed Ferrante into coming to terms and putting pressure on Orsini over the Cibò castles, by making a monetary composition to retain them.

Such manoeuvres were practicable within Italy, where states were small and the balance of power could alter quickly, but when the great powers of Europe became involved, the situation changed. War aims became more far-reaching, with the combatants seeking a resolution of issues rather than an adjustment of an existing balance of power, while the invasions broke up the relations of patronage and dependence between the larger Italian powers and the smaller *signori*. Furthermore, whereas within Italy the papacy had been of comparable power to its rivals, within Europe as a whole it was small compared with the invaders of the peninsula, and it was no longer practicable to use methods of diplomacy, such as marriage alliances, which had served previously. It is also possible that whereas the Italian states were accustomed to papal activity in secular politics and might oppose the pope politically without challenging his position in the Church, the great European powers, particularly France, were accustomed to put pressure on the papacy through ecclesiastical means.

It was the succession in Naples, and the French claim inherited from the Angevins, which finally prompted the invasion of 1494 and the subsequent decades of fighting which ravaged Italy. Alexander recog-

nised the title of Ferrante's son, Alfonso, thereby securing a Neapolitan alliance, but in face of the imminent French invasion he was losing
support in the higher ranks of the Church. Cardinal Giuliano della
Rovere had always been hostile, and Ascanio Sforza, his most influential supporter at the conclave, had moved into opposition when Alexander came to terms with Naples, in line with his Milanese relatives.
Rovere and Sforza, former rivals, but now both allied to France, were
both prepared to assert that the pope should be deposed. Against
Italian enemies, a papal-Neapolitan alliance would have been powerful, but against the French it was inadequate. Colonna opposition,
Orsini defection, alternate negotiation and attempted force by the
pope allowed Charles VIII a virtually uncontested march to Rome and
beyond. Italian politics, however, were as volatile as ever, and
although Alexander was militarily powerless his political shrewdness
was unimpaired. Charles did not secure papal investiture with Naples,
but did abandon talk of Church reform and the pope's deposition.
There was soon a hostile reaction in Naples, when the conqueror
conferred favours too freely on his countrymen, and after some three
months occupation Charles retreated with half his army, leaving the
rest to hold his conquest. Although the battle at Fornovo was indeci-
sive, the French retreat continued and after some thirteen months in
Italy, Charles returned home with no profit. At first sight the French
withdrawal represented a return to the conditions of the previous forty
years, but the support given by the Spaniards and the emperor to the
Italian league against the French [11] had been a major cause of Charles's
departure. These powers remained involved in the peninsula, the
Spanish army under Gonsalvo of Cordoba playing a major part in the
reconquest of Naples for Alfonso's son, Ferrantino, and Maximilian
invading Italy, though with no result, in 1496.

The Italian powers did not recognise the changed situation, because
after the withdrawal of the immediate threat, they soon resumed their
mutual hostilities. Ludovico Sforza came to terms with the French,
perhaps in order to undermine the danger of Charles supporting his
cousin and heir presumptive, Louis of Orleans, who had a claim on
Milan from his grandmother Valentina Visconti. He felt sufficiently
secure not to maintain his army and fortresses adequately, but this was
short-sighted, as became apparent when Orleans succeeded to the
throne in 1498. The pope seems to have felt that he had weathered the
storm of the invasion, surviving the attempts of his ememies within the
Church to depose him, being generally on good terms with the Italian
powers, and no longer being in danger from Naples, where fighting
continued. His main difficulty was that hardy perennial, the Roman
nobility, and his measures against the Orsini, in revenge for their
retention of the Cibò castles and their desertion in 1494, were similar

to the actions of popes before 1494. He recovered the castles of Anguillara and Cerveteri, though the new diplomatic situation and foreign influence limited his success when Spanish and Venetian pressure compelled him to come to terms with the Orsini. A new development in Alexander's policy was his attempt to establish his son Juan, Duke of Gandia, whom he appointed captain-general of the Church and leader of the papal army, in the Orsini lands. Earlier attempts at Borgia dynasticism were based on marriage alliances and the endowment of papal relatives in Naples and Spain rather than in the lands of the Church. Gandia did not secure the lands, but did obtain the greater part of the indemnity paid by the Orsini as part of the settlement.

It was in these years that the Borgia family became really prominent at the papal court, with Gandia as the main beneficiary of his father's policies. When Ferrantino of Naples died without an heir, his uncle and successor, Federigo, requiring papal investiture, dared not protest when the pope conferred on Gandia as hereditary fiefs, Benevento and Terracina, lands disputed between the kingdom and the papacy. The only objection came from Cardinal Piccolomini, although Spain was displeased. A week later, before open trouble arose, the duke was murdered by an unknown assailant. Who was responsible for this need not concern us; what matters is that the killing was a major setback to Borgia dynasticism. The pope's immediate emotional reaction, leading to the establishment of the reform commission was admittedly short-lived, and although the pope kept his family at a distance during the summer of 1497, he was also taking steps to annul Lucrezia's first marriage. Giovanni Sforza had been of little value as an ally to the pope, who may well have been planning to destroy the Romagnol vicariates and impose direct papal rule rather than to pursue the old policy of enhancing the Church's temporal authority through alliances. Moreover, the Sforza marriage represented alignment with Milan, and though this had made sense when it was concluded, it was less apropriate in 1497, even although Duke Ludovico, who did not wish to quarrel with the pope, brought pressure on his cousin to agree to the divorce. Alexander's policy was now oriented towards an alliance with Naples, and therefore with Spain, as the new king depended on a Spanish army. Lucrezia's second husband, Alfonso, Duke of Bisceglie, was an illegitimate representative of the Neapolitan royal house.

Gandia's death and the apparent incompetence of the Prince of Squillace seemed to weaken the prospects for Borgia dynasticism as a diplomatic weapon. Alexander resolved the problem by releasing Cesare from his clerical status so that he might marry, and for the rest of the pontificate Cesare was even more conspicuous than his father in the politics of the Papal States. These years revealed both the strength and the weakness of a policy of nepotism. Though a *condottiere* who was the pope's son might be more reliable than a freelance adventurer, there was always a danger that the growing power of the family might be too high a price for the Church to pay.

Cesare's career was closely bound up with the renewed French threat after the succession of Louis XII, whose claim to Milan, as heir of the Visconti, shifted the emphasis of French ambitions to the north, which was more vulnerable to them because of its geographical proximity. The pope exploited Louis' desire for an annulment of his first marriage in return for a duchy for Cesare, to whom the king promised military assistance in the Romagna, after Cesare had joined him in a campaign against Milan. Charles VIII's fiasco may have led Italian opinion to underestimate French capacity, and possibly the pope and the Venetians, both of whom joined Louis against Milan, hoped to exploit his support in the expectation that he could not secure any permanent gains. However, this time the French were victorious and Ludovico Sforza fled to Maximilian. This freed Cesare for a campaign in the Romagna in the winter of 1499–1500 in which he captured the old Riario lands of Imola and Forlì, ruled over by Girolamo's widow, Caterina Sforza. A brief Sforza recovery compelled him to abandon an attack on his former brother-in-law at Pesaro, but Ludovico was soon deserted by his Swiss mercenaries and fell into French hands.

For the rest of this pontificate Naples was again in the forefront of politics, being eventually united under Aragonese rule after an unsuccessful partition treaty between Aragon and France. So within a decade of 1494, two major Italian states had passed under foreign control and a third, Florence, was closely allied to France. As Naples was still technically a papal fief, its fate, in which Alexander had to acquiesce, marks the political weakness of the Church against the great powers of Europe. By contrast, the pope had considerable success in extending his control in the States of the Church. He dispossessed the Colonna after the fall of their ally, Federigo of Naples; betrothed his great-niece, Girolama Borgia-Lanzol, to Fabio Orsini in 1498 and her sister, Angela, to the Rovere heir of Urbino in 1500, though this last marriage did not take place, when Cesare's capture of Urbino in 1502 made the alliance politically superfluous. Lucrezia's son by her second husband, whom Cesare murdered, was given lands she had purchased from the Gaetani and some forfeited Colonna properties, and other members of the family also received land grants.

The main Borgia advance was in the Romagna, where the Venetians acquiesced in Cesare's campaign, probably because they wished papal support against the Turks. The promotion of the Venetian Cornaro to the cardinalate may also have been a favour to the Republic. Cesare

relied on mercenaries, largely Spanish, and soon captured Pesaro and
Rimini, though at Faenza Astorre Manfredi put up a protracted resistance till April 1501. This left Bologna as the most important survivor
of the northern cities in the States of the Church. After the fall of the
Sforza it had come to terms with the French, on whom the Bentivoglio
had to rely if they were to survive against Cesare. Louis' actions
represent a balance between Borgia and Bentivolio, for Cesare was
unable to attack Bologna in 1501, but Giovanni Bentivoglio had to
refrain from helping his grandson, Astorre Manfredi, at Faenza.

Shortly afterwards, Lucrezia's marriage to the heir of Ferrara consolidated Cesare's position by providing a screen against Venetian
intervention in the newly captured towns. By this time Borgia interests
were obviously being given priority over those of the Church, because
the pope remitted to the Duke of Ferrara the annual *census* owed to
the Church, as well as paying a considerable dowry. What is uncertain
is how far Cesare was now acting without his father's knowledge. A
feint at Florence in the summer of 1501 was probably a bluff, as the city
could expect French support, and all that he gained was a treaty and
the promise of a *condotta*, which was never paid, but the occupation by
one of Cesare's captains in 1502 of Arezzo, which had revolted against
Florence, was probably planned to test French reactions, even
although the Borgias denied complicity and later withdrew the force.
1502 saw Cesare's most successful campaign, in which he captured
Urbino and Camerino, and later overcame a plot by his own *condottieri*, negotiating to keep them loyal until the surrender of Senigallia
made them less necessary to him. They were then arrested, two being
strangled forthwith and two more, both members of the Orsini family,
being executed later. Cesare was diverted from Bologna, but soon
after reoccupied Città di Castello and Perugia. The pope then summoned his son back to Rome, where he turned his forces on the Orsini,
two of the leaders of whom had to retire to France. With this, the pope
could reasonably feel that the power of the Roman nobility had been
broken.

Cesare's actions strengthened Borgia power in the States of the
Church, but French protection for the Tuscan cities was limiting his
ambitions. At the same time, the French defeat in Naples and increasing Spanish influence was leading the pope to another possible diplomatic realignment. Probably he was making offers to both sides,
hoping that they would pay his price, of a permanent hereditary state
for Cesare, to give him greater security than that afforded by his
existing position of papal vicar in the Romagna. The policy of military
advance was pursued in the interests of the Borgia family rather than in
those of the papacy as an institution.

At this point, Alexander's death upset the political situation and showed that Borgia power rested primarily on his tenure of the papacy. It would have been surprising if Cesare had not laid plans for preserving his position, and as the pope was over seventy, Cesare could not have expected support for many years more. What he could not reckon on was that the fever which killed his father would also disable him at the crucial moment. For all his very real influence, he was now merely one party in the struggle and not the decider of papal policy. French and Spanish armies were both poised within easy march of Rome, and the cardinals in the city were trying to reassert their authority against the Borgias and their adherents. Outside Rome, the deposed *signori* in Urbino and Camerino returned to their towns, and the Venetians assisted Giovanni Sforza at Pesaro and the Malatesta at Rimini. But in both the north and Rome, the eventual outcome would depend on the conclave.

In fact it required two conclaves to clarify the position. The elderly and infirm Cardinal Piccolomini survived his election for less than a month, and Giuliano della Rovere, so long one of the most influential members of the college, eventually secured the supreme office to which he had probably aspired ever since the death of his uncle Sixtus IV. Under the former, Cesare still preserved verbal support for his rule in the Romagna, but although he came to terms with Rovere before the second election, this was more an attempt by a desperate man to salvage something from the wreck of his fortunes than a settlement between equals.

From the start, Julius II was determined to restore papal control over the Church's lands in the Romagna. He was willing to safeguard Cesare's person and goods, but was resolved that he should return his lands to the Church. This aim was simpler to state than to fulfil: Cesare still had troops under loyal commanders in the Romagnol fortresses and, more serious, the Venetians were exploiting the changed political situation by infiltrating into the area. Gradually the pope improved his position, with Cesare's castellans surrendering to him while their master was in captivity, at first in papal hands and then in those of the Spaniards in Naples. When Forlì, the last place where his forces surrendered, passed into papal control in August 1504, Cesare was sent to Spain where he died in an obscure skirmish, fighting for his brother-in-law, the King of Navarre.

Cesare's fate shows again how an individual pope had effective power to influence the policies of the papacy as an institution. While he had Alexander's support, he could expand his power and dominate Italian war and politics, but without it he was almost totally vulnerable. His career, however, had certain long-term results, for not all the expelled Romagnol despots were able to return . His removal created a power vacuum into which Julius II could move, though sometimes only with difficulty because of competition from other powers, notably Venice. This largely explains the hostility, for most of the pontificate, between the papacy and the republic, the one secular Italian power still effectively independent of the non-Italian states. The Treaty of Blois of 1504 between Louis XII and Maximilian had papal support, and although this alliance did not lead to the contemplated action against Venice, it foreshadowed the later attack after the conclusion of the League of Cambrai in 1508.

Before this, however, the pope had enforced closer control on Perugia and Bologna. The conquest of the latter was his main objective, but Perugia fell sooner, when Gianpaolo Baglioni came to terms with the pope. Alone of the northern cities acknowledging papal suzerainty, Bologna had not fallen to Cesare, but when the pope came in person it could not hold out. The *de facto* ruler, Giovanni Bentivoglio, tried to lay down terms, that Julius should not bring an army, but he no longer had the French support which had saved him against Cesare, except in the form of refuge in Milan. When he departed, Julius entered the city in peace. The conquest was not permanent, because the pope refused to accept the limitations on his power contained in the capitulation agreed with Nicholas V, and his first two cardinal legates were both guilty of serious misgovernment. Although the first, Ferreri, was deprived of his office and imprisoned, the second, Alidosi, was equally oppressive. This led in 1511 to a reaction in favour of the Bentivoglio.

Before this, however, international wars were renewed in northern Italy, and involved the papacy for the remainder of the pontificate. The changes in alliances and the policies pursued by the pope and the secular powers alike represent international politics at their most cynical and opportunist, notably in the combination of the great powers against Venice. All, admittedly, had some grievance against it: the French at its advance into the Milanese lands; the emperor at its occupation of Fiume and Trieste; the Spaniards at its retention of Brindisi and ports in Apulia since the expulsion of Charles VIII, and the pope at its refusal to surrender refugee members of the Bentivoglio family or to allow him to make a provision to the see of Vicenza. Plans for a league were put forward in February 1508, and an agreement was concluded between France and the empire at Cambrai in December, with the pope adhering to it in the following March. The opportunist character of the league was soon shown by the course of events; once Venice had been defeated and surrendered all that the league had desired, disunity re-emerged between the allies. After obtaining the surrender of Rimini, Faenza, Cervia and Ravenna, the pope came to terms. At the same time, he quarrelled with Louis XII over the appointment of a new bishop of Avignon, and the king stopped the payment of ecclesiastical revenues from Milan to clerics in Rome, clear evidence of how political changes affected Church administration.

The League of Cambrai enabled the pope to make the maximum gains possible at Venetian expense, after which he turned on the next serious threat to his power in the north, namely France. This had given additional offence by granting protection to the Duke of Ferrara, a papal vassal who had served as captain-general of the Church in the war of the League of Cambrai, but had persisted in the anti-Venetian alliance with French support. The duke's excommunication in August 1510 marked the start of a new struggle, which lasted until the pope's death, and was waged both on the battlefield and in ecclesiastical politics, when Louis gave support to the rebel cardinals who called a council to Pisa against the pope. The details of the struggle are less important than its outcome, and there is little doubt that Julius out-manoeuvred his opponents. The convocation of his own council to the Lateran in July 1511 undermined the assembly at Pisa, and the conclusion of an anti-French alliance in October prepared the way for the victories of the following year. The French success at Ravenna was transitory and costly, and before long an attack by the Swiss compelled them to abandon even Milan. Moreover, the return of the Medici to Florence ended its alliance with France, which had been a constant factor in diplomacy since 1494. When Julius died in February 1513, he had repulsed the French effectively and extended the Church's real control in lands where its power had previously been only nominal.

The historian's judgment on Julius must depend, above all, on the criteria by which he is assessed. Certainly he was anathema to spiritual men, and Erasmus in the *Julius Exclusus* depicted him as a fierce and an arrogant military leader. There is much truth in this, and indeed he served in this role even before he became pope. Guicciardini's comment that he would have deserved the highest glory if he had been a secular prince provides the best basis for judgment, because in the early sixteenth century it was impossible for the papacy to be detached from its temporal problems. However much one may deplore his political methods, and there is much to deplore, such as the use of ecclesiastical sanctions against Venice or Ferrara in temporal matters, it is hard to see what other course was open to him. Provided that it was considered desirable that the Church should possess temporal power, and this was generally accepted, it was necessary to defend it and presumably also recover lands which had slipped from control. Also, where his predecessors had endowed their relatives richly from Church lands in return for military service, Julius brought back the conquered territories under the direct rule of the Church. Compared with Sixtus IV, Innocent VIII or Alexander VI, Julius II was more single-minded and disinterested, with the result that the state which he handed on to his successor was faced only with external threats and not with the same internal unrest which had existed a decade earlier. While one may describe his Italian policy as a series of expedients, beneath these one can see the fundamental object of strengthening papal power. Who his allies were mattered little, if an alliance met immediate problems. He could use the French against Venice, turn to Spain when the French threat became too powerful, and in the last year of his life became concerned with excessive Spanish influence in Naples. Many of his actions involved a response to the policies of other powers stronger than himself, and he cannot be regarded as the sole shifting element in the kaleidoscopic political scene. Indeed his aims remained consistent behind the apparent inconstancy of his actions.

Julius' death was fatal to the rebel council. Already undermined by the convocation of the Lateran council, it lost its *raison d'être*, the aim of deposing Julius, when Giovanni de' Medici became pope as Leo X. In Italian politics, Leo's main aim was to maintain family intersts in Florence and his expulsion of Francesco della Rovere from Urbino in 1516 and the investiture of his nephew, Lorenzo, with the duchy was reminiscent of the nepotism of Sixtus IV or Alexander VI, particularly as the finances of the Church suffered seriously from the resulting war. In relations with France he did not, however, follow a policy of open hostility, because his primary concern was to secure the return of French obedience after the schism, this being eventually secured at the eighth plenary session of the council in December 1513. During the French attempt to recover ground in Italy earlier in the year, which culminated in the defeat of Novara in June, Leo pursued a policy of neutrality.

When Francis I invaded Italy in August 1515, the pope again vacillated. Although in July he had adhered to the league for the defence of Milan, he remained in friendly correspondence with the French king, and no papal contingent fought against the French in the decisive battle of Marignano. Before the battle, Leo's policy was inconsistent, and after the French victory he rapidly came to terms with them, and wrote to his former allies justifying his conduct. At first he pleaded that he had no other course open, but later he praised Francis's merits and his devotion to the idea of a crusade. He conceded Parma and Piacenza to the French, obtaining in return a promise of support for Medici rule in Florence and a pledge to pay for salt from the papal mines of Cervia. In December the pope and the king met a Bologna, an encounter which led ultimately to the concordat which, in return for French abandonment of the pragmatic sanction, provided a basis for governing the French Church very much on the king's terms. On political issues the pope procrastinated in face of the king's demands, despite the latter's dominance after Marignano. He held out a possibility of eventual investiture with Naples on Ferdinand's death, but when this occurred in January 1516 the French king was in no position to enforce his claim.

The mixture of political and ecclesiastical issues in these negotiations gives some impression of Leo's priorities. Even when he was at considerable military disadvantage, he was sufficiently determined to stand firm on political questions, whereas he surrendered effective control over the French Church in return for the comparatively slight concession of the abandonment of the Pragmatic. At first sight this might indicate that the secular concerns of the papacy were more important to him than the preservation of his power in ecclesiastical matters, and there is some truth in this. Two reservations may, however, be made: the French king already had a large measure of control over the Church in France, so the surrender was less drastic than might at first appear, and Leo's conduct must be seen as the result of the role which the papacy had been compelled to take because of its temporal power in Italy. Since 1494 successive popes had had no option but to take sides in the European power struggle, because the States of the Church lay between Milan and Naples, the two main areas of conflict in the 'scramble for Italy', and the conflicting powers would not leave them untouched. Traditional links between the Holy See and Naples intensified the problem, because whatever the *de facto* position was, it was understood that *de jure* the right of investiture with the kingdom lay with the pope, as it had done for generations. Admittedly some popes entered the political struggles without reluctance, even with avidity – Alexander VI in pursuit of Borgia interests, Julius II in attempts to consolidate the temporal power to the Church's advantage – but one may doubt if they could have stood aloof even if they had so desired. The popes must not bear the entire blame for the abuses resulting from their political preoccupations. The secular powers, as much as the papacy, did not distinguish between ecclesiastical and political matters, as can be seen in Louis XII's support for the cardinals who rebelled against Julius II, and in Maximilian's threats in the winter of 1515–16, just when Leo came to terms with Francis, that the reform of the Curia was necessary before any crusade could be undertaken. The European powers recognised the vital role of the pope in politics and were anxious to obtain his support. The pope, on the other hand, was primarily concerned with preventing any of the great powers becoming more powerful, and this largely explains Leo's attempts during the imperial election of 1519 to have a candidate elected other than Charles of Habsburg or the French king.

One possible candidate was the Elector Frederick of Saxony, and this explains the approaches made to him by Rome, including the conferment of the Golden Rose, and the failure to take action against

Martin Luther, that dissident professor of Frederick's university at Wittenberg. Only the future would show how papal preoccupation with politics here would have repercussions in every aspect of the Church's life.

PART THREE

Secular Rulers and the Administration of the Church

CHAPTER 7

Spheres of Conflict, I: Benefices and Provisions

During the schism, the secular rulers had secured gains in certain jurisdictional and administrative matters at the expense of the central authority of the Church. The struggles between the papacy and the councils in the first half of the fifteenth century left them favourably placed to consolidate these gains, which in many cases they held, either by concession or by usurpation, until the Reformation crisis. The growth of princely power did not, however, go unchallenged, and an examination of the relations between the secular and the spiritual powers during the century shows where the main points of dispute lay, and how they were resolved in accordance with changing political circumstances and the respective power of the parties concerned.

Foremost among contentious questions, as before the schism, was that of appointments to benefices. Secular rulers naturally wished some say in this, particularly when the benefice concerned was a bishopric or a great abbey, in view of the part played by leading churchmen in the secular affairs of their countries. The over-riding authority of the pope in this field was certainly acknowledged in theory and in practice men might look to the pope for a confirmation of title, even if this had no apparent flaws in it. In 1429, Patrick of Cardross, prior of the Augustinian house of Inchmahome, petitioned Martin V to ratify his election so as to remove any doubt about his title. This he did ten years after canonical election by the house and confirmation by the ordinary. Even before the schism, however, the secular rulers had secured some successes in controlling appointments, as can be seen from the tacit concordat between the Avignon papacy and Philip VI of France, by which the pope promoted candidates with royal support, although not always as rapidly as the king wished. A notable assertion of royal power was the English Statute of Provisors of 1351, which had in practice confirmed the king's effective control, in which the papacy had perforce to acquiesce. It was regarded, along with the later statute on the same subject, as the basis for appointments in England during the Council of Constance. When, at the end of the council, concordats were concluded between the reunified papacy and the nations of Christendom, provisions to benefices were treated at length in those with the Spanish, German and French nations, but were not mentioned in that with England. The subsequent attempts by Martin V to have the statute revoked also suggest some recognition of its validity.

Nevertheless, although the pope might be reduced to pleading with a secular ruler, his powers over benefices remained considerable after the schism. When Martin V reissued the chancery regulations in the February after his accession, among the first were those which maintained papal rights of reservation over various benefices.[1] The concordats also show the extent of papal powers, in his right to fill benefices falling vacant at the Curia, or vacated by the death of a cardinal or of certain named papal officials. With other benefices, elaborate schemes were worked out to strike a balance between contesting interests. In abbeys and cathedral churches, canonical election was to be restored and the rights of ordinary collators recognised. In the German concordat there were stipulations to allow chapters to appoint only men of noble or knightly rank, and conditions to give special rights to graduates. The most notable feature, however, about these concordats is that they do not show any concern with the right of the secular ruler to influence appointments. To this extent they must be regarded as unrealistic, because power had already passed into secular hands. In 1408 a council of the French Church had formulated a scheme by which a commission investigated claimants for provisions, setting them in order of merit, in a list which collators would have to follow. Late in 1413 the pope granted the king the disposal of 530 important benefices, an action which provoked this comment from Jouvenel des Ursins; 'le roy et les seigneurs au regard des prelatures estoient pape'. In March 1418, shortly before the concordat, a royal ordinance upheld free elections in France and the Dauphiné and rejected papal reservations and expectatives.

The omission of any reference to royal influence in the concordats may arise from the presence at Constance of numbers of academics, who were more sympathetic to a system of free canonical election than to one in which the king was dominant.[2] There were varied pressures in both ecclesiastical and lay society, and a consultation of 1417 between members of the Parlement of Paris, the Great Council, the prelates and the University of Paris suggested that many in the French Church were willing to accept royal support against the pope. Political changes, however, could alter attitudes to Rome: the ordinance of March 1418 was repealed in the same autumn; the services due to the pope were reaffirmed, and the blame for the earlier measure cast on Bernard of Armagnac. Such changes probably had little practical effect in the life of the French Church, although the continual bargaining between the Crown and the pope in succeeding years suggests that the latter's favour was always regarded as desirable by the king. Even if he paid only lip-service to papal superiority, this still indicates his doubts about taking independent action in Church affairs. It may also, after 1422, reflect Charles VII's desire for papal support against English claims to the French throne.

In a series of instructions to his ambassadors to the pope, probably from 1422, Charles requested the power to nominate 500 persons to benefices in the kingdom, as had been granted to his predecessors. Similar requests were made in negotiations in 1426, and one of the bulls issued by Martin V on 21 August deals largely with the question of benefices. Predictably this reasserted papal rights: it laid down that elections and dispositions of benefices, where the election had devolved to the Holy See, should have free effect, and a list of the reserved benefices was given. Other benefices should be filled by the ordinary collator, subject to certain restrictions. So far there had been no mention of the king's influence, but the bull then mentions a royal request for the nomination of fifty persons to sundry dignities, and a confirmation of their position by special grace. The pope granted the king twenty-five.

The form of the grant shows that the king did not have any recognised legal title to such nominations, but the fact that it was made shows that the pope was willing to admit his influence and meet at least part of his request. This bull foreshadows the later willingness of the pope and the king to come to terms over Church government and to disregard the wishes of the Gallican party, who looked in vain to the king to protect the Church against Roman domination. The Gallicans' sentiments were made clear in a remonstrance presented to Charles VII in 1430 by a Parlement at Poitiers; he was urged to implement old ordinances asserting the independence of the French Church and to work for the success of the general council, which was to meet at Basel, in reforming the Church.

The secular power, however, could disregard such demands unless it wished to bring pressure on the pope for further concessions. But there is no doubt that the king was concerned that benefices should be held by reliable men, as is evident from letters issued by Charles VII in March 1432. There are complaints in the preamble that an ordinance debarring foreigners from holding benefices in the realm had been ignored, and that these had been conferred on them by the pope. Accordingly the old regulation was renewed. In the ensuing decade the advantage passed to the king in his relations with the pope: his power within the realm increased as that of the English declined, while the struggle between Eugenius IV and the Council of Basel introduced a new element into the relationship between the papacy and the secular powers, whose attitude could determine whether or not the council would obtain the political support essential for it to resist the pope. Eugenius was effectively muzzled by the danger of antagonising the king, who could extend his influence under the pretext of defending the liberties of the French Church. The council's decrees on elections in 1433 and 1436 were among the reform measures adopted in the Pragmatic Sanction of Bourges of 1438, although their original form was modified in the king's interest. It was accepted that kings and princes were entitled to seek favours for deserving subjects, but it was laid down that even when the pope named a bishop or abbot at the Curia, the latter should take his oath of obedience to his own superior.

Although the king secured no specific legal right to make appointments, he was however able to influence the choice of candidates for major benefices. It is harder to judge how far the king might accept papal encroachment on the letter of the pragmatic, if this over-rode free election in favour of a candidate with royal support. Haller has shown that most episcopal vacancies in French between 1439 and 1450 were filled in accordance with the pragmatic, but this does not necessarily contradict the view of Valois that the king and his officials observed it only when it suited them. Certainly papal interference was sometimes accepted, and on other occasions the king may have obtained his wishes more easily by putting pressure on the electors. An examination of the elections by the cathedral chapter at Paris illustrates the conflicts which could arise. The capitular candidate for the deanery, elected in 1440, had to contend with a papal nominee, who had been Charles VII's proctor in Rome and a royal councillor, and who had the king's support. The dispute was not finally resolved until 1456, by which date the original papal provisor had disappeared from the scene and been succeeded by another man acceptable to both pope and king. In the end the deanery was conferred on a third party by the papal legate. In the episcopal vacancy of 1447 the king originally supported the pope's nominee, but the chapter refused to elect him, choosing instead Guillaume Chartier, a royal servant and former receiver general of finances, who could by no means be antipathetic to the king. After some four-and-a-half months the king agreed to the election, but a further year passed before the pope accepted it, and then only when alternative provision was made for his own candidate. Clearly the wishes of the king and the pope were not invariably opposed, and in particular cases there was scope for negotiation and compromise. More generally, too, the king was willing to make concessions to secure papal good will: in 1441 royal letters declared that the pragmatic was not retroactive and that provisions made before 1438 were to be regarded as valid, while between 1442 and 1450 there were a number of negotiations for a concordat, although without success.

Not all the lands within the territorial limits of France were affected by the pragmatic. Most notably in Brittany the duke pursued an independent policy from the king in relations with Rome and indeed reached his own agreement with the pope. Under Martin V, the pope appointed various persons named by the duke, and although he made the formal provision, his choice was limited to clerks acceptable to the latter, who normally enjoyed the *regalia* of the see during the vacancy and handed them over to the new bishop when he presented his bulls and took an oath of loyalty. The precise jurisdictional situation in Brittany was not clear, but seems to have been determined by the concordat with the French nation at Constance, which was adopted in Brittany, and which continued to apply even after other agreements had been reached for the rest of the kingdom. Duke Jean V exploited the struggle between Eugenius IV and the Council of Basel, generally giving his support to the pope in return for concessions. These included the right to confer benefices on forty persons, granted in 1432, and although the duke had an embassy at Basel for a time in the middle of the decade, from 1436 onwards his renewed adherence to the pope was again rewarded with grants of benefices. He was still prepared to play off conciliar claims against Rome but his flirtation with Basel was short-lived, and despite attempts by Felix V to hold the duke's loyalty by nominating Bretons as cardinals, the latter eventually came round to Eugenius's party.

One result of this was that the pragmatic did not apply in Brittany, and a formal settlement was reached between the pope and the duke in the concordat of Redon on 14 August 1441, which ended the uncertainties of the previous decade. Though the papal envoys did not take any binding pledges in their master's name but merely promised to procure concessions, Eugenius ratified most of the promises made. First and most important was that the pope would nominate to bishoprics only persons specially recommended by signet letters, or persons agreeable to the duke who had been canonically elected. There was also the promise to concede forty-five nominations to the benefices to the duke, a figure increased by the pope to fifty. When Jean V died in 1442, he left the Breton Church obedient to Rome, when Gallicanism was rife elsewhere in France. On the question of benefices, only the broad lines of a settlement were reached, and trouble continued, although Eugenius did choose men who were *persona grata* to the duke to fill vacant bishoprics. This did not end tension, because the duke did not always make his position clear. When Nicholas V provided Robert de la Rivière to the see of Rennes, he chose a member of the ducal council who had a general recommendation from Duke Francis I. Clearly he intended to choose someone acceptable, but the duke had an alternative candidate in Jacques d'Espinay, the son of the master of the ducal household. This led to protracted trouble, aggravated when the duke died and his successor, Pierre II, was hostile to the Espinay family. It was not until 1454 that Jacques d'Espinay after many vicissitudes eventually secured possession of his see.[3] By then the end of the Council of Basel had left the papacy better able to assert its claims, although in practice the duke remained influential.

Similar problems arose also in the French lands under English control in the first half of the century. While the Duke of Bedford, as regent for the infant Henry VI, ruled in Paris, he tried to maintain the traditional claims of the French Crown on his nephew's behalf, and in 1424 the chancellor delcared to the estates that the duke wished the liberties of the French Church to be maintained according to the ordinances. This made it clear that whoever the secular ruler was, he was concerned with curbing papal rights – the 'liberties' of the Church were strictly limited by the power of the prince. More than twenty years later, in 1447, when English influence was far less widespread, Henry VI showed that he was still interested in Church appointments, when he issued letters patent, warning any person who claimed a benefice within his territories by papal gift, that it would not be tolerated. The ordinance gives the impression that an attempt was being made to extend to the French lands the principles behind the statute of Provisors. These lands had not been affected by the pragmatic. A chronicle of Bec Abbey, referring to the election of John of Rouen as abbot in 1446, states that it took place, *pragmatica sanctione in Normannia minime locum habente*. When he died in 1452, Normandy had passed into French hands, and his successor was elected, confirmed and blessed *secundum pragmaticam sanctionem*.[4] The influence of political changes upon ecclesiastical administration could hardly be more clearly indicated.

In Burgundy, too, there was virtual autonomy in ecclesiastical matters, although to some extent the pope's hand was strengthened by the duke's wish to secure recognition of his independence from the French Crown and support in his struggles against it. Control over the episcopal cities was one means of extending political influence, and Bishop Jean de Thoisy, and older councillor of John the Fearless, strengthened Burgundian influence at Tournai, where French sympathies were strong. On his death in 1433, the papal choice for the see, Jean d'Harcourt, was potentially neutral in the Franco-Burgundian struggle, but his appointment did not satisfy Philip the Good, who maintained pressure on the pope until he translated Harcourt to the archbishopric of Narbonne, and provided the ducal candidate, Jean Chevrot. The comment of Monstrelet on the struggle is a fair statement of how the papacy sought secular goodwill: '*Si fist le pape ceste transla-cion pour contenter les deux parties, et part espécial ledit duc.*' Philip's importance in European politics can be seen in the efforts of both Eugenius and the council to secure his support. When he withdrew his envoys from Basel and accredited an embassy to the papal council at Ferrara, the pope thanked him and held him up as an example to Charles VII.[5] He also gave grants of benefices to the duke's subjects, and granted to the duchess the right of collation to twelve benefices. In 1441 a concordat was agreed for the Burgundian lands outside France, and in the following year it was extended to include the dioceses of Besançon and Cambrai. But Philip did not impose on the pope any Burgundian equivalent of the pragmatic sanction, a fact recognised by Pius II in 1461, when he wrote that the duke had deserved well of the Holy See. Papal appreciation of the duke's deserts was often shown in grants in benefices, but it is noteworthy that the favours granted to ducal familiars were more numerous during the conciliar crisis than later in the century, when the pope's title was uncontested. However, in both periods the relatives of the duke, both legitimate and illegiti-mate, secured episcopal appointments for which they were far from suited, thereby helping to strengthen ducal control in their lands.[6]

The examples of France, Brittany and Burgundy show how the secular princes of the second quarter of the fifteenth century could influence appointments to benefices, either by a general agreement with the pope or by unilateral action, which might be modified in particular cases. In England, the situation was rather different, because the question of appointments had been effectively settled before the schism by the Statutes of Provisors. The concordat between the papacy and England at the end of the Council of Constance was more limited in scope than those with the other nations, and makes no mention of provisions. In practice the king already had legalised his power over appointments, and it was Martin V who attempted to upset the *status quo* and recover influence after the schism. Henry V tried to warn Martin off attempting to confer English benefices, but in 1419 a papal envoy was instructed to try to secure the abandonment of the Statutes of Provisors. This was unsuccessful, and there was a further clash in 1421, when the pope refused to promote the king's am-bassador at the Curia, Thomas Polton, from the see of Hereford to that of London, but instead shifted round a number of the English bishops. Further negotiations had no result, and it seems probable that Henry had no serious intention of making concessions, and that when he hinted at them, it was with the aim of securing papal support to consolidate his political gains in France.

During Henry VI's minority, Martin continued putting pressure on England to give way on collations, and Humphrey of Gloucester made an unsuccessful attempt to exploit this, by allowing the pope free disposition of benefices in return for favour in his marital affairs. This *ad hoc* concession did not interrupt papal attempts to secure a more definitive settlement, but an embassy in 1426 under the future cardinal Cesarini had no more success than any earlier ones, as the English continued to reply that nothing could be done until the next Parliament.[7] At this point the pope lost his patience, and in December 1426 he warned both English archbishops to observe papal reservations under threat of excommunication. Archbishop Chichele was suspended from his legatine powers and forbidden to take the spiritualities of vacant sees, apparently because the pope regarded him as the main upholder of English customs. He was urged to use his influence against the statutes, but his first reaction was not to comply but to appeal against his suspension from the pope to a general council, and to remind Martin of the circumstances of his election. Later he wrote to an unknown cardinal with a bribe of 50 nobles for wine, and rallied support from his suffragans and from Oxford University, who both wrote to Martin in 1427 to praise Chichele's loyalty to the Roman Church. In January 1428 the archbishop spoke in Parliament in favour of the pope's rights, but nothing was done about the statutes.

In the end the papacy had to accept the English situation, and a few years later it was recognised by the curial canonist, Roselli, who declared that the pope alone could grant *spiritualia* to a layman and by adding that this was why the kings of England and Hungary conferred prebends in their kingdoms implied that they did so by papal concession.[8] The papal collector in the mid-1430s, Piero da Monte, wrote in 1436 that no one would be admitted as a bishop in England, unless he was one of those on whose behalf the king had petitioned the pope. In another letter of the same year, he transmitted the wishes of the English government, and in all cases the pope authorised the desired appointments. This was to be the pattern of English Church appointments, not only during the years of the Council of Basel when the pope was weak but also after the restoration of an unchallenged papacy. Although the popes occasionally failed to obliged the king, they generally made the desired appointments, and the chapters were excluded from any active part in choosing their bishops. The system called down the criticism of Thomas Gascoigne later in the century, and about 1510 Edmund Dudley declared that it would be a gracious act if the king restored free elections, because royal letters of recommendation were in practice commands. It is noteworthy that Dudley made no mention of the pope's part in appointments, because this reflects not only Dudley's sycophancy to the king but also the practical elimination of papal influence despite the absence of any formal agreement between England and the Curia. Perhaps the clearest indication of royal power is seen in the assumption that its nominee would obtain the see, as can be seen from the bestowal of its temporalities on him before his translation or 'election'. Even the wording of the headings in some episcopal registers implies that royal nomination played a vital part in the appointment.

In Brandenburg, too, one can see the development of princely power over the Church between the Council of Constance and the middle of the century. Martin V was able to assist the Elector Frederick I in asserting his influence over the bishoprics in his lands, while Frederick II exploited the confusion during the Basel crisis to extend this further. He secured a promise from Eugenius that he would appoint as bishops only those whom Frederick recommended as suitable, a concession which enabled him to act against the independence of the chapters. He also secured an increase in his rights of patronage over the Church. This may reflect the position of the prince in other German states also, despite the activity of conciliarists in Germany who attacked the system of provisions as such, because it stood in the way of Church reform.[9] In practical terms, however, their influence appears to have been slight.

With the re-establishment from the middle of the century of an uncontested succession of popes, Rome might have hoped to curb princely encroachments on church appointments. In fact this did not occur and the princes continued to make practical gains, greater than those to which they might be entitled in theory. The Concordat of Vienna of 1448 between the pope and the German nation did not grant to the emperor or to the secular princes within the Empire power to confer benefices, and indeed collations were divided between the ordinary collators and the pope by alternation of months. The princes, however, secured the promotions of their candidates without difficulty: Nicholas V allowed Frederick II of Brandenburg to depose clerks who had adhered to Felix V, and those appointed to replace them were to be *personae marchioni acceptae*. A bull to the Archbishop of Salzburg, who was a prince as well as an ecclesiastic, confirmed his right to appoint three of his suffragans, and in Saxony and Bavaria the princes gained control of the bishoprics. Many vacancies were filled by members of the princely families or by the officials of the ruler. Secular influence continued later in the century at both the imperial and the princely levels. In 1473 Sixtus IV granted Frederick III rights of presentation to 300 benefices, and confirmed bulls of Eugenius IV and Nicholas V giving him rights of patronage over certain bishoprics. In 1478 he granted him temporary patronage over other sees.

Sometimes the princes had to compromise with the canonical electors, although they were usually able to exercise effective influence. In 1471 the chapter of Brandenburg elected Arnold von Burgsdorff from among themselves and the Elector Albrecht accepted him, provided that he withdrew and was re-elected as the elector's nominee. After this, he lent Burgsdorff money when he went to Rome to secure confirmation. The elector wished not only to have the power to select the prelates in his lands but also to have it visibly recognised. Not all elections could be settled by compromise: Albrecht's successor could compel the withdrawal of Günther von Bünau, elected bishop by the chapter of Lebus, and make the canons take a new vote, in which they chose Dietrich von Bülow, a trusted councillor of the elector, who remained active in state affairs. Below the level of bishoprics, the electors secured papal grants of the presentation to major prebends in collegiate churches, including that of St Nicholas at Stendal, the richest in the Mark. The provost was almost always a councillor of the Margrave, who also had the right to present to several major prebends. During the period of papal weakness Eugenius IV had conceded five, but the elector was faced by capitular resistance and in 1452 this figure was cut to three.

Similar princely activity can be seen elsewhere in the empire: the Elector of Saxony demanded, as part of the price for accepting the Concordat of Vienna, the right to confer a third of the prebends at Naumburg, Merseburg, Zeitz and Wurzen, and in 1476 Sixtus IV granted to the Saxon duke the right of presentation to certain dignities in the chapter of Meissen, a favour extended by Innocent VIII nine years later. The Elector Philip of the Palatinate exploited Church resources to support his family, his second son being nominated to a prebend at Köln in 1484 (at the age of four) and securing the provostship of Mainz by 1491. He was appointed Bishop of Freising in 1499, although his consecration was delayed until he reached the canonical age in 1507. Three of his brothers also became bishops. Even this princely influence did not exclude papal nominees entirely, because one still finds complaints against them and resistance to the employment of German benefices for Italian political ends in the protests of Archbishop Berthold of Mainz in the 1480s. Nor was it only the princes who extended their influence over the Church: similar gains were made in some cities, as at Nuremburg, where in 1474 Sixtus IV granted to the council the right to present candidates for the two parish churches in the city during the 'papal months' as defined in the Concordat of Vienna. In 1513 the council negotiated with the local bishop to extend this power over the remainder of the year, and in the following year Leo X granted it full rights of patronage over these churches. In Hungary Matthias Corvinus in 1482 asked for the

appointment of a co-adjutor for the Archbishop of Esztergom, Johann
Peckenschlager, with whom he was in conflict, but although he obviously expected that the Curia would accommodate his wishes, he
secured no more than the translation of Peckenschlager to Salzburg,
with the administration of Esztergom being granted to the Cardinal of
Aragon.[10]

Here clearly papal influence survived in the later years of the century, and elsewhere in the Slav lands, in Poland, a balance existed
between papal and royal powers. In the aftermath of the schism Italian
officials could seek benefices by papal grant, and exploit their knowledge of local conditions. Jacobinus de' Rossi, papal collector in
Poland, was much concerned with his own advancement. In 1428, on
the promotion of Stanislaus Czoleck to the see of Poznan, he sought
provision to one of the benefices vacated in consequence, sending a list
of these and of their value to a friend at the Curia. In 1429 he sought
the provostship of Breslau, where the incumbent was *in extremis*, and
in 1432 the deanery of the same church, offering to resign a less
valuable benefice in exchange.[11] Later in the century a struggle broke
out between the Curia and the king, the crucial point being reached in a
contest over the see of Cracow in 1463. After this a typical fifteenth-
century compromise was reached, by which the Crown nominated high
church dignitaries, with the assumption of curial consent. Although
Sixtus IV and Innocent VIII threatened excommunication of those
who prevented free elections, and although a dispute over the see of
Ermland in 1489 led to an exchange of letters between King Casimir
and Cardinal Marco Barbo, statutes of 1496 and 1505 laid down that
benefices should be granted only by the will of the king. Relations
between Poland and the Curia improved in the pontificate of Leo X,
and when the Poles acceded to the Fifth Lateran Council, the way was
cleared for a concordat which divided the rights of collation between
the pope and the ordinary collator, by alternation of months as in the
Concordat of Vienna. The bull of 1519 was amplified by another six
years later. Effectively such a concordat left much power in the king's
hands, although formally the pope conceded less than he had done in
the French concordat of 1516.

Indeed a more explicit concession to the secular power than that in
the Concordat of Vienna may be seen in a grant only four years after it,
the indult of Nicholas V to the Duke of Savoy in 1452. The lengthy
preamble affirmed that the pope wished to favour the duke, so that he
might not suffer from promotions to benefices within his lands. The
grant specified that promotions would not be made to metropolitan
and other cathedral churches or to abbatial dignities within the duke's
lands, as long as they remained within the pope's obedience, unless the
pope had obtained the duke's consent to them. Similar concessions

were made about promotions to lesser benefices. This favour to a
secular ruler was greater than the papacy normally granted, and the
explanation for this may be found in the condition to the grant, that it
would be operative as long as the duke's lands remained within the
pope's obedience. This may well allude to the close ties of Savoy to the
schismatic party during the Council of Basel, when the former duke
was chosen as the conciliar antipope, Felix V. The indult would bind
Savoy closely to Rome and go far to prevent any danger of a renewed
schism, so Nicholas V probably felt that the price which he was paying
was worthwhile if it could guarantee Church unity. These grants were
confirmed and elaborated by Sixtus IV, who stated that no foreigners
should obtain benefices in Savoy by letters or expectative graces, and
later there were further confirmations by Innocent VIII, Julius II and
Leo X.

These concessions by the papacy may be paralleled elsewhere. In
1487 Innocent VIII granted an indult to James III of Scotland, in
which he promised that he would refrain from making any provision to
cathedral churches or monasteries valued at more than two hundred
florins a year, for a period of eight months, while he awaited the king's
recommendations. In the Spanish lands, too, the last quarter of the
century saw disputes over benefices culminating in papal concessions.
In 1475 Sixtus IV protested to King John of Aragon about the king's
refusal to admit Cardinal Mila to the see of Lerida and in 1478 a papal
provisor to the see of Tarragona was compelled to resign. An attempt
by the same pope to confer the see of Cuença on his great-nephew,
Cardinal Sansoni, in 1482 also failed when it was granted to Queen
Isabella's confessor, Alfonso de Burgos. The Spanish rulers coerced
Rome by breaking off communication and by threats of a council, and
Sixtus conceded the right of the monarchs to propose candidates for all
metropolitan and cathedral churches. This grant was extended with the
growth of the power of the Spanish monarchy, first into the recon-
quered lands of Granada and later into the New World. In the particular circumstances of Spain, where Isabella was queen of Castile in her
own right, tension might arise over church appointments quite irrespective of the papacy, and there seems little doubt that it was the queen
who was more influenced by spiritual considerations. She secured the
appointment of Ximénez de Cisneros to the see of Toledo, when her
husband wished it for his own illegitimate son, who was already
archbishop of Saragossa. The Portuguese king also could influence
episcopal appointments and in 1514 Leo X granted him the
patronage of all bishoprics and benefices in the overseas lands of the
Crown.

Here the papacy asserted at least a nominal authority by the very
fact that it conferred privileges on the king, but in Hungary the kings

extended their claims to partonage over all churches without obtaining curial approval, although in practice the papacy had to acquiesce. A king who visited Rome, as did Christian I of Denmark in 1474, could take advantage of this to secure favours, including concessions on benefices, over which he gained considerable influence, particularly through the demand that ecclesiastical posts should be held only by natives of the realm.[12]

Even in Italy, where one might expect papal influence to be greatest, the secular powers made considerable gains, and political hostility might well be intensified by problems of Church appointments, as in Florence in the 1470s, when hostility was developing between Sixtus IV and Lorenzo de' Medici. The pope's nephew, Cardinal Pietro Riario, had held the archbishopric of the city, and after his death in 1474, the see went to Lorenzo's brother-in-law, Rinaldo Orsini. Shortly afterwards, the pope appointed an unsuccessful aspirant to the position, Francesco Salviati, Archbishop of Pisa, although it was evidently known that this would not be welcome to the Medici, and for three years the Florentines would not admit him to his see. In the end Salviati became involved in the Pazzi conspiracy, and was put to death after its failure. In Milan the secular power had considerable influence over benefices, as was recognised by the French in 1489 when they recommended the king's Italian doctor to the duke for the first important benefice falling vacant within the duchy.[13] In Sicily, too, the secular power made gains: Innocent VIII granted it a right of nomination to major benefices in 1487 and the kings claimed the same for bishoprics under Leo X.

In view of the political difficulties between the papacy and Venice, it is hardly surprising that crises arose over provisions. Even if the pope intended favour to the Republic, he might inadvertently give offence. In 1459 Pius II conferred the see of Padua on the Venetian, Cardinal Barbo, the future Paul II, but the Senate favoured Gregorio Correr for the post. The Cardinal was given twenty days to renounce the see, under pain of his revenues from Venetian territory being sequestrated, and pressure was also put on his brother to induce him to resign. In the end the cardinal gave way, though the man appointed, Jacopo Zeno and not Correr, had to pay him an annual pension of 2,000 ducats. A quarter of a century later, in 1485, the same see was disputed between Cardinal Michiel, also a Venetian, and the Republic, and again the latter was victorious. The most important factor in Venetian history at this period, the territorial advance on the mainland, had direct influence on ecclesiastical matters, not merely because of conflicts with the papacy, but also because the government wished to ensure that dioceses would be in the hands of trustworthy men. From 1363 nominations to bishoprics in Venice had been by senatorial vote, a practice gradually extended to the mainland dioceses. In 1491 a decree laid down procedures for sending letters of commendation to Rome concerning benefices, to ensure that they were generally approved.[14]

The Italian wars in the early sixteenth century affected appointments to benefices in the Venetian lands. In 1507, after a two-year dispute, the Venetians could enforce the withdrawal of a papal candidate, Cardinal Galeotto della Rovere, from the see of Cremona with only money compensation, and this was followed by an even more bitter quarrel over the see of Vicenza. Despite Julius II's refusal to confirm the nomination, the Venetian candidate, Jacopo Dandolo, took possession of the see, styling himself 'Bishop-elect of Vicenza by grace of the Senate of Venice'. In view of these struggles, it was hardly surprising that after Julius and his allies defeated the Venetians at Agnadello in 1509, the capitulation imposed on the Republic in the following February included a recognition of the pope's right to collate unchallenged to benefices in its territories. The papal victory was, however, limited, because although senatorial voting and public discussion was brought to an end, the men who filled the mainland sees in the sixteenth century were almost all drawn from Venetian noble families.[15]

Far more successful was the papal reassertion of control in Naples, perhaps the one country in Christendom where secular power over the Church actually declined in the second half of the fifteenth century. There is little doubt, from the evidence of the registered letters of Alfonso V's chancery in the early 1450s, that at that date there was active royal influence in ecclesiastical appointments, although the nominal right of the pope to make provisions was recognised. Letters to the pope requesting appointments were accompanied by others to the king's proctor at Rome and to various cardinals lobbying them for support.[16] Royal efforts to have the Abbot of S. Stefano at Dertona appointed Bishop of Trivento encountered papal resistance, because of insults offered by his men to the orator of the French king, even though the abbot himself knew nothing of the offence. The king seems to have made a successful *démarche* on this matter for within three months he was thanking the pope for making the appointment. He also lobbied the College of Cardinals collectively and wrote to three members of it individually, as well as to his resident proctor.

In these cases it is clear that appointments were made on royal initiative, in others it is less certain, but one has the impression of a system which worked by co-operation between the secular and the spiritual powers, with the former playing an active part. Only one case in the register shows any disagreement when a papal provisor found that he had been inhibited in the possession of his benefice by a rival who held it in virtue of a royal rescript (allegedly obtained surreptitiously). A petition to the king by the ousted provisor, however, sufficed to win his case, and there is no evidence of pressure from Rome to bring the king to heel, although the petitioner, who was chaplain to Cardinal Orsini, could presumably have obtained influential support there. It is presumably a sign of royal power over the Church that the claimant sought justice from the king.

Later in the century the political problems of Naples led to papal intervention there, in virtue of Holy See's temporal overlordship of the lands. The popes could play off rival claimants to the kingdom against each other or countenance the resistance of the nobility to the king. By these means the papacy sought not only political advantage, but also administrative gains in the matter of benefices. A settlement in 1486 proved of short duration and Ferrante defied papal demands, but in 1492 a further peace agreement renewed the 1486 terms as far as the Neapolitan Church was concerned. These represented the full papal claims: elections were to be free, saving papal rights of reservation, and it was laid down that neither before, during nor after the election would the consent or counsel of the king be required. All that was preserved for the king and his heirs were the rights of patronage which had previously been exercised and of receiving oaths of fealty according to ancient custom from those prelates who were accustomed to give them. The king promised to give peaceful possession to papal provisors. How effectively the pope maintained his control over these benefices during the Italian wars it is impossible to say, but it is likely that this was maintained for some time, as it is not until the pontificate of Clement VII that the king again secured a right of nomination to a number of bishoprics.

It was through political concerns that the pope could coerce the Neapolitan kings, because he had the threat of withdrawing their enfeoffment with the realm. The other power with an interest in the kingdom was France, and here, too, the history of provisions can be seen clearly only in the light of wider political considerations. In theory the conditions for filling benefices had been laid down in the Pragmatic Sanction of Bourges. This, because it also contained an affirmation of conciliar superiority, was anathema to the papacy, and attempts to secure its abolition were a constant feature of papal policy for three-quarters of a century. The kings did not adhere to it constantly, but regarded it as a useful weapon in negotiations with Rome, and if the price paid by the pope was sufficiently high, its operation could be suspended in practice, or it could even be abolished. Essentially, there were two main ways in which the papacy could oblige the king: political co-operation with his interests in Italy, which were considered in the last chapter; and support at home for the centralising royal power, both against the semi-independent feudatories such as Burgundy and

Brittany and the lesser, though still turbulent, nobles of the south, and over the Gallican faction in the French Church, which saw the best prospects for ecclesiastical reform in restoring free elections for bishoprics and other elective benefices, and patronage by the ordinary collators for lesser ones. These two classes of opposition to the monarchy could unite, as local nobles supported a chapter, which probably contained a number of their relatives, in its attempts to elect its bishop rather than acquiesce in the appointment of a royal nominee. The filling of vacancies was carried out after a triangular tug-of-war between the pope, the king and local interests, and the whole issue was complicated further by political factors affecting the relationship between the king and the pope, or the king and his subjects, at any particular time. This occurred notably at Pamiers and Carcassonne.

Negotiations between France and Rome were frequent, but they were never purely about benefices, even when ecclesiastical issues bulked larger than political ones. In 1452, when Cardinal d'Estouteville was sent to France as papal legate, his tasks included an investigation of the rehabilitation proceedings for Jeanne d'Arc, which had strong political overtones, and the possibility of a pacification between France and England, as well as an attempt to have the pragmatic withdrawn. In the end the king agreed to Nicholas V having slight extra rights of collation, as well as concessions on taxation, but the pragmatic remained in force. During the next twenty years, however, it was abolished twice, although on both occasions it was subsequently restored. The earlier of these was in 1461, shortly after the accession of Louis XI, when the new king's probable motive for this concession to the pope was a hope of recompense by political support in Naples. This restored the government of the French Church to the conditions operating before 1438, one aspect of this being the renewal of the practice of issuing expectative graces. Pius II failed to comply with the king's wishes. By 1463 Louis was clearly moving towards reasserting his power over the Church, and in the following year two ordinances effectively restored the terms of the pragmatic.[17] After this, disputes concerning benefices re-emerged between the king and the pope. In a disputed election at Comminges, the pope set aside both claimants and provided his own, and although Louis attempted to secure the promotion of one of his councillors, he eventually had to accept the pope's provision.

The second abolition of the pragmatic in 1472 was probably the price paid by Louis for support against the baronial coalition headed by the Duke of Burgundy. A working agreement was reached between the king and the pope, who was prepared to make a number of concessions. The bull publishing this concordat laid down that the collation of benefices falling vacant in the even months should pertain to the ordinary collators, and there was some restriction of reservations. An accompanying writ from the pope to the king mentioned the royal request that cathedral churches and consistorial benefices should not be conferred without his consent, and the pope said that he was always prepared to await the king's letters, for he believed that the king would suggest only suitable persons, who would be a credit to him and to the Holy See. When Louis ratified the concordat by letters patent, his tone was equally conciliatory and insincere.

In practice, when relations between the king and the pope were friendly, nominations to benefices did not raise any great difficulty, and between 1472 and 1475 only two cases of disputed nominations to bishoprics were unresolved after some negotiations. In minor benefices there were some conflicts, but generally these were appeased. Clearly the effect of the 1472 agreement was to supersede free canonical election to the common advantage of king and pope. Such conflicts as took place at this time were those between papal provisors and claimants elected by the chapters. Indeed this co-operation in appointments even persisted despite some sharp exchanges in 1473 over the pope's failure to promote Charles of Bourbon to the cardinalate, and may suggest that Louis was more concerned with dominating the Church in France than with the elevation of his cousin.

From 1475 onwards relations between the king and the pope deteriorated, and Sixtus was less co-operative over various provisions in that year. He refused to translate the Bishop of Avranches to Coutances, although later he did promise to grant him an abbey *in commendam*, and he turned down the king's request to confer the church of Clermont on Charles of Bourbon, though he attempted to produce explanations which might conciliate the king. Papal favour to the Duke of Burgundy may well have been one factor in this ill-feeling. In 1476 threats of a general council were put forward, the king's right to intervene in matters relating to benefices was asserted in a pleading before the Parlement of Paris, and according to one chronicle there was talk of restoring the pragmatic. Probably the most bitter alienation between Louis and Sixtus followed the latter's participation in the Pazzi conspiracy of 1478,[18] but even during periods of political tension, correspondence continued between the two rulers over appointments to benefices, with each requesting favours from the other. The same situation prevailed in the last years of the reign, and there are numerous references to this subject in the king's letters. Both parties stood to gain from this entente, the pope in so far as the exercise of his rights of provision represented a restoration of papal overlordship against the principles of the pragmatic, while the king secured the appointment of men on whom he could depend to major benefices. The episcopate in

particular owed its appointment to royal favour, and ecclesiastical
independence was virtually suppressed.

There was a reaction after Louis' death. At the Estates-General at
Tours in 1484, a *cahier* presented to the king and council by the Three
Estates affirmed that the decrees of the Councils of Constance and
Basel, as modified at Bourges, should be maintained, and papal reservations and provisions were explicitly attacked. In a speech on 21
February it was declared that under Charles VII the Church had
flourished in sanctity and devotion, but under Louis it had been
dishonoured, and unworthy persons had been promoted to bishoprics
and other benefices. The bishops present were described as the crea-
tures of royal power, who had been named despite the pragmatic. The
assimilation of royalist and papalist attitudes is seen in the fact that
these prelates took a pro-Roman line, attacking the attempts to curb
the power of the Roman Church, and suggesting that these were not
without an element of schism and heresy.

These objections had little result, and before long there was a
reversion to the practice of Louis XI's reign, by which the papacy,
subservient to royal policy, provided the Crown's candidate. A case of
this may be seen in 1487, when there is record of an unsuccessful
appeal to the pope for a provision to the see of Agen, but in the years
which follow there are traces of resistance to Roman action. A disputed election at Beauvais, where the canons opposed the papal
choice, was remitted for judgment to the vicars of the Archbishop of
Reims, in accordance with the pragmatic. In the end, however, the king
threw his support behind the papal provisor, who obtained the see.
Above all, royal concern was with the maintenance of the king's
power, as at Clermont in 1488–9, when the attempt of the chapter to
elect its own candidate was over-ruled by the king, without the papacy
being involved. From 1490 onwards, however, there are numerous
references to provisions and expectatives being granted by the pope at
the king's request, and the instructions given to French envoys in
Rome in 1491 include clauses dealing with benefices. After the outbreak of the Italian wars in 1494, ecclesiastical matters were affected
by the immediate political relations of king and pope, although on
occasions the king issued instructions concerning benefices without
reference to Rome.[19]

In the early years of Louis XII, despite difficulties which led to talk
of a possible general council in 1502, relations between France and
Rome were generally friendly, as king and pope had reasons for
desiring mutual support, the former because he wished papal assent to
the annulment of his marriage with Louis IX's daughter, Jeanne of
France, so that he would be free to marry Anne of Brittany, and the
latter because he wanted French support for the advancement of his

son, Cesare. This co-operation ·affected benefices, where there was considerable bargaining, which continued into the next pontificate: three bishoprics were filled in 1504 by candidates with royal support, and in the following year when Julius informed the king of the promotion of pro-French cardinals, Louis had to pay a price in accepting the nomination of Italians to French sees. This compromise policy had the support of the greatest figure in the French Church, the legate Georges d'Amboise, who secured the right to dispose of collative benefices.

Louis XII's relations with the papacy deteriorated about the same time as the legate's death, when Julius II formed the Holy League with Venice, Spain and the Swiss cantons, with the aim of expelling the French from Italy. In reaction, a royal ordinance of August 1510 reasserted the principles of the Council of Basel and the pragmatic sanction, and imposed strict limitations on papal powers of provision. This was clearly a piece of royal propaganda designed to rally Gallican support for the king's policy. From this time, until the negotiation of the concordat, Franco-papal relations were hostile, and nothing was done about provisions, although early in the reign of Francis I the new king made some attempt to come to terms with the pope, with promises of benefices for certain cardinals. The Fifth Lateran Council tried to abrogate the pragmatic, but this meant nothing in practice. Only after the French victory at Marignano on 14 September 1515 was it possible to take serious steps towards a settlement. By then it was the French king who was negotiating from strength, so the agreement which emerged represented, above all, a view acceptable to the secular power. Negotiations were lengthy, and though one draft was agreed by January 1516, the settlement was not finally promulgated as a bull until the following December.

By the concordat the pragmatic was abrogated, and the French Church effectively handed over to the power of the king. In the agreement the question of benefices occupied no less than the first nine clauses. The first of these contained the most important stipulation, that when in future a vacancy occurred in a bishopric in France, the king had six months within which to make a nomination to the pope for provision. Only if the king failed to do so could the pope make the provision on his own initiative. If the pope refused the royal candidate, the king was given a further three months to nominate an alternative. There were stipulations as to the age and academic status of the nominees, but these could be waived when the nominee was related to the king, came from a noble family, or was a member of a reformed religious order. A similar system was laid down for monastic houses, where election was suppressed in favour of nomination, though the head of the house there could be as young as 23.

Clearly this measure strengthened royal control over the Church, but it did not go unchallenged. On 21 March 1517, the chancellor, Antoine Duprat, made a speech justifying the concordat, as a measure taken to obviate the Lateran Council's attempt to revoke the pragmatic. He had to admit that it abandoned elections, but justified this on the grounds of *la malice du temps*. This was the first royal apologia for the concordat: when the papal ambassador presented the bulls approving it and revoking the pragmatic, the king sent representatives to the Parlement to argue the case for their publication, and when the Parlement refused to publish the concordat, the king commanded it to send councillors to him to explain the failure. Duprat put forward a lengthy case justifying the concordat, criticising the abuses which, he claimed, resulted from free elections and suggestions that these would be ended by the royal right of nomination. He justified royal claims by reference to the powers of other rulers, accurately in his allusions to Scotland and Spain, but not so in his reference to England, where he alleged that the king had a written privilege of nominating to bishoprics and archbishoprics, with the pope making the provision. Even after this, pressure was required before the Parlement registered the concordat, including a threat that the king might establish another Parlement at Orleans. Eventually registration was secured on 22 March 1518, and with this, the French Church passed effectively into the king's hands.

One limitation of the concordat was that it was not applicable in Brittany, a fact which serves as a reminder that the king's power had geographical limits, even within the lands over which he claimed superiority. In Brittany the dukes had held the effective whip-hand over appointments and could negotiate directly with the pope. In 1453 the pope reserved five cathedrals in the duchy, Nantes, Rennes, Dol, St Malo and Vannes, and promised to promote only persons acceptable to and named by the duke. Later Pius II attempted to reserve the Breton bishoprics without any such pledge, and not until 1479 did Sixtus IV grant the duke the right to nominate to the five sees. Two years later the pope declared *motu proprio* that he would appoint to the other four Breton sees also only candidates acceptable to the duke.

Relations between France and Brittany complicated the question of provisions in the Breton Church. When Louis XI came to terms with the pope in 1462, the Breton abbey of Redon was among the benefices to which he was granted a right of nomination, and ducal rights were disregarded. The duke's response was to forbid the execution of the papal letters, put the abbey under sequestration, and name commissioners to administer it. The secular power in the duchy was as effective as that in France; when Pierre Landais, the powerful treasurer, fell in 1485, seven of the nine bishoprics were filled by men under his influence. The duchess, Anne, Brittany's last independent ruler, resisted the promotion of Robert d'Espinay to the see of Nantes, when Innocent VIII had followed the recommendation of the French Crown rather than her own, and also refused to accept the provision of two cardinals, one a nephew of the pope. Even after she became Queen of France, she acted independently in appointments to Breton benefices, and only after her death in 1514 did royal power dominate the duchy. Francis I did obtain the right to appoint to consistorial benefices there, but by a separate indult, and the concordat was not regularly applied in the duchy until 1553, although some attempt was made to enforce it at Nantes in 1532.

In the Burgundian lands, too, political questions complicated Church appointments. The early Habsburg dukes tried to forbid the receipt of papal acts concerning nominations to benefices, and in 1492, when Innocent VIII attempted to provide Cardinal Pallavicini to the see of Tournai, the orator sent to the Curia by Maximilian and the Archduke Philip presented a lengthy justification of his masters' opposition to the proposal, claiming that bishops should be considered as servants of the prince, who should be consulted before their appointment. In the parts of Burgundy which owed obedience to France, some residual power remained with the king until the early sixteenth century. Not until the years 1515–30 did the papacy grant any formal concessions to the dukes, and legalise the power which they already possessed. A bull of 1515 granted to Charles V that no provision should be made to monasteries in his lands, except Naples and Spain, without his agreement; an act of 1522 recognised his rights of nomination to abbacies and other dignities, and an indult of 1530, reserving a prebend to him in each cathedral and college, gave him extensive patronage over lesser benefices.

This survey of papal provisions and of secular intervention over the whole of Western Christendom shows, above all, that there was no unified system in operation. The details of how promotions were made varied not only between countries but also from time to time within the lands of a single ruler and even from one vacancy of a benefice to the next. There can be little doubt that effective papal influence was severely limited by the early sixteenth century, sometimes by formal concession, sometimes by no more than a realistic acquiescence in the *de facto* control exercised by a secular prince. It is fair to say that the developments of the fifteenth century were the logical conclusion of the efforts of the privileged classes to dominate the Church, but there is little doubt that the circumstances of the period gave these classes greater opportunity than at any previous date since the great Church reforms of the eleventh and twelfth centuries. It was essentially the aristocracy who gained from papal weakness, and papal sympathy for them is well typified in those concordats where special privileges were allowed to those of noble birth. The princes, at the head of aristocratic society, were in the strongest position of all, because they could pay the price which the papacy wanted in the form of political support. Whether this represented an alliance against conciliar forces in the Church or one against the secular enemies of the papacy in Italy is hardly relevant when one considers the effects of their actions. For the princes, control over appointments was a means of strengthening their power over all their subjects, and it was to be one of the foundation stones of the new relationship between the secular and spiritual powers which developed amid the strains of the greater crisis of the Reformation.

CHAPTER 8

Spheres of Conflict, II: Taxation

Disputes over appointments to benefices arose from the position of churchmen as subjects of both a prince and the pope, and the former's desire to secure favours for loyal servants; the resources of the Church and of churchmen provided a second important and recurrent cause of tension between the papacy and secular powers. Contention over taxation was not new, either in secular claims to tax the clergy or in princely resistance to the flow of money to Rome, and probably went back at least as far as the twelfth century. As is well known, at the end of the thirteenth Boniface VIII attempted to prevent lay taxation of the clergy, but had to admit defeat, so even before the schism the balance of advantage lay with the secular power. During the forty years of crisis there had been an undermining of papal powers and a break-down of the normal adminsitrative machinery. Besides the attempts of the papacy to restore this to effective working order, it also concerned itself with seeking some *modus vivendi* with the secular power. As with benefices, this was not easy, because both the papacy and the lay rulers were subject to various pressures which affected their mutual re-lations. The conciliarists attempted to limit papal rights of taxation, thereby giving a weapon to the secular princes, but these themselves might have to face individuals and groups whose particular interests were not always compatible with the concerns of the monarch. On the papalist side of conciliar controversy, however, Torquemada asserted that the pope, through his dispensing power, could make fiscal con-cessions to the laity on special occasions for just causes, although not in perpetuity. The cardinals, another group with an interest in the resources of the Church, also attempted to limit grants to princes, including those of taxes. This was done in the election capitulation of 1471, and repeated thirteen years later.

Fiscal relations between the secular and spiritual powers fell into several different classes: both the papacy and the lay rulers claimed a right to tax the clergy, and each could resist the other's action, the kings by imposing a ban on the export of currency from their lands, the popes by forbidding churchmen to pay taxes to the lay power. These matters, however, were negotiable, and in the bargaining between the two powers the main concern of both was to secure for themselves as high a proportion as possible of the revenues from clerical taxation, irrespective of who had initiated the tax. Besides this, kings might wish to limit gifts made to the Church by their lay subjects, as such grants in mortmain might withdraw potential revenues from themselves; in this princely power was more effective, because the papacy could not intervene before lands had passed into clerical possession. In this chapter the negotiations over different taxes will be considered together, and mortmain will be discussed separately at the end.

In considering clerical taxation one must remember that a simple examination of revenues and assessments can be misleading, as many benefices were burdened with debts which were not allowed in the assessment and, on the other hand, the deferment of payments could ease pressures on the clergy. Nevertheless there is ample evidence of complaints about papal impositions, and during the schism the lay power became involved in resistance to payments to Rome and to Avignon. This can be seen in France, although the complaints put forward by Jean Petit in 1406 were not always justified. After the schism, the French were prepared to bargain recognition of Martin V for the settlement of various problems in relations between the papacy and France, and on 25 November 1417 a meeting of members of the Parlement of Paris, the University, the Great Council and the prelates put forward views on various matters, including taxation. It was agreed that some form of financial support for the papacy was necessary, and that the French Church should make moderate contributions to support the pope and the Universal Church, such as were made by Churches in other kingdoms, but at the same time it was suggested that the king should put an end to papal exactions in matters connected with provisions to benefices.[1] The question of these payments was settled, at least temporarily, by the concordat agreed in the following year, but in the intervening months there was clearly some suspicion of the new pope, and questions about the payment of taxes to him. The doubts about Martin were essentially political, arising from his relations with the King of the Romans. The alliance between Sigismund and Henry V of England could not but be regarded with hostility in France, and Sigismund's important part at Constance led to suspicions that Martin's election might not have been entirely free. It was feared that money taken by the pope from France might pass into the hands of Sigismund, an enemy of the French king. Such counsel was acceptable to the king, if not inspired by him, because royal ordinances of this period also tried to limit the outflow of money, although the reiteration of these prohibitions, with the complaint that money was still leaving the realm, suggests that they were not entirely successful.

These measures may have been part of an attempt to put pressure on the pope in negotiations for the concordat, because when agreement was reached on this in April 1418 certain limitations were set on the payment of dues liable in connection with appointments to benefices. Service payments were halved, and it was stipulated that if a vacancy in a benefice occurred twice within a year, services were to be paid only once. This last restriction is found also in the Spanish and German concordats, although a longer period was allowed to complete service payments in these countries than in France.[2] As the Concordat of Constance was due to last for only five years, negotiations soon began on the form of an agreement to succeed it, and the dauphin, Charles, sent an embassy to the pope in 1419. The concordat seems to have been taken as the basis for discussion, and certainly on taxation the idea of the half annate was accepted, on condition that this would also take account of reductions in assessment previously allowed. This basis for payment persisted, although there were problems connected with outlying parts of the kingdom such as Brittany, which had accepted the 1418 concordat but did not regard itself as subject to the Concordat of Gennazzano of 1426. In fact Martin V granted the tax reduction in Brittany, but declared that this was an act of grace. Under Eugenius IV the reduction became the rule, but some bishops still had to pay the full sum in dues.

Until the Council of Basel and the renewal of a struggle within the Church which could give additional advantages to the secular ruler, disputes over taxation were not particularly serious, although several episodes suggest the basic weakness of the papacy. In Aragon the persistence of claims by the Avignon line of popes gave the king a weapon to resist Martin and exploit the Church to his own advantage. This can be seen in the way in which the embassy of Cardinal Adimari had to concede heavy clerical taxation to the young Alfonso V. In England the secular power was able to get the better of a dispute over taxation. In 1427 Martin laid a tenth on ecclesiastical revenues to meet the threat from the Bohemians, and in the following year a papal envoy notified this to both the regency council and the Archbishop of Canterbury. When convocation met, the king also asked for a subsidy. The taxes were discussed, and no decision was taken on either before the assembly was adjourned. When it met again, expressions of papal displeasure were read to it, but although it granted a half-tenth to the king, and a subsidy at the same rate for Bohemia, the payment of the latter was made conditional on it not offending the king or the laws of the kingdom. The council effectively, although indirectly, blocked the tax, and limited the payment to the pope to money given for devotion to the cause, that is, for indulgence.[3] Even money raised through indulgences might be misapplied. Although an agreement was reached for the raising of troops under Cardinal Beaufort for a Bohemian crusade, the defeat of the English at Patay led to the diversion of the army to France to aid Bedford, with the indulgence revenues being used to meet the pay of the troops. The lords of the council gave surety that the money due to the pope would be repaid, and in the end this was done, although proceedings connected with this taking of what was in effect a forced loan from the pope were not finally cleared for the best part of half a century.

If the restoration papacy had weaknesses even when it was unchallenged, the quarrel between Eugenius IV and the Council of Basel could only aggravate its difficulties. In the spring of 1432 there were again affirmations that money was leaving France and in the autumn an embassy from the council to Charles VII asked that the king, like other princes adhering to the council, should grant that collectors who owed money to the Camera should in future account for it to the treasurer of the council. Charles agreed to offer no impediment to this. This action by Basel was an open invitation to the secular princes to interfere with ecclesiastical finances, and to choose where payments might go, and the pope's need for support made him liable to bargain away his rights of taxation. The abolition of annates by the council in June 1435, a blow aimed at Eugenius, was a further incentive to, or at least an excuse for, the princes to curb the outflow of money to Rome. Although some reformers accepted that some subvention should be made to support the pope, to replace the taxes which were being abolished as sacrilegious, they did not suggest how this could be raised. Undoubtedly it was the princes who stood to gain from this situation, and while Sigismund paid little attention to the struggle over annates, being at that time more concerned with Bohemia, Charles VII seems to have tried to exploit the pope's difficulties. Instructions sent to his ambassadors to Eugenius in March 1436 included complaints about papal taxation and requests for its reduction. When in 1438 in the pragmatic sanction the French adopted the reform decrees of Basel as law, the suppression of annates was one of the clauses, although there was at least theoretically recognition that some provision should be made for the pope. It was, however, stipulated that any payment of taxes was not to prejudice Gallican liberties, and that it was to be a life grant, stopping on Eugenius's death. In fact, during the next pontificate, in 1452, the question of annates was raised by a papal embassy, and later in the decade it is clear that papal attempts to levy taxes in France were continuing.[4]

In 1439, the German princes also adopted the decrees of Basel in the *Acceptatio* of Mainz, following their declaration of neutrality of the previous year. By this, annates were annulled, and it was declared that no financial exaction of the Curia was to be sanctioned in Germany without the consent of the German rulers. There was not, however, an unqualified alliance between the princes and the fathers at Basel, because the pretensions of the council were not directed solely against the pope. The assertion of the Church's freedom in the financial sense could easily be turned against the secular power. From this there arose the ambivalence so characteristic of princely attitudes; they sought to exploit conciliar ideas to the advantage of the lay ruler without at the same time undermining his authority over the Church in his own territories. The terms of the *Acceptatio* made it essential that when in the following decade there were negotiations for a settlement between Germany and the pope some agreement should be reached on taxation, and in the last resort the pope was more willing to oblige the princes than the council. In the indult granted by Eugenius IV to the German nation in 1447, the so-called Concordat with the Princes, the pope remitted all debts due to him or to the College of Cardinals in annates or services. A year later, in the Concordat of Vienna, the financial needs of the papacy were recognised and annates were restored, although provision was made for a reassessment of rates if the sums demanded were excessive. As in 1418, two years were allowed for the payment of services on major benefices, although annates on less valuable ones were to be paid within a year and the poorest benefices were exempted. After the agreement, the popes were prepared to reward their secular allies with grants of clerical taxation and Frederick III was a notable beneficiary of such favours, obtaining a grant of a tenth on clerical incomes from Nicholas V in 1452 and from Calixtus III in 1455.[5]

In the end the pope emerged from these negotiations with his financial rights reasonably well secured, in marked contrast with the concessions made during the years of crisis. An ally of the papacy at a critical moment might well receive financial favours in return. It was probably Eugenius who exempted the diocese of Liège from paying a tax imposed by the council in 1435, because the bishop had been resisting conciliar pressures.[6] The clergy of Liège were less fortunate in 1442 when Eugenius granted a tax on clerical goods to Philip of Burgundy, committing the execution of it to the Bishop of Tournai, and they sought exemption from it on the grounds that they had been faithful supporters of the pope, because although Eugenius granted the exemption, the duke over-ruled it by force. The initial grant of the tax to the duke itself shows how papal favour could benefit a territorial ruler, and the chronicler, Cornelius Zantfliet, had no doubt that the pope's motive in making it was to reward his fidelity. These actions of the pope show the extent of his initiative in fiscal matters – when the tax was an ecclesiastical one, he could intervene, but when payment was due to the secular power, papal influence was severely limited by princely force. The agreement of 1441 between the duke and Eugenius touched on payments to Rome, and here the pope secured rather better terms than in some other settlements with secular powers, because the first half of annate payments had to be made within six months, and the second within the same period afterwards.

In Brittany the papacy compromised with a sympathetic secular ruler. When the council attempted to levy taxes for its negotiations with the Greeks, Eugenius forbade the collection of the money, and what had already been gathered was divided between the duke and the pope. Later, however, when Eugenius tried to levy the tax himself, its rate led to hostility among the Breton clergy, and although he attempted to conciliate the duke by choosing as collectors men closely connected with him, disagreement over a provision to a bishopric as well as over the tax moved the duke's sympathies towards the council. In 1441 financial matters were among those included in the Concordat of Redon. During the negotiations the duke asked for a grant of a tenth, but although the papal envoys accepted the demand verbally, the grant was not ratified by the pope before the duke's death. His successor Francis I, was, however, able to obtain a grant of clerical taxation by papal authority, when a bull of March 1445 authorised him to levy three-tenths on all clergy of the duchy, with the exception of cardinals and certain regulars. The initiative in this grant appears to have come from an assembly of the clergy themselves with the papal confirmation following later, but the duke had probably put some pressure on the clergy to make it.

Even princes with little real power could benefit from a grant of taxes on the clergy. The future Louis XI, while dauphin, negotiated in Rome for a tenth in 1443, to be applied to the ransom of the governor of the Dauphiné, whom the English had captured, and in 1446 Eugenius IV ordered the Archbishop of Aix to pay Louis 20,000 florins from the tenth imposed on the revenues of the French Church. This latter may well be connected with the pope's appointment of Louis as gonfalonier and protector of the Church earlier in the year, in which case the grant must be seen as an attempt to bind the French prince more closely to papal service.[7]

Relations between the papacy and the secular princes were not always so amicable, and the lay power often went its own way, both in taxing the Church without papal authority and in resisting papal attempts at taxation. French royal letters of November 1440 refer to the levy of a tenth on the clergy, but no mention is made of papal permission, and in 1445 the king made his claims even clearer, stating that while clergymen were not to be compelled to contribute to the provision of soldiers, *'toutesfois Nous entendons en autre manière requérir lesdicts Gens d'Eglise qu'ils aideront à supporter les charges de nosdits gens d'armes, & pour cette cause leur escrivions en chacun Diocèse Lettres particulieres'.* This seems to have been assumed as a royal right, and no mention was made of papal authorisation. A good example of the blank wall of resistance which the papacy could encounter in its attempt to raise a tax can be found in England. In 1443, Eugenius IV attempted to levy a tenth on the revenues and receipts of all ecclesiastical persons, for a crusade in support of the Greeks. Collectors were named in 1444, and Henry VI was informed of the tax in the following year. The English produced an alternative proposal of a subsidy of ld in the mark, and this was approved at various diocesan synods. Attempts were made to cajole, or even bribe, the king by the grant of the golden rose, but although Archbishop Stafford thanked the pope for it on the king's behalf, no concession was given on the tenth. The whole episode shows that without royal consent the pope could not obtain any tax on English clerical incomes, whether mandatory of voluntary.

When the Council of Basel was defeated, the papacy was strengthened within the Church and in its relations with the outside world. No longer faced with a rival power to which the lay powers could threaten to transfer their support, the pope could intervene more effectively in relations between princes and the clergy of their realms, as can be seen in 1451, when Nicholas V asserted his influence in a dispute between Alfonso V of Aragon and the churchmen of his states. The fact that the pope was Alfonso's feudal superior for Naples probably strengthened his hand in taking action, but the agreement which was reached, so far from being confined to the king's lands in Italy, was primarily concerned with his Spanish territories. The king had to promise to annul letters concerning the seizure of clerical goods over a question of taxation and to refrain from imposing such a tax in future. The agreement also provided for setting up machinery to assess the liability of such goods for general taxation. The whole form of the agreement illustrates the balance of forces between the secular and the spiritual powers. The king had taxation rights over the clergy as he had over laymen, and this was a far cry from the heyday of papal claims under Boniface VIII. On the other hand churchmen could establish that the particular form of taxation imposed was unacceptable, and the king was prepared to withdraw it, Such concessions were not agreeable to all circles in the Church, and criticism of them by the cardinals led to an attempt to prevent it in the election capitulation of 1458.

Crusade proposals also led to papal taxation in the provinces of Christendom, and such money might be misappropriated. Calixtus III granted the Duke of Burgundy a tenth in 1455, on the assumption that he would lead the crusade, but when he had levied it he kept the money. After long opposition, Charles VII ordered his subjects to pay the tax, but in Brittany there were protests about it. The Breton dukes also resisted other crusading taxes. An attempt to raise them in 1460–1 was maintained until the death of Pius II and the abandonment of the crusade. After the suspension of demands for the tenth, money collected for crusading purposes was seized by the chancellor of the duchy and handed over to the treasurer, who used it for the repair of castles. In later years negotiations on financial issues sometimes involved other questions also. When the powerful treasurer-general of the duchy, Pierre Landais, was wishing papal support for the depostion of Bishop Jacques d'Espinay of Rennes, he was prepared to concede some of the bishop's confiscated goods to the papal Camera. Here there was a link between the monetary concession and the other matter, but very often diplomatic interchanges between Rome and the princes might include financial matters not connected with other problems: when the Burgundian cleric, Antoine Haneron, went to Rome in 1460, his duties included the explanation of the difficulty in raising taxes, certain matters of ecclesiastical promotion, including the suggestion that the Bishop of Arras should be created a cardinal, and topics relating to the crusade.

Papal attempts to levy crusading taxes in England were further complicated in the years around 1460 by the internal problems of the kingdom, the more so as the papal legate became involved in these as a Yorkist partisan. In 1460–2 nothing was done about payment, but eventually in 1464 Edward IV accepted the idea that some subvention be made to the pope. He was not, however, willing to allow the tax to be imposed by papal authority, and proposed that in its place the English clergy should make a voluntary gift to the pope. At least the gift was voluntary on the king's part, for payment was enforced on the clergy by royal command. The rate of assessment, a quarter of a tenth, was small compared with that which the pope had originally demanded. Later in Edward's reign too, the papacy had difficulty in collecting money due from England, for in December 1474 Cardinal Bourgchier, the Archbishop of Canterbury, was asked to assist the papal collector who had been unsuccessful in his attempts to levy Peter's Pence.

The Turkish threat was, of course, more menancing in Italy and in the Balkans than elsewhere in Europe, and it was used as a pretext for taxation by the secular powers as well as by the pope. In 1466 the Venetian Signoria imposed taxation on clerical property, without papal permission, on this excuse, although in 1499, when there was a renewal of the Turkish war, the pope did consent to Venetian taxation of the clergy. Nor was Venice the only Italian state where the secular power antagonised Rome by imposing taxes on churchmen – there were clashes between Paul II and the Florentines in 1466 and 1469.

The German territorial princes also made gains in their financial relations with the Church. They obtained papal grants which enabled them to exploit eccesiastical revenues, by removing clerical exemption from taxation. Clerical tenths were diverted into the princely treasuries, and special taxes, such as those for the crusade were likewise taken over. Furthermore, they could exclude the preachers of an indulgence, unless they obtained a share, which meant that their encroachment on spiritual funds was not merely confined to taxes, but even affected the voluntary offerings of the faithful. The background to this secular interference may be seen in the recurrent German opposition to the levy of money for supporting papal policies in Italy. Perhaps the most vitriolic expression of this was the appeal of the far from disinterested Gregor Heimburg, who complained that money raised on the pretext of a military expedition against the Turks was being converted to support the bastard Ferrante against the lawful king of Naples, René of Anjou. In 1487, when Innocent VIII was trying to raise money for a crusade, his legate in Germany had no success. Archbishop Berthold of Mainz and the electors of Saxony and Brandenburg appealed to the pope for exemption from the proposed tithe, and clerical opposition was so great that Innocent abandoned the attempt to levy it. In 1500 the Diet of Augsburg resolved that the pope be required to refund part of the money sent to Rome for annates and indulgences, because the empire had been drained of its coin.[8]

Faced with such opposition, the popes could do little beyond hoping that concessions to the princes might purchase support. Examples of papal approval of lay taxation of the clergy can be seen in Bavaria and Saxony, while in Brandenburg there was lay encroachment, when the bishops had to share the proceeds of a tenth with the territorial lords. A Liège chronicle tells how a grant of taxation to the emperor in 1471 was allowed to lapse when news came of the pope's death, but that the Duke of Burgundy continued to make exactions from the clergy in his lands. Ten years later a papal legate, who had been commissioned to levy a tenth for campaigning against the Turks and to conduct a monastic visitation, faced such opposition that he could collect only a fraction of the tax. It was not only the emissaries of Rome who encountered resistance; the secular prince also faced opposition from his clergy and even papal support might not help him. When Albrecht Achilles, the future elector of Brandenburg, was ruling the Hohenzollern lands in Franconia, he faced passive resistance to attempted taxation, and pressures from the nobility whom the clergy supported against him meant that he had to renounce various papal concessions. Nor was it only the secular princes who asserted such rights: the spiritual princes acted in a similar manner and followed secular means to attain material ends. This is hardly surprising, because the higher clergy were generally drawn from the ranks of the nobility and the princes, whose attitude to clerical property was generally one of attempted exploitation. This is exemplified in the *Dispositio Achillea*, the dynastic settlement of Albrecht Achilles of Brandenburg, who laid down that in future there was to be no permanent alienation of family lands, and that younger sons must either receive only pecuniary support or become prelates and obtain their livelihood from the resources of the Church.

In the 1460s there were a number of financial disputes which caused tension between the papacy and France, and in 1464 the king refused to authorise the levy of a tenth. The interaction of fiscal and other issues is shown in a letter from the Milanese ambassador to his master where he wrote that the best course for the pope would be to oblige the king by translating two prelates from the Dauphiné, whom Louis wished to have removed. If this were done the king might be more amenable to the levy of taxes. In the following spring Louis bargained for the grant of the legateship of Avignon to his nominee in return for the settlement of a debt which the king claimed was owed to him. With this background, it is perhaps surprising that when the concordat of 1472 provided a brief settlement between France and the papacy, it contained little about taxation, apart from an affirmation that the half rate of annate payments agreed at the time of the Council of Constance should still be followed. It is not unfair to say that it solved none of the real problems, and certainly four years later, when the Dean of Lyons was sent as an ambassador to the pope one of the king's demands was for a moderation of papal taxes on vacant benefices. In practice the pope had to co-operate with the king, for if he did not he had little chance of securing the payment of clerical taxes due to him. On the other hand, Louis was not much concerned with securing papal consent for taking money from the clergy– in 1471 he demanded a loan of 600 écus from the Abbot of Bec to meet the cost of arms when he was politically threatened by Charles of Burgundy.

With the outbreak of sharp political disagreement between Louis and Sixtus IV after the Pazzi conspiracy against the Medici, the king reiterated the old complaint about the outflow of money to Rome. An ordinance of 16 August 1478 contained a lengthy preamble attacking the pope for diverting revenues which ought to be used for the defence of the faith into attempts to usurp the lordships of Italy and a letter five days later to the chapter of Troyes, summoning it to send envoys to an assembly of the clergy to discuss relations with Rome, included the king's compaint about the outflow of money. This accusation was renewed at the meeting of the Estates-General at Tours in 1484, when it was alleged that the money was merely going to finance the pope's

Italian wars. In the years which followed the majority of Charles VIII, this particular issue appears to have lapsed, perhaps because the king and the pope were at times in alliance during the Italian wars, and when they were not the king could easily prevent the flow of cash to Rome. Charles, however, was quite prepared to use the financial resources of the clergy for these campaigns, but he possibly had to face resistance to this. Certainly, in 1494 he had to renew a demand to the Bishop of Troyes for a loan of 1,500 écus from the diocese, an action from which one may reasonably infer a lack of co-operation. In fact, there was little difference in attitude between the two powers, both of which regarded the resources of churchmen as something to be tapped whenever required. The old complaint about the outflow of money to Rome was renewed in 1510, when Louis XII was threatening a council against Julius II, and two years later the king imposed a tariff on imported alum, which could well have affected papal interests.[9] These measures are best understood as political manoevres, and financial matters were negotiable in precisely the same way as any other issues. This can be seen clearly in the concordat of 1516, when the veto on annate payments, part of the pragmatic sanction, was not revived. This aroused Gallican opposition, notably in the Parlement of Paris, but the king probably conceded that a payment should be made to the pope, in return for greater influence in provisions to benefices. Furthermore, the king may have been made more complaint by the concession to him of a tenth on all churchmen of the realm, and a jubilee indulgence to last for two years.

In Naples, the feudal rights of the papacy complicated fiscal relations between Rome and the clergy of the kingdom. From this, the king was the loser, because the pope could impose severe restrictions on him, which afforded some protection to ecclesiastics there. In the settlement of 1486, renewed in 1492, the king had to agree not to impose any tallage or levy on churches and churchmen and their goods, and also had to give up claims to take profits from vacant benefices. This situation, where the pope had a special political status, was of course exceptional, but it does emphasise the impossibility of drawing clear lines between fiscal questions and the political power of the papacy. In Naples, it was the papacy as an institution which had such interests, while during the pontificate of Leo X it was the pope as an individual and as a member of the Medici family who was concerned with the affairs of Florence, and his grant to the city in 1516 of certain taxation rights shows how the secular concerns of a particular pope could affect the Church's resources, although in this case the lay power may have received no more than its due. The preamble to the bull related that the city was in financial difficulties because various citizens had transferred their goods to churches, hospitals and pious places, where they were exempt from impositions. The pope decreed that the city might lawfully tax such goods made over to the Church, and that these taxes were to be paid, notwithstanding consitutions to the contrary. One may, however, doubt if Leo would have rectified such an abuse of ecclesiastical immunity in any other city or state.

There were also certain spheres where the popes might make tax concessions to secular rulers whose policies were in accord with the aims of the Roman See. Most notable of these was the struggle against Islam particularly in the Danube valley and in the Iberian peninsula. In 1476 Sixtus IV informed the Voivode of Moldavia that the subsidy against the Turks was to be sent to Matthias of Hungary, while from 1479 the pope regularly authorised grants to the Spanish sovereigns of clerical taxation to finance the campaigns against Granada. Money was raised by a crusading indulgence and a 10 per cent tax on benefices and tithe revenues. The pope demanded one-third of the proceeds for the war against the Turks, but Ferdinand and Isabella were reluctant to agree to this, possibly because they had doubts about whether the money would actually be used for this. Throughout the 1480s there was tension over payments to Rome, in which the secular power was successful in retaining the money levied, partly perhaps because christian successes in the war were gratifying to the pope. Some of the revenues collected were, however, delivered to Rome. That some part of the funds was not devoted to the crusade is certain, a fact which caused distress to the pious Isabella, who provided in her will that recompense be made for them, but probably by far the greater part was disbursed on expenses to which the pope could not object. It was perhaps after the Moslem threat became less immediate that the clergy were more reluctant to pay such taxes, and an agreement between the king and the prelates of Portugal, submitted to the pope for confirmation in 1516, may reflect this change. It was noted that certain taxes – thirds of tithes – had been conferred on the king by the pope, for the purpose of fighting the Moors, but that the prelates had asked the king to renounce the concession. This he did, and in return the clergy promised him certain sums of money. The pope agreed to the new form of payment, empowering the Archbishop of Lisbon and another bishop to enforce payment by imposing an interdict or by calling in the secular arm. The most noteworthy feature of this agreement is the fact that the pope was brought in at all, because the practical compromise between the king and clergy had been reached without him. Nevertheless, it was clearly felt desirable that Roman approval should be obtained, a sign that however much papal claims were flouted in practice, some form of lip-service was still paid to them.

There was yet another sphere where one can see increasing royal and princely interference with clerical resources, namely grants in mortmain. Here the papacy did not try to secure greater liberty for benefactors to alienate lands to the Church, perhaps because the property concerned was not yet in ecclesiastical hands, but was only potentially its concern. The actions of the secular power, however, illustrate the practical extent of its gains and the limits of papal action. Secular rulers had taken measures against mortmain from an early period – there was mortmain legislation in England since the reign of Edward I, although this did not impose an absolute veto on land acquisition by the Church but merely enabled the king to control it and obtain money in return for licences to alienate land to the Church, the cost of these being perhaps higher when the king was in financial difficulties. Similar restrictions were applied even when there was no specific legislation against mortmain, as in the Palatinate where permission was always required to sell land to a church, although there was no law against amortisation. Similarly, endowed masses could not be financed from property revenues, but only from money or movables.

In places, although regulations on mortmain existed they were applied with little rigour. For example, the dukes of Burgundy treated the Church quite generously in this, although when they took measures on it there were varying reactions in the different parts of their domains. An ordinance of Philip the Good for Brabant in 1446 did not arouse any opposition, whereas his *placards* in Holland, issued in 1439 and 1446, provoked lively resistance. The reason for this may be that each territory had its own customary practices and that the Brabantines did not regard the duke's action as overstepping his rights, while in Holland, where Philip had made good his claim to rule by conquest, the issue provided a pretext for opposition to an alien importation. Legislation, however, was not the same as effective law, and goods continued to pass into ecclesiastical hands without much attention to the ducal measures. In 1474 Charles the Bold ordered a new declaration of goods acquired in the previous sixty years without being amortised. Receivers were appointed to collect the tax and the amounts paid – the taxes in Brabant alone were worth over 16,000 livres – show that there had been negligence in implementing earlier mortmain legislation. Thereafter state intervention again declined until the early sixteenth century, but in 1515 Prince Charles, later the Emperor Charles V, followed his predecessors' examples in seeking a declaration of acquisitions made in the previous forty years but not amortised. The period stipulated shows clearly that he was looking back primarily to the steps taken by Charles the Bold.

In France, too, there is no lack of evidence for royal concern with questions of ecclesiastical landholding. In 1463 Louis XI ordered an investigation of the titles to land held within the *prévôté* of Paris by prelates and chapters, and the royal ordinances show numerous letters

licensing grants in mortmain.[10] Royal letters also reflect the interest of
the king. In 1470 Louis XI instructed the Parlement of Paris to ratify
royal letters permitting the dean and chapter of Orleans to acquire
property to the value of £100 *tournois*, while in 1480 the *chambre des
comptes* was ordered to verify an amortisation of lands. In 1482 the
king himself amortised 1,500 livres of rent to the chapter and college of
St Gilles in the Cotentin. In the following reign in 1492, the inhabitants
of Lyons were ordered to take an inquest and make a return to the
chambre des comptes about the amortisation of lands for the building
of an Observant house there.

When one surveys the whole field of fiscal relations between the
secular and spiritual powers, one sees that the former could secure
considerable influence. In some matters, such as mortmain, its freedom of action was more or less complete, while in others, such as the
taxation of the clergy and the payment of money to Rome, the limitations on lay action were slight. There must have been some recognition
of papal claims, because otherwise a prince would not need to seek a
grant of taxation from Rome, but it is likely that such grants were
regarded primarily as a means of bringing additional pressure to bear
on reluctant clerical taxpayers. If a king wished to tax his clergy the
pope could do little to stop him, nor could any check be put on the
diversion into the royal revenues of taxes originally levied for
ecclesiastical purposes. Furthermore, financial matters could be bargaining counters when other issues, such as appointments, were being
negotiated between the two powers, and they should be understood in
the context of the whole relationship between the papacy and the
secular princes, which depended so much on the immediate circumstances at any particular time.

CHAPTER 9

Spheres of Conflict, III: Jurisdiction

One field in which the growth of papal authority had been very marked in the central Middle Ages had been that of Roman jurisdiction over the Western Church. Appeals to the Curia, where alone final decisions could be made on points of canon law, had been a powerful force in ecclesiastical centralisation, but such jurisdictional developments also provoked bitter clashes between the papacy and the secular rulers, who attempted to maintain control over all their subjects, lay and clerical alike. Even before the schism, however, there had been some recognition of separate spheres of jurisdiction; some were left within the uncontested rights of the pope while in others the secular powers established their control. The last century of the medieval Church did not see such fierce nor such widespread disagreement as there had been earlier, although some issues still aroused a clash of jurisdictions, particularly when rival litigants attempted to exploit unresolved dissensions between contesting judicial bodies. The problem of churchmen who had recourse to secular judges in matters which properly belonged to the ecclesiastical courts provoked a threat of penalties from Martin V shortly after his accession. Secular objections to litigation in Rome were often connected with its financial implications as much as with strictly legal issues, and when there was political tension between the pope and a particular lay ruler, it was not surprising that the outflow of money to Rome should arouse protest, as in letters patent issued by Louis XII in 1510, after the overthrow of the French alliance by Julius II. In disputes over benefices, which often caused recourse to Rome, one may again see factors other than the strictly jurisdictional being the reason for trouble, notably the concern of the ruler to secure the appointment of some reliable individual or to exclude a papal nominee.

Despite disputes over details, it was generally accepted that there were limits to the scope of ecclesiastical jurisdiction, and writers made some attempt to define these. Roselli stressed that the keys which were given to St Peter were those of the kingdom of heaven, and argued that certain matters could not belong to papal jurisdiction, unless some question of sin was involved. He pointed out that the pope had refused to judge a feudal issue between the kings of France and England. Although the spiritual power was greater than the temporal power, and the pope had plenitude of the former, the *argumentum a maiori* did not apply. Biel declared categorically that the pope was not bound by position law, though his pronouncements were limited by Scripture, divine law and natural law. This suggests that he set no limits to the jurisdictional rights of the papacy, but he does not state this explicitly, and one should recollect that this *Defensorium* was written in the context of a dispute over ecclesiastical jurisdiction. Piero da Monte declared that the pope was sovereign judge in all ecclesiastical causes, as universal ordinary, and the only limitation which he would accept was that the Church hierarchy must be respected and that appeals could be made to the pope only from the sentence of an archbishop. Wessel Gansfort was more critical, holding that papal jurisdictional power was exercised in warning, teaching and edifying, and in administering the sacraments, but denying to the pope the right to issue commands under pain of mortal sin, unless the offence was itself a mortal one. More specifically he denied the power of Pius II to issue his decree on alum under pain of mortal sin. That clerical writers, such as these, should assert the spiritual jurisdiction of the papacy is hardly surprising, but lay opinion might also accept that there were some matters with which only the Church could deal. An English case recorded in the Year-book for 21 Henry VII (Hilary Term 1506) noted the affirmation of Justice Kingsmill that a statute could not make the king a parson, for the law could not give a temporal man spiritual jurisdiction; no one could give him this except the supreme head.[1] Papal rights were clearly upheld, although it appears that Kingsmill would not have objected to the king exercising spiritual jurisdiction if it had been conferred on him by the pope.

If one turns from theories to practical attempts at regulating questions of law, one sees that the Concordats of Constance were fairly general in their terms. Those with the Spanish and French nations were identical, declaring that causes which did not pertain to the Church courts were not to be received at the Curia, except with the consent of the parties, while those which did, could be heard in Rome or remitted to the place of origin, depending on the importance either of the case or of the persons involved. Normally matrimonial causes were not to be brought to the Curia except on appeal. Attempts were made to curb frustratory appeals, made before a definitive sentence in the locality, by providing that frivolous offenders would be fined and would not be allowed a second appeal. The German concordat lacked the clause dealing with frivolous appeals, but otherwise was the same. Later these provisions were reiterated in Martin V's chancery regulations. The 1426 agreement between Martin V and France dealt with churchmen who had recourse to lay courts in matters properly pertaining to those of the Church and despised the spiritual penalties which they thereby incurred. Such offenders were to lose all graces conferred by the pope, unless they had received some special concession from him. In the same bull, Martin affirmed that he did not intend to derogate from royal rights in matters pertaining to the king's jurisdiction, provided that this was genuinely ancient custom. The terms of this made it clear that the issue at stake was that concerning appointments to benefices, but the pope's grant was not explicit. The concordat of 1442 between Eugenius IV and Philip of Burgundy set certain limitations to the right of recourse to Rome, although it was stipulated that litigation concerning revenues of more than fifty florins annually should go to the papacy eventually.

Some concordats do not elaborate on judicial matters, except for regulations on cases arising out of appointments to benefices for example; the Breton Concordat of Redon of 1441 and the French concordat of 1472. Eugenius IV's concordat with the German princes in 1447 was concerned with judicial matters only so far as was necessary to resolve problems which had arisen during the German neutrality between the pope and the Council of Basel, and the settlement indeed abandoned most of the provisions of the German Concordat of Constance, which was not even mentioned in the Concordat of Vienna between the pope and the emperor.[2]The most systematic attempt to lay down general rules for judicial proceedings was that in the French concordat of 1516. There it was made clear that judicial causes should be completed within the realm, except for major cases specially named in law. Appeals were to proceed up the hierarchy and were not to be taken to the Holy See until all the lower courts had been exhausted. Even when one party was immediately subject to the Holy See, cases should be referred to France by rescript until they had been heard, although appeals could still be made to Rome thereafter. In all these cases, the secular power would probably be well placed to interfere in matters of ecclesiastical jurisdiction, and only in Naples, where the popes had rights of feudal overlordship as well as of spiritual superiority, was the Church able to demand effective independence from secular judicial interference.

In some spheres, however, the secular power accepted papal rights, most notably in penitential jurisdiction. The secular rulers do not

appear to have questioned Rome's unique authority to grant absolution in major spiritual cases, and the activity of the Penitentiary was
virtually unaffected by political issues, apart from certain rights to
grant dispensations, notably for marriages within the prohibited
degrees. However, certain administrative developments within the
Penitentiary display a concern with the practical realities of linguistic
differences in Christendom. In the fourteenth century, the minor
penitentiaries were drawn from various parts of Europe, but when in
1435 Eugenius IV issued new regulations for the office, limiting the
number of minor penitentiaries to eleven, he laid down how they were
to be divided by nations, two each from Italy, France and Spain, and
one each from England, Hungary, Upper Germany, Lower Germany,
and the Slav lands.

Jurisdiction in the general field of ecclesiastical organisation was
also indisputably a papal responsibility. In 1500 the pope transferred
the Channel Islands from the diocese of Coutances to that of Win-
chester, so that political divisions could be brought into line with the
area of ecclesiastical obedience.[3] Discrepancies between political and
ecclesiastical boundaries could undoubtedly raise problems, which
might lead to political intervention in basically ecclesiastical struggles.
The margraves of Brandenburg supported the struggles of the Bishop
of Havelberg against Mecklenburg, because this might lead indirectly
to the extension of the boundaries of the Mark. When there were
disagreements over rights between secular powers, the pope was better
able to exercise influence, because he alone could be regarded as
neutral between the contenders. After the fall of the Burgundian
duchy, such a dispute arose over the right to nominate to the church of
Tournai, and in 1492 orators from Maximilian and his son Philip
argued the right of the heirs of Burgundy to make the appointment. A
similar question of general ecclesiastical organisation lay in disputes
between religious orders. In 1490 Henry VII of England wrote to
Innocent VIII for a ruling concerning a certain Cistercian monk who,
after having transferred to a Carthusian house and remained there for
seven years, returned to his former house, after his former abbot had
claimed that the privileges of Citeaux made it impossible for a monk to
pass to another order, even one with a severer rule.[4] This episode
served as a test case, and what was sought in Rome was a judicial
definition of dubious points. Such recourse to the Curia may well have
been normal in doubtful cases, particularly if they might give rise to
precedents. This is shown by the action of London in sending orators to
Rome to defend a citizen who had been prosecuted for the non-
payment of certain tithes, and to secure a settlement of the issues in
dispute.

Jurisdiction over doctrine also was generally recognised as an ecclesiastical responsibility, although the only serious doctrinal schism of the century, that of Hussite Bohemia, was complicated by its contemporaneity with the struggles of pope and council. Sigismund's support for the Council of Basel, though an acknowledgement that doctrinal matters should be settled through ecclesiastical channels, was prompted primarily by the political implications of the Bohemian revolt and the hope that conciliar pacification of the Hussites might assist him in asserting his claim to the kingdom. After the end of the conciliar struggle, Rome continued to show concern at the doctrinal deviations of Bohemia, but had little effective power to suppress them, particularly during the reign of the Hussite, George Podebrady. Elsewhere princes showed varying attitudes to doctrinal questions – Albrecht Achilles of Brandenburg held that matters of belief should be settled by the pope, but the Landgraf Ludwig II of Hesse, became implicated in 1479 in the struggles of the mendicant orders over the doctrine of the Immaculate Conception. Earlier in the same decade there was a case of secular intervention in France in a theological dispute concerning divine foreknowledge and future contingents. The University of Paris was drawn in, charges of heresy were cast about, and the case was referred to Rome, where the theologians reversed the anti-nominalist verdict of the Sorbonne. So far papal rights to define doctrine had been left unchallenged, but in 1474 Louis XI in a royal ordinance condemned the nominalists' teaching, and commanded that the doctrines of the Thomists and the Scotists rather than those of the nominalists should be taught in the Arts and Theology faculties. In 1484 Jean Laillier appealed to the Parlement against the Faculty of Theology for refusing to confer a doctorate on him, because his views on clerical celibacy were suspect. Parlement, however, remitted the case to the bishop's official. When theological divergence developed into heresy, there was no doubt that this was the province of the Church courts, but in cases of relapse, when the heretic had incurred the ultimate penalty, this would be inflicted by the lay power. The secular authorities were prepared to assist the Church in pursuing heretics, notably if they had been involved in sedition, but if they had not been rigorous enough, the pope might exhort a prince to act against offenders.[5]

Spiritual jurisdiction was always vulnerable to secular pressure, and kings could be arbitrary in resisting it, as in 1478 when Louis XI commanded the Parlement of Paris to annul an interdict imposed by the Bishop of Chartres. There was a considerable measure of lay encroachment also in matters of family law, where both secular and spiritual powers might have interests. In France the king might grant letters of legitimation, and in a case of 1498 it was noted that although the petitioner had already received a grace of legitimation from the pope he was also seeking one from the king. In an earlier grant, in 1485, the king's action was less concerned with legitimation, with which the Church was concerned, than with his own right of ennoblement, when he granted the rights of nobility to a man whose father had not been legitimate. In England the laws concerning legitimation had diverged from normal continental practice in the thirteenth century, and in the fifteenth Sir John Fortescue gave a long justification of the English custom.

It is hardly surprising that the secular power was concerned with questions of legitimacy, because these might affect matters of inheritance. It is for this reason perhaps surprising that the Church kept control over probate jurisdiction. In another sphere of spiritual jurisdiction, which could have implications for property and in politics, there was far more tension between the two powers, namely in matrimonial causes, more particularly over the grant of dispensations from observing prohibitions for consanguinity. The right to dispense undoubtedly belonged to the supreme spiritual authority, as was recognised in a letter of Louis XI to Sixtus IV in 1475, trying to secure a dispensation for the marriage of Alfonso of Portugal to Juana of Castile. Of course when papal action might lead to a marriage of which a king disapproved, he could discourage the pope from making any grant. Even this, of course, emphasised the fact that the right to dispense rested with the spiritual authority.

Dispensations could, however, lead to difficult situations, because political circumstances might change between the time of the grant and the fulfilment of the marriage. In 1425 a dispensation was obtained for the marriage of the Duke of Anjou and Isabeau, daughter of the Duke of Brittany, and the wedding had been celebrated, but only by proxy. When the Duke of Brittany wished to break his alliance with Anjou, the pope at first refused to nullify the dispensation. In the subsequent negotiations the pope could drive a hard bargain, because his jurisdictional rights were indisputable, and eventually in 1430, when the duke gave way on the question of paying a tax to support a papal army against the Hussites, Martin V found a technical excuse for nullifying the marriage and dispensed Isabeau to marry the Count of Laval. The papal treasury gained from these political complications, for the various bulls cost 1,500 *écus*. Nor was this an isolated case – in England too Martin attempted to exploit his dispensing power as a political weapon. In the course of trying to secure the annulment of the Statute of Provisors, he delayed granting a dispensation sought for the marriage of the Earl of Huntingdon and Anne Mortimer, widow of the Earl of March, but in the end the marriage took place without any concessions being made on provisions.[6] An earlier attempt at bargaining benefices for a marriage dispensation was made by Humphrey,

Duke of Gloucester, when he had attempted to make concessions to the pope. The pope was, however, unwilling to pay Humphrey's price, and issued a rebuke to him. He also sent a bull to Duke John of Brabant, denying reports that he had confirmed Humphrey's marriage to Jacqueline of Hainault and nullified her previous marriage.

Towards the end of the century, the marriages of Anne of Brittany to two successive French kings throw further light on the problems arising from the dispensing power. The danger that the Pragmatic Sanction of Bourges might be extended to the duchy had made Innocent VIII reluctant to make the original concession, and the general feeling among the cardinals had tended to favour Anne's rival suitor, Maximilian of Austria, to whom she was married by proxy in 1491. This marriage was, however, annulled and the dispensation for that to Charles VIII was granted. At the same time the pope forbade the introduction of the pragmatic into Brittany, and the king complied with this command. On Charles's death, his successor, wishing to consolidate the union of the kingdom and the duchy, required an annulment of his previous marriage to Jeanne of France in order to marry Anne, and Alexander VI exploited the situation to secure political advancement for his son Cesare, who was granted a duchy and married the sister of the King of Navarre. By temporising over the grant of Louis XII's dispensation, the pope delayed the dangers arising from the break with the other Italian powers which an alliance with France involved. It was Louis XII's good fortune that the pope's political interests were compatible with his own; a generation later, when Henry VIII wished for his divorce, he had to deal with a pope in very different political circumstances.

The political background to such cases should be stressed, because, as far as can be seen, the papacy generally obliged princes in their requests, particularly if they could make incidental gains for themselves, either political or financial. Henry VII of England received permission for his marriage to Elizabeth of York in July 1486 and Henry VIII was allowed to marry his brother's widow. Such grants by the pope show that matrimonial causes were primarily a spiritual matter, but one can also see an attempt, in France at any rate, to introduce some concept of a civil impediment to marriage. This is found in the case of Jeannette Roland, whom the Parlement of Paris refused to allow to go with her betrothed to England, even although there was no canonical impediment. By the sixteenth century jurists were using a distinction, originally made by theologians, between the contractual and sacramental elements in marriage, in order to withdraw matrimonial causes from ecclesiastical jurisdiction. It must, however, be remembered that cases which had political implications were rare, and that when proceedings concerned only individuals the lay

power would await the decision of the spiritual court. A Neapolitan
case of 1451, dealing with doubts as to whether a marriage was lawful,
shows the king commanding that the parties should be left unmolested
until the case had been properly heard by the apostolic commissioner.
It appears that the normal procedure was for such matters to be heard
in local church courts, or for them to be referred back to the locality,
because only a few came to the highest tribunal in Rome, the Rota.

In such fields, the recognition of papal authority meant that a
practical system of jurisdiction was established. Besides the claim of
the Church to have cognisance over particular types of case, there was
also the equally long-standing and even more tricky question of legal
authority over the persons of the clergy, and clearly the fifteenth-
century popes made little attempt to assert the inviolability of the
clerical order. In some cases the secular powers made a token gesture
of recognising the Church's claims, but it might well be no more than a
token. At the time of the fall of Savonarola, the Florentine government
requested from Rome powers to try the arrested religious, but it
declined to comply with a papal request to send the prisoners to Rome.
The pope compromised by sending two judges-delegate to participate
in the trial, but by the time that they arrived they were too late to play a
significant part in it. In England, during the struggles of Lancaster and
York, various prelates were imprisoned for their political activities,
without this provoking any apparent reaction from Rome.[7] In France
the Parlement of Paris in 1418 took cognisance of cases of *lèse-majesté*
committed by clerks, and later in the century Louis XI was able to
arrest and imprison his former adviser, Jean Balue, Cardinal Bishop of
Angers. Papal intervention may have protected Balue from a worse
penalty than imprisonment, but it could not secure his liberty, and he
remained in custody for several years. In the reign of Charles VIII, the
pope was able to intervene rather more effectively in defence of the
clergy, although even then there were delays before this had results. [8]
In general, however, the papacy was weak or impotent against a
determined secular ruler, at any rate outside Italy.

If prelates could be treated so cavalierly, the lower clergy were even
more subject to princely authority, and even where tradition guaranteed them certain protection, attempts were made, and sometimes
successfully, to limit this. In 1455 a petition to the English Parliament
sought for restrictions to be placed on benefit of clergy, and under
Henry VII petty treason was declared not to be 'clergyable'. Probably
the political instability of fifteenth-century England gave the Church
an opportunity of recovering some of its jurisdictional influence over
the clergy, which had been lost since the thirteenth century, and only
after the firm establishment of the Tudors was the secular power able
to renew its encroachment on Church privileges. In places the papacy

even upheld the secular power against the local ecclesiastical authority. In Saxony, ducal proceedings against a priest at Jessen, who was suspected of a robbery, aroused the opposition of the bishop, but the duke's envoy to Rome, himself a churchman,[9] secured papal vindication of the proceedings. The pope allowed the offender to be stripped of his priestly dignity, so that the secular power could prosecute him for a criminal offence. There were variations in the effectiveness of secular action between different territories, even those ruled by the same family: when Albrecht Achilles, the future ruler of Brandenburg, was ruling over the Franconian lands of the Hohenzollerns, he exercised stronger control over offending clerks there than he could in the Mark, although even there a monk could be punished for an offensive sermon.[10] One must not, however, assume that the secular power automatically opposed ecclesiastical jurisdiction in criminal affairs; that the reverse might be true is shown by a French example of 1481, when the Bishop of Luçon complained that a clerk, who had been guilty of murder and whose correction pertained to him, had appealed to Parlement, thereby delaying the fulfilment of justice. The king instructed the Parlement to uphold the bishop's right in the case. Much, however, depended on the arbitrary will of the secular ruler and on the relations existing at a particular time between him and his clergy. When Bishop Guillaume Le Ferron of St Pol-de-Léon in Brittany quarrelled with Duke Francis II over the right of spoil on a stranded whale, the duke's men acted forcibly against him, banning recourse to the episcopal tribunal except for cases of marriage, testamentary dispositions, and leprosy. When a notary of the bishop's court drew up an instrument in defiance of the ban he was compelled to eat it, seal and all, and eventually the bishop's temporalities were seized. The pope's reaction was to appoint investigators with power to pronounce canonical censures, despite the papal privilege to the Bretons that they should not be cited outside the duchy. It shows that the papacy might on occasions undermine even its own grants if circumstances appeared to warrant such action.

The synodal statutes of a number of bishops also asserted ecclesiastical authority against the secular power. In 1468 Cardinal Jean Rolin, Bishop of Autun, not only laid down penalties for those impeding ecclesiastical jurisdiction but also dealt with the more specific problem of secular lords imprisoning clerks, and he commanded that action be taken to transfer them to the episcopal prison, under threat of interdict. Similar provisions can be seen at Avignon in 1451 and in the synodal statutes of Tréguier, in 1439, 1440, 1469 and 1493. On some occasions sanctions were applied to general offences, impugning the liberty of the Church or impeding the bishop's jurisdiction, but in other cases specific topics were raised. In 1469 sentence of excommunication was laid on secular powers who tried to prevent the seeking of apostolic letters and compelled men to have recourse to the secular judge in matters pertaining to the ecclesiastical courts. This reference to Roman jurisdiction is unusual, and it seems that many judicial questions were resolved locally.

How far was there a clash of jurisdictions? The reiteration of sanctions against impeding episcopal authority suggests that the secular power paid little heed to ecclesiastical fulminations, but there is little sign of prolonged conflict on many jurisdictional issues. Churchmen might well take a responsible attitude to their powers, and prelates would caution against their abuse. A Tréguier statute of 1450 declared that men who were leaving their parish should seek licence to do so, and state publicly to which parish they were going, so that they should not escape their creditors, and another from the same diocese in 1493 laid down sanctions against those (clerks and others), who vexed simple persons by citations to ecclesiastical courts. Other churchmen, however, were less restrained in their attitude to lay jurisdiction and provoked secular reaction. Undated royal letters from the reign of Louis XI forbade lay causes from being transferred to ecclesiastical tribunals to the prejudice of royal jurisdiction in the *sénéchausées* of Velay, Vivarais and Gévaudan. Possibly the most sensitive matter was that of penal action by the lay power against criminous clerks, but even here there was less trouble than might have been expected, and a treatise written about 1500 by Bernard Lauret, president of the Parlement of Toulouse, laid down the occasions when a secular judge might lay hands on a clerk without fear of excommunication. The author assumed that lay and ecclesiastical jurisdictions were distinct and that the latter was the greater of the two. Lauret allowed the secular power to act when a clerk had acted contrary to the duties of the clerical order, by assuming military attire, abandoning his clerical habit, or by frequenting taverns. Nor were punishments to be inflicted on laymen who laid violent hands on clerks whom they found acting improperly with their wives, sisters or mothers. Lauret did, however, stipulate that penalties on clerks should be imposed *pecuniariter* rather than *corporaliter*. Lauret also left to the lay power possessory matters relating to churches. Much of what he wrote had been expressed more than half a century earlier by William Lyndwood in England, who had agreed that lay public authority could act against a clerk guilty of sedition, highway robbery and other offences, if he had not accepted canonical correction. Lyndwood also accepted that a private individual could take action, provided that he was personally concerned in the case, as for example if a clerk were found acting improperly with his wife, mother, daughter or sister. When the layman did not have such a personal concern, however, Lyndwood held that he was not entitled to arrest the clerk without authorisation from an ecclesiastical judge.

Such theoretical writings seem to reflect actual practice. In 1453 Cardinal d'Estouteville, as legate in Brittany, decided that clerks who lived unworthily could under certain conditions be abandoned to the secular judge. In England, for practical purposes, secular and spiritual jurisdictions were co-operative rather than competing, and the Church acquiesced in lay action against clerks guilty of moral offences. Such offenders were often in only minor orders, and in 1516 Leo X attempted to curb this, by commanding that ordinands should receive all orders to the subdiaconate simultaneously, or be provided with a benefice. The secular power was to have the right to punish offenders. He apparently hoped that this might control the admission of dubious persons to orders and the protection which they afforded. The Church could also draw on lay assistance to enforce its own authority, and to take action against offenders who had been excommunicated. In mid-fifteenth-century Naples, lay attitudes to the Church courts varied; Alfonso of Aragon could order his officials to capture a fugitive Carthusian monk, who had abandoned his religious habit (in letters also containing platitudes about the king's duty to the Church) and command an abbot to expedite proceedings against a monk guilty of certain unspecified crimes. On the other hand he could resist papal action which threatened encroachment on his own jurisdiction, when he wrote to the pope asking him to revoke the excommunication of a knight who had failed to appear in a case concerning the castle of Rofrano, as the case was being heard in the royal court. Towards the end of the century the papacy extended its influence in the kingdom. The peace of 1486, renewed in 1492, between Innocent VIII and Ferrante included a provision that no ecclesiastical person would be brought before a secular judge on any matter, except a feudal one.

The possibility of the papacy laying down such conditions in Naples shows its greater influence there in virtue of its feudal superiority, whereas elsewhere there was little consistency of practice and individual cases were treated according to their own circumstances and in the light of other issues between the secular and the spiritual power. In 1492 Alexander VI complained to the Chancellor of Brabant about his summoning of churchmen before his tribunal, at a time when there was a general deterioration in relations between the Curia and the ducal court, with attempts being made to limit papal nominations to benefices. However, in 1515 Leo X made concessions to the secular power by setting severe limits to the citation of subjects of the Low Countries to courts outside the country, even those of Rome, and in 1522 an imperial edict forbade the citation of laymen before ecclesiastical judges in various cases. In the town states of north Italy, the papacy not infrequently was at loggerheads with the civic authorities, and political disputes between the two powers probably exacerbated the jurisdictional ones. In 1496 the Florentine Signoria commanded Savonarola to preach, in defiance of a papal prohibition, and in 1498, after the friar's excommunication, it threatened severe action against the Church authorities when they tried to prevent the people from attending his sermons. In the time of Julius II the Venetian government forbade appeals to Rome in ecclesiastical matters and churchmen were brought before secular tribunals without papal permission. At this time and shortly afterwards the Council of Ten expanded its penal powers to take cognisance of cases of sacrilege and blasphemy, and in 1517 the Senate condemned the taking of legal proceedings before an ecclesiastical judge in cases pertaining to the secular courts. Similarly there was opposition to the withdrawal of cases from the civil to the ecclesiastical courts on the pretext that the person concerned was a churchman.

Where the papacy had little direct influence, as in Germany, the lay power could extend its power without serious opposition. In the Palatinate, Würtemberg and Bavaria, the princely courts secured control of almost all ecclesiastical cases. The bishops may have claimed independent jurisdiction, but they did little to resist the princes. The secular control of most civil litigation in the Palatinate was aided by the fact that the elector's court provided speedier and more effective justice, and churchmen preferred to have recourse to it, while the presence of legally trained clergy there softened any prejudice against secular jurisdiction. Property suits had to be heard before the court of the place where the property was situated, and the classification of benefices and tithes as property brought these before the secular courts. Nor was it only the princes who disregarded clerical immunity. In the Brandenburg towns ecclesiastical privileges were infringed, and the councils demanded the right to exercise authority over places of worship and over the lower clergy and their followers. A large town, such as Berlin, was able by payment to secure exemption from being cited to Rome. In the imperial cities of southern Germany, the councils claimed the right to control civic morality and punish blasphemy, in order to avert the possible hostility of God from the city. Such an attitude of corporate responsibility in religious matters led naturally to actions to control the clergy.

Not all lay intervention was unwelcome to the Church authorities, and indeed secular powers could make a major contribution to enforcing ecclesiastical discipline. The attitude of the laity to Church reform was inconsistent and depended on particular circumstances. In some cases the lay power would co-operate with the efforts of the reformers, in others it would be the main stumbling block in their way. Albrecht of Austria, later the Emperor Albrecht II, worked for the reform of the monastery of Melk, and appealed to Martin V for help, which was forthcoming in the form of a group of six monks from Subiaco. In 1451, during his visitation of Germany, Cardinal Nicholas of Cusa threatened to appeal to the secular arm for help in enforcing enclosure on a group of nuns, although later in his own diocese he was gravely hampered by the support that Duke Sigismund of the Tyrol gave the Abbess of Sonnenburg in resisting his reform measures. In the quarrel with the duke, the cardinal was totally unable to enforce papal claims of jurisdiction. The lay power assumed a right to intervene in such matters, without any infringement of its own rights: a letter to the Council of Basel from the Emperor Sigismund in 1434 urged it to invoke secular aid, although at the same time he asked that *causae prophanae* should be heard in secular and not ecclesiastical courts. In France, while Jean de Bourbon was attempting to reform the abbey of Cluny, Louis XI agreed to his request that the Parlement should not hear appeals from Cluniac monks. Here one can see a churchman who accepted the king's right to limit legal actions by the clergy and a similar attitude, although in a different field, can be seen in the churchmen deliberating at Tours in 1493 on the reform of the French Church, when they asked the king to request from the pope revocation of *commendams* and, if the pope did not act, to command the monasteries to make elections in disregard of papal rights. Such an attitude among his leading clergy would greatly strengthen the king in any disagreements which he might have with the pope.

Issues of sanctuary occasionally caused tension between the secular and the spiritual powers, but the worst difficulties of this were obviated by papal acquiescence in lay restrictions on it, and indeed by positive assistance to the prince. In England, bulls of 1493 and 1504 limited privileged immunities, while earlier in the century a compromise solution had been reached in Castile. In 1459 there was serious antagonism between the king's officials and the bishops, as the latter retaliated with excommunication for any violations of sanctuary. Theoretically the ultimate authority on such questions was the pope, but it would have taken too long to consult him on every case. At the king's request, Pius II empowered the Archbishop of Seville to determine the validity of the censures in each case. By so doing, he ensured the maintenance of ecclesiastical control, in a way more acceptable to the secular power. In Brittany, there was a ducal complaint in 1430 about an extension of the *minihy* or sanctuary at Tréguier, but in 1452 various papal bulls on disputed issues included one to abolish the privileges of *minihys* for those guilty of major crimes, although the rights of sanctuary were maintained for lesser matters.

There was, however, one area of jurisdiction where it was harder for the two masters of the Church to reconcile their interests. This was when litigation arose over disputed appointments and contested elections. Even when the pope had not himself claimed the right to present to a benefice, he could claim cognisance of any case arising out of an election dispute, and such judicial action was resisted by the lay power. The *Journal* of Clément de Fauquembergue shows that during the pontificate of Martin V the Parlement of Paris not only protested against appeals to Rome but also applied this principle when issues concerning benefices came before it.[11] For those who defied the Parlement and took proceedings at Rome, action might be taken against them. The Parlement's strongly Gallican point of view might not be shared by the king, and the Concordat of Genazzano of 1426 showed temporary agreement between Charles VII and Martin V over disputes concerning benefices. This bull was confirmed in 1429 following a futher period of tension during which the pope had asserted his claims against lay judges who usurped his claims against lay judges who usurped possessory suits.[12] It was impossible to reach a permanent agreement and the split between Eugenius IV and the Council of Basel gave the king a weapon for putting pressure on the pope. Ambassadors were sent to him in 1436, in a renewed attempt to limit access to Rome, but the negotiations had no positive result, and Charles threw his support behind the council. In January 1438 it passed a decree limiting recourse to curial tribunals, although it still accepted that certain cases, including those dealing with disputed elections to sees and abbeys, should be reserved to Rome. When in the pragmatic sanction the French adopted those decrees of Basel which seemed to their advantage, they made some small amendments to this decree, setting further limitations on recourse to Rome.

If the issue in France involved rival pressures from the pope and the king, in Brittany the particularism of the local courts added further complications. The duke asserted an ancient right of jurisdiction over benefices, which was eventually accepted in a papal bull in 1453. Unsuccessful litigants, however, might appeal from the Breton Parlement to the Parlement of Paris, and as by the middle of the century this meant that they were being taken to a court where the hated pragmatic was law, the papacy was prepared to uphold ducal rights against those of the king. Even after the recognition of the duke's rights, cases concerning bishoprics might still be 'evoked' to Rome. One such, taken to Rome in 1458, was resolved only in 1462, and then not by papal decision but by the death of one of the claimants, an indication of the intractability of some of the problems. Papal support for Brittany against the French king could be renewed at times of Franco-papal tension, as in 1478–9, when ducal rights in possessory cases relating to benefices were confirmed, saving a right of appeal to the Holy See. The Parlement of Paris was excluded, no doubt to the satisfaction of duke and pope alike.

By this time the French secular courts certainly exercised authority over questions concerning benefices, despite various attempts by interested parties to appeal to Rome. Between 1462 and 1483 there were not less than sixty proceedings before the Parlement concerning elections to benefices, and between 1483 and 1516 at least fifty-five for the possession of bishoprics and over eighty for the possession of monasteries. Royal letters show regular interference over benefices: sometimes judges-delegate were appointed to hear cases, on other occasions they might be heard by the Parlement or by the Great Council. There was, however, no consistency in royal policy, and each case must be seen strictly in its own context. In 1482 Louis XI ordered the chancellor to uphold a sentence given at the Curia. The pressures involved can be seen in two protracted disputes over bishoprics, at Carcassonne and Pamiers. Some aspects of these were noted in Chapter 7 but the cases are worth considering in the jurisdictional context also. The former crisis lasted from 1456 to 1462, when the candidate postulated by the chapter and supported by the local nobility, Geoffroi de Bazillac, who, because he was under age had to appeal to the pope for a dispensation, had his postulation annulled, with the benefice being given by Calixtus III to the king's nominee. When the canons resisted the latter, the suit went to the court of the ecclesiastical superior, the Archbishop of Narbonne. The proctor for the papal provisor, Jean du Chastel, the brother of the king's favourite, Tanguy du Chastel, claimed that the case should be remitted to Rome, while the chapter claimed that they were acting in accordance with the pragmatic sanction, and that the bull of provision was contrary to the royal ordinances. The case eventually was referred to Rome. However, concurrently with these proceedings, Jean du Chastel was cited before the Parlement of Toulouse for breach of the pragmatic. The king intervened on his behalf, ordering the transfer of the suit to the Parlement of Paris, even although Carcassonne lay within the jurisdictional sphere of Toulouse. The pretext given was that Bazillac and the canons had too many allies and relatives at Toulouse and that the Parlement of Paris would be more impartial, but more probably the king's motive was to have the case heard where he himself could exercise stronger influence. Attempts to put Chastel in possession of the bishopric were faced by physical resistance, with some success, and Bazillac, with considerable effrontery, appealed again to the Parlement of Toulouse against the royal commissioner who had resisted his possession. In the end Chastel secured the see, and helped to secure a small bishopric to compensate his rival.[13]

The Pamiers crisis was even more protracted. In 1467 the pope attempted to reserve the see, but the canons disregarded his commands, elected Mathieu d'Artigueloube, the nephew of the previous bishop, and sought recognition of him, not only from their metropolitan but also, perhaps over-optimistically, from the pope. The suit was taken to Rome, where the elected candidate was persuaded to renounce his claims and support a papal nominee. However, he went back on his promise and the Parlement of Toulouse intervened to take cognisance of the case. The king asserted his interest, the case was 'evoked' to the Great Council, and despite the pope's attempts to employ spiritual sanctions in favour of his candidate, it seemed as though the canons' choice had prevailed. Then the king changed sides and the canons followed his example, but Artigueloube continued to pursue his claim by seizing the episcopal fortress and securing a favourable verdict from the Parlement. The affair dragged on for decades, complicated by a struggle for the county of Foix in the 1480s and by the Gallican reaction after the death of Louis XI. The death of the original papal provisor was followed by a renewed provision. An attempted appeal to Rome was adjourned *sine die* by the pope, and only after the death of the second papal nominee did Artigueloube, in 1498, secure provision from Alexander VI, along with absolution for irregularities incurred in the previous thirty years. The old pro-Roman party in the chapter had, however, elected their own candidate, who in effect then became the new champion of Gallican claims. Before long the pope dropped his support for Artigueloube, and when the rival claimant died during a period of Franco-papal alliance, Alexander provided to the see Amanieu d'Albret, whose sister Charlotte was married to the pope's son Cesare. Only when the Albret allied themselves with Spain against France, and when the accession of Julius II brought to the papacy a man hostile to all with Borgia connections did Artigueloube gain control, with support from the courts of both Paris and Toulouse, and remain as bishop until his death in March 1514. Even then tensions were renewed with the return of Albret, and after he demitted the see in 1519 the canons made a futile attempt to resist the provision of a royal nominee under the terms of the concordat.

These two disputes show clearly that issues of principle played a much smaller part than questions of politics. The courts, notably the Parlement of Toulouse, tended to Gallicanism, but royal policy alternated between a pro-Gallican position and support for the papacy. It was actual authority rather than its appearance with which the kings were concerned, and according to the needs of the moment they would accept or resist Roman control. In a disputed election at Beauvais in 1489, a royal letter to the Parlement of Paris commanded that the matter be remitted to the appropriate judges, the vicars of the Archbishop of Reims, in accordance with the pragmatic sanction. Royal policy was markedly more flexible than might be imagined from the arguments put forward during negotiations. In 1452 Teodoro de Laelio had claimed a general right of appeal to the pope in cases concerning benefices, and affirmed that he could either take direct cognisance or refer to the judges-delegate, while the king's reply was that he was too busy to take any decision in the matter. In the negotiations before the concordat of 1472 the question of jurisdictions was a factor in delaying a settlement. Eventually it was conceded that cases concerning benefices would be heard initially in France, but would go to Rome on appeal, apart from certain special cases, such as those concerning cardinals, which would be heard at Rome in the first instance. Stipulations were made concerning the settlement of suits already in progress. Despite the compromises which the king might make, Gallican feelings persisted elsewhere, and in the *cahier* concerning the Church presented by the Three Estates in 1484, one demand was that nothing should be done prejudicial to the pragmatic by citations to Rome and other ecclesiastical citations, prejudicial to collators and ecclesiastical judges.

In the arguments for accepting the concordat of 1516, one justification was that it provided a more certain form of government for the Church than the pragmatic had done, and a speech made by Antoine Duprat, chancellor to Francis I, included a reference to the pleading of cases in Rome among the abuses which the agreement would obviate. In a later speech Duprat returned to the same theme, pointing out that the pragmatic had been abrogated by the Fifth Lateran Council[14] and that the French were faced with defying the council, unless they could find some form of compensation. This abrogation might lead to papal interference and to legal proceedings in Rome, which would draw money from the realm, with a drastic diminution of royal rights. Admittedly these speeches cannot be taken at face value, when one remembers how kings had acquiesced in papal action when it suited them, even under the regime of the pragmatic, but they still emphasise that the secular power made vigorous efforts to assert its rights over jurisdictional issues. In the end, the concordat gave effective control over such cases to the king, by laying down that they were to be heard within the country, and that appeals were not to go to Rome until all higher courts in turn had taken cognisance of the case. In practice, this gave the king ample opportunity to influence proceedings, and as the concordat also gave him effective control over appointments, such jurisdictional powers merely strengthened his hand. The pope had in practical terms to abandon considerable influence to the king. Although his competence to hear major cases was recognised, the importance of this tended to be theoretical, particularly as cases con-

Table 2 Chronological table of persons and events

Popes (dates of election unless otherwise stated)	Councils and assemblies	Secular rulers (dates of accession, unless otherwise stated)	Other important events
1417 Martin V			
		1410 Sigismund (Emperor) (disputed election; unanimously re-elected in 1411)	
		1416 Alfonso V (Aragon)	
	1418 End of Council of Constance		1418 Concordats with France, Germany, Spain and England
		1419 Philip the Good (Burgundy)	
		1422 Henry VI (England) and Charles VII (France)	
	1423–4 Pavia-Siena		
			1426 Concordat of Gennazzano (France)
1431 Eugenius IV	1431 Basel (Nov. papal dissolution)		
	1432 Council defies dissolution		
	1433 Pope revokes dissolution		
	1434 Pope recognises council	1434 Death of Joanna II (Naples)	
	1437 Council declares pope contumacious		
	1438 and suspends him	1438 Albrecht II (emperor)	1438 Pragmatic Sanction of Bourges
	1438–9 Florence		
1439 Felix V (Antipope)	1439 Council deposes Eugenius		1439 Acceptatio of Mainz
		1440 Frederick III (emperor)	
			1441 Concordat of Redon (Brittany)
		1442 Alfonso of Aragon secured	

Popes	Councils	Rulers	Events
			1453 Fall of Constantinople
1455 Calixtus III			
1458 Pius II		1458 Ferrante (Naples) John II (Aragon)	
	1459–60 Congress of Mantua		1460 Bull *Execrabilis*
			1461 Abolition of pragmatic
		1461 Edward IV (England) Louis XI (France)	
1464 Paul II			1464 Restoration of pragmatic
		1467 Charles the Bold (Burgundy)	
			1469 Marriage of Ferdinand of Aragon and Isabella of Castile
		1470 Henry VI (England) restored	
1471 Sixtus IV		1471 Edward IV (England) restored	
			1472 Concordat with France
		1474 Isabella (Castile)	
		1477 Death of Charles the Bold	
		1479 Ferdinand II (Aragon)	
			1480–1 Turks occupy Otranto
1484 Innocent VIII		1483 Edward V, Richard III (England) and Charles VIII (France)	
		1485 Henry VII (England)	1486 Barons' War in Naples
1492 Alexander VI		1493 Maximilian I (emperor) Alfonso (Naples)	
		1494 Louis XII (France)	1494 French invasion of Italy
		1498 Louis XII (France)	
1503 Pius III Julius II			
		1509 Henry VIII (England)	1508–9 Treaty of Cambrai
1513 Leo X	1511–13 Pisa-Milan	1515 Francis I (France)	1516 Concordats with France and Portugal
	1512 Fifth Lateran	1516 Charles I (Spain, later Emperor Charles V, 1519)	1517 Luther's 95 Theses
			1519 Concordat with Poland

cerning those exempt from normal jurisdiction were to be heard within France by judges-delegate.

It was probably due to the close interest of France in Italian politics that the spiritual and secular powers established so well-defined a system. Elsewhere in Christendom, there were variations in the extent of secular influence over the Church, but such influence was general, and the variations lay in the details. In Germany, indeed, they can be seen between different principalities. After the Concordat of Vienna, which, one must remember, was concluded by the emperor and not by such corporate bodies as the Reichstag or the electoral college, individual princes demanded from the pope their own price before accepting the agreement, and full obedience was restored only gradually – the Bishop of Strassburg did not return to obedience until 1476. Part of the price paid to the Elector of Saxony was the limitation of spiritual jurisdiction in his territories, and in Brandenburg and Austria also the papacy made specific concessions to the princes. Elsewhere the process of princely encroachment was less formal, but even when there was no specific papal grant, the Church found it necessary to acquiesce in the increase of lay power. Chance factors, such as differences in personality between individuals, may explain the variations, but these do not affect the basic fact that in German lands the state had taken over much of the place of the papacy in the Church's administrative system in the century before the Reformation.

Clearly, therefore, in the judicial field, as elsewhere, lay influence extended at the papacy's expense in the century between the Council of Constance and the Reformation. Equally certain there was no consistent aim on either side beyond that of securing the maximum advantage obtainable in any particular situation, and the gains of the lay power resulted simply from its greater willingness to regard its judicial authority as something which might be sacrificed when it was wishing to bargain for advantages elsewhere.

CHAPTER 10

The Working of the System

When one views the relationships between the spiritual and secular powers of Christendom between the ending of the Great Schism and the start of the Reformation, one may wonder if the historian is justified in describing it by the term 'system'. Certainly the willingness of both sides to haggle over details on a particular issue, or to exploit some temporary weakness of the other for immediate advantage, leaves an impression of confusion which contrasts strongly with the apparently clearer positions of popes and princes in the twelfth and thirteenth centuries, although even then one may feel certain that the practical operation of ecclesiastical polity diverged from the theoretical claims to authority put forward by the rival powers of Church and State. In the fifteenth century there was even willingness to compromise in theory and to attempt to determine spheres of influence by negotiation, and certainly beneath the changing methods of ecclesiastical administration there was an understanding of the practical realities of power within the Church, and some consistency of policy on the part of popes and princes alike.

The historian of the fifteenth-century Church must not let his view become too coloured by his knowledge of events in the sixteenth century, nor interpret events of this period in terms of post-Reformation orthodoxies, of any colour on the spectrum between the Tridentine and the Genevan. It is more important to try to understand events in the light of what preceded the restoration of unity in the Western Church in 1417, because it was the circumstances of the schism which moulded the outlook of both secular princes and popes on the question of how the Church could be ruled and their rival claims to authority reconciled. Many of the problems which the papacy inherited from the schism have been noted in earlier chapters, but one should remember that the prolonged crisis had influenced secular attitudes also. It was not that the fifteenth-century princes were more unscrupulous than their pre-schism forerunners (although for cynicism and insincerity Louis XI would surely be hard to match) but rather that they had gained confidence from the situation in which they could play off rival popes against each other. It is hard to overestimate the revolutionary character of the French withdrawal of obedience of 1398, which in effect implied that it was not necessary to have a pope at the head of the French Church. The German neutrality between Eugenius IV and the Council of Basel in the *Acceptatio* of Mainz in 1439 was a comparably drastic step. Even after the end of the Basel Schism there was still persistent ecclesiastical particularism, and there was some truth, admittedly expressed in rather rhetorical terms, in Aeneas Sylvius Piccolomini's statement in 1454: 'Christianity has no head whom all wish to obey. Neither the Pope nor the Emperor is rendered his due. There is no reverence, no obedience. Thus we regard the Pope and Emperor as if they bore false titles and were mere painted objects. Each city has its own king. There are as many princes as there are households'. Such an attitude to the papacy made it easy for men to regard it purely in political terms, as a factor to be considered because of the power at its disposal but without regard to its claim to be inherently different from other powers in virtue of its spiritual rights.

This was an easy attitude to take, because the popes themselves were uncertain of their role. They had long abandoned, in practice if not in theory, the grandiose claims of men such as Boniface VIII, and although the Avignon period had seen the reforms of governmental machinery in the Church which increased its administrative effectiveness, the long absence of the papacy from Rome may well have weakened its psychological appeal to the mass of the faithful. As long as the papacy was associated with Rome, with all the city's spiritual associations, these could strengthen it against its critics, but at Avignon there was no such emotional appeal which could soften hostitlity to the powerful and vigorous bureaucracy. In consequence, men were likely to regard the papacy as a jurisdictional rather than a spiritual force, and the pope as a chief administrator rather than as the Vicar of Christ. In the early fourteenth century, Dante, for all his hatred of Boniface VIII, could describe the French attack on the pope's person at Anagni as 'Christ being made captive again in the person of his vicar', but no comparable comment seems to have been made about Eugenius IV's ignominious flight from Rome in 1434 or the military pressures applied to the papacy during the wars after 1494. The divided headship of the Church between 1378 and 1417 set limits to both practical power and theoretical claims, and the popes of the Restoration period were left with the difficulty of turning into an effectively organised system of Church government the undoubted belief that there was some basic unitary character in the Church, the sentiment which had played a vital part in turning conciliar ideas into an effective programme of action against the division of Christendom. A purely spiritual unity might coexist with administrative division, but it is hardly surprising that the popes wished to reverse the separatist tendencies of the schism. Furthermore, besides the roles of spiritual leader and administrative head, the pope was also the ruler of the States of the Church in Italy, and there is little doubt that the return of an unchallenged pope to Italy intensified the part which the papacy, as represented by the Roman line of popes during the schism, was already playing in the politics of the peninsula. The resources of the States of the Church were regarded in the same light as other papal revenues when it came to meeting the expenses of the Roman See, but to ensure that these could be raised, the popes had to develop further their role as territorial princes.

The situation of the papacy in the century after 1417 changed in response to circumstances, and one may identify different phases in its policies. The popes had no option but to meet immediate problems, however much this might mean concessions with serious long-term implications. There can be little doubt that in 1417 the papacy's greatest weakness lay in its relations with the rest of the Church. Only through the action of the Council of Constance had unity been restored, and however true it is to say that the members of the council were not conciliarists in the sense that they would uphold the superiority of a council over an undisputed pope, there were equally opponents of the papacy who realised that the implications of what had been achieved at Constance could be turned to their advantage. This can be seen in the changing attitudes to councils in later years: whereas in the early fifteenth century the question of unity had been the over-riding concern of the councils, by the time of Basel conciliar authority was seen more as a possible means of controlling the pope, and therefore as a weapon which the secular power could exploit for political ends.

Without allies, the popes could not reassert their control over the councils, and this need for assistance during the first two pontificates of the Restoration drove them into bargaining with the secular powers. The princes' importance in Church affairs was already clear, as it was the decisions by the secular rulers to support rival contenders to the papacy in 1378 that hardened the divisions among the cardinals into a split in Christendom, while without secular acceptance of conciliar action, attempts to restore unity would have been futile. The princes could assist the pope, at a price, although they, too, had weaknesses which set limits to the pressures which they could apply. The wars between England and France, and the participation in these of the Burgundians, gave the popes some choice of allies among the secular rulers. Nor could kings who wished to strengthen their authority at the expense of their subjects really acquiesce in the constitutionalism of the conciliarists, who wished to set limits to papal power comparable to those that their own more powerful subjects might wish to impose on them. The co-operation of kings and popes in the fifteenth century was a factor tending towards the growth of absolutism, just as the rivalries of spiritual and royal power in the twelfth and thirteenth centuries had tended to assist constitutional movements within the feudal state. Furthermore papal rights in ecclesiastical administration were nego- tiable, and provided a basis for co-operation between the pope and the princes. With papal support a king could increase his control over his clerical subjects and exploit ecclesiastical resources to reward his servants. As long as the papacy's main concern was to recover the influence which it had lost to the councils, the lay power could apply pressure in its own interests, and it is hardly surprising that the greatest opportunity for this occurred during the Council of Basel. Not all princes followed the same methods, as can be seen by comparing Charles VII of France and the imperial electors with Duke Philip of Burgundy; the two former exploited papal weaknesses to encroach on Church rights, but the third obtained advantages for himself by agree- ment with the pope. The difference, however, was one of method rather than of basic aim. The princes did not concern themselves much with the principles of the conciliar struggle, but merely exploited the opportunities which it gave to them. They might use the council for different reasons according to their own particular interests, whether this was negotiation with the Hussites, as in the case of Sigismund; securing control of the national Church, as with the French adoption of the reform decrees in the Pragmatic Sanction of Bourges, or with support in the political struggle in Naples, as in the actions of Alfonso of Aragon.[1] At the same time it is noteworthy that the princes were not prepared to create a comparable schism to that of 1378 by supporting the conciliar antipope against Eugenius IV. This suggests that there was still a desire to preserve some unity within Christendom, and that the princes did not wish a repetition of the chaos which followed the events of 1378.

The princes were aided in their actions by the council's efforts to act as an independent agent, not merely in Church government, but also through its interventions in European diplomacy as for example, in its sending of an embassy to the Congress of Arras in 1435. In this it was attempting to undertake the role of peacemaker in Christendom, a part frequently played by the papacy, although one might note that parties to negotiations sometimes stipulated that the pope should mediate as a private person and not *ex officio*.[2] Yet a further advantage for the princes may have been that the pope was not fully aware of the political situation outside Italy, while they were more aware of papal difficulties. Certainly Eugenius IV did not appreciate conditions in the empire and the weakness of the emperor *vis-à-vis* the territorial princes.[3] The princes' gains during the Basel period and in negotiations with the pope at the time when conciliar resistance was breaking down left them with much real influence over the Church in their lands, and it is worth considering how far the fifteenth-century Church should be considered as a unitary body under the pope and how far as a loosely linked collection of independent national churches. In theory, there is no doubt that it was the former, but one may wonder how far theory and practice coincided. Certainly growing sentiments of nationalism under royal authority ran parallel to increased secular influence over the Church, which left the princes with the powers of ultimate decision in ecclesiastical matters. The situation to some extent resembled one in which former colonial territories, which had achieved independence, still preserved certain links with their former imperial power.

From the time of Nicholas V onwards the ecclesiastical problems of the popes altered in character, because by 1450 the most serious phase of conciliar activity was over and the survival of conciliar ideas in the ensuing period had only limited practical consequences. The failure of the rebel council of Pisa-Milan in 1511 was the result of inadequate secular support, this being due to the political isolation of France, rather than of any general acceptance of the anti-conciliar ideas upheld by papal propagandists. But despite the decline of conciliarism, the papacy still feared a council, unless it could control its proceedings, as it did equally in the cases of Ferrara-Florence and Fifth Lateran, and this probably explains papal resistance after 1517 to demands for a free council in German lands. Besides this fear of having its power limited, the papacy also had to negotiate with the secular powers to restore other aspects of its position, in the practical details of administration, which had been undermined both by the schism and by the quarrel with the council.

Concurrently with the struggle against its rivals within the Church, the papacy had the problem of its temporal power in Italy, which had been gravely undermined by the struggles of the schism. This involved it in diplomatic manoeuvres and the search for allies, and was a protracted difficulty which continued long after the Reformation. There were two kinds of problem, that of immediate control over the Papal States and that of the broader field of peninsular politics, as the other powers of Italy tried to exploit papal weaknesses. This in turn drew in some non-Italian powers, notably France and Aragon and in Franco-papal relations ecclesiastical issues were often employed as bargaining counters in political disputes. This was true both in the conciliar period and later in the century, notably over the question of Naples, although other territorial interests did exist and could give rise to clashes even outside Italy. Avignon was territorially a part of the Papal States but was contiguous to France and an area into which the

French kings wished to extend their influence. A prolonged crisis over it, from 1465 to 1476, though not in itself of first rate importance, shows clearly how the cross-currents of politics and administration affected relations between a secular prince and the papacy. From 1465 Louis XI was trying to secure for his cousin Charles of Bourbon, the Archbishop of Lyons, appointment as papal legate of Avignon and from 1469 also his promotion to the cardinalate, in the hope that this would strengthen royal influence in the area. Paul II procrastinated, but shortly before his death offered the king either the legateship or the cardinalate for his cousin. After the accession of Sixtus IV, during the negotiations for the abolition of the pragmatic sanction, one concession which the new pope offered the king was the delivery of the legatine bulls to Charles, and on the day when the concordat of 1472 was published he wrote to Louis promising to grant Bourbon the red hat at the next creation of cardinals. This promise was not fulfilled, and subsequent correspondence between the king and the pope showed that the latter was trying to bargain the red hat for the renunciation of the legateship. The Avignonese complained that Bourbon was preparing the union of the county to France, and the pope attempted to remove him from his position, appointing his own nephew Giuliano della Rovere as successor. Violence broke out, and Louis complained that the pope's attempt to seize Avignon was open support for his Burgundian and Savoyard enemies. In the struggle the king exercised effective power, although eventually there was a compromise. Rovere had to tell the Avignonese to submit, his right to the legateship was recognised and he was allowed possession of various French benefices to which he had been provided. In return the Avignonese had to promise to do nothing to help the king's enemies, and Charles of Bourbon at last received his red hat. In this crisis one sees many of the factors in the relationship of popes and princes: the initial tension arose out of the political concerns of the king and the territorial rights of the pope, these being complicated by the desire of the former to secure a cardinalate for a protégé and that of the latter to advance a relative. The pressure applied by the secular power in withholding benefices from the pope's nephew typifies both how the pope could make such grants and how secular power could nullify their practical effect.

In this crisis, and in many others, political considerations were prominent, and its complexities reflect much papal activity in the latter part of the century. Another factor which posed serious problems for the papacy after 1450 was the advance of Islam. This had been highlighted by the fall of Constantinople, and much of the activity of Calixtus III, Pius II, Paul II and Sixtus IV was directed to meeting it. The second of these had the most ambitious schemes, but it was the first and last who actually succeeded in sending fleets against the Turks. The unwillingness of the Italian powers to give support limited Paul's activity to financial subsidies for the Hungarians and Albanians. Pius' attention was also diverted from the East by the renewed struggle for the Neapolitan succession, his attempts to secure the withdrawal of the pragmatic sanction, and serious trouble in Germany, where the rebellious Archbishop of Mainz, Diether von Isenburg, was threatening an appeal to a future council, as was Duke Sigismund of Austria, who had expelled Cardinal Nicholas of Cusa from his diocese of Brixen. However much Pius was concerned with such residual conciliarism, the papacy was still not endangered by it as it had been a quarter of a century earlier – the appeals were tactical moves rather than expressions of any real hope that constitutional curbs would be set on the pope. The real importance of the German troubles was that they diverted the pope's attention from his other aims.

The period from the accession of Nicholas V to the death of Paul II was the most stable in the history of the Restoration papacy. These years were not without problems, particularly in Italian politics, but nothing really threatened the fundamental strength of the papacy. One reason for this may have been a better financial balance, with the resources of the temporal power showing a profit to the papal budget. Paul II's abolition of the venal college of abbreviators may also indicate an improved financial position, although equally possibly this pope may have had higher moral standards than his predecessor in matters of Church administration. However, at the beginning of Sixtus IV's pontificate Giovanni Tornabuoni wrote to Lorenzo de' Medici that the pope was living beyond his means and expected his bankers to cover his deficit, though it is not clear whether this statement was a reflection on the general financial problems of the papacy or a comment directed specifically at the new pope. Certainly this period was already seeing a decline in alum revenues and in this pontificate venal offices reappeared as a major factor in papal finance, thereafter becoming increasingly important as a means of anticipating revenue rapidly.

In many ways the pontificate of Sixtus IV was the turning point of the fifteenth-century papacy. Even before it, the central organisation of the Church had become increasingly Italian in character, despite the demands made at the Council of Constance for the representation of different nations of Christendom in the Curia and the College of Cardinals. Already Italians dominated the latter body, both in new appointments and in those present at conclaves. In the Curia the Italians held most positions of importance, and around 1480 Italian supplanted Latin as the normal language there, although not until the time of Leo X was the latter replaced as the vehicle of communication between the papacy and its diplomatic agents. By then the Curia had become more homogeneously Italian in character. These factors help to explain why Sixtus was much more concerned with peninsular affairs than with those of ultramontane Europe, although the Avignon crisis discussed earlier shows that he did not totally neglect the world beyond the Alps. Possibly, too, he was generally left in peace to engage in Italian politics by the European powers, at any rate early in his reign, because those states with the greatest interest in Italy were themselves distracted by internal crises, Louis XI by the wars with Burgundy, and Aragon and Castile by the succession struggles which culminated in the creation of the united Spanish monarchy under Ferdinand and Isabella. Certainly the re-emergence of active French interest in peninsular affairs, after the Pazzi conspiracy, came after the death of Charles of Burgundy. In the early years of the pontificate the most important aspect of external politics was the Turkish threat, in meeting which it was essential for the papacy to secure support from its fellow Italian powers, and the inability of Paul II to mobilise sufficient forces may have been one factor in encouraging Sixtus to pursue more strongly and systematically his policy of strengthening the Papal States into a more effective political force.

The main reason for the developments in papal policy at this time must however be sought in the pope's character. His affection for his relatives led to the reconquest of the Papal States from the territorial *signori* being pursued more in the interests of the Rovere family than in those of the Church, and the resulting financial problems were aggravated by the pope's activity in Rome itself. Here he was clearly concerned with the creation of a court comparable with the other princely courts of Italy, and the whole programme, particularly those works set in motion before the jubilee year of 1475, was calculated to impress visitors to Rome with the grandeur of the papacy. Sixtus was hailed by the humanists as *restaurator urbis*, and there is no doubt that the pattern which he set was one which his successors followed. In learning this reign saw an important landmark – from the time of Nicholas V the popes had extended at least intermittent patronage to scholars but the foundation of the Vatican Library, and the appointment of Platina as its prefect in 1475, was one of the papacy's most important contributions in this field.

Both political activity and support for scholarship and art were expensive, so the pope had to develop various fiscal expedients, which affected not only the lands in Italy but also the Church as a whole. Changes in the cameral tex books were particularly frequent during this pontificate, and evidence from various countries in Christendom bears out that there were increases in the sums paid for services. Here clearly papal interests were liable to clash with those of secular rulers, the more so as services, being a tax payable at the Curia and not in the country of origin, were less easy a target for princely encroachment than those other taxes levied by resident papal collectors in their lands. The coincidence of rising fiscal demands with the more Italian character of papal policy was obviously a potential source of resentment in an age when the awareness of nationality was increasing, although as yet papal ambitions did not far impinge on the political concerns of non-Italian rulers. For this reason, resentment was not yet as bitter as it would become after 1494. At a more popular level too, there was always the danger that papal attempts to impress by the grandeur of his city would indeed create an impression, but of the wrong kind. New architectural styles might emphasise to the sophisticated society of Renaissance Italy that the papacy shared its cultural aspirations, but the visiting prelate from northern Europe who was paying heavy taxes might justifiably question the ways in which his money was being spent. In this psychological sense, as well as in politics and administration, a breach had been opened between an Italian papacy and the rest of Christendom.[4]

By comparison with Sixtus IV, Innocent VIII was perhaps less dangerous to the reputation of the papacy, but only because he was less effective. His Cibò relatives did not have the same enthusiasm for pursuing long-term gains as the Riario and Rovere kinsmen of Sixtus IV, although he himself may have tried to utilise their services in a similar manner to his predecessor. Undoubtedly his main problems were those of Naples, which was in a state of unrest for much of his pontificate, and certainly his response to this determined many of his political actions. It involved him in negotiations with France, and even actions apparently unrelated to Italian politics may have been indirectly connected. His concessions over the control of the Scottish Church in 1487 may have been in part intended to secure the benevolence of Scotland's ally France, as well as to obtain a better defined system of provisions to benefices, so that he could obtain with less delay the taxes payable when appointments were made. The ultimate importance of this pontificate lay in Innocent's willing participation in international politics, as this helped to set the scene for the invasions from 1494 onwards, although it would be unfair to blame him too severely for this, as previous foreign intervention in Italy had been on a comparatively small scale and it was presumably military action of that kind which he envisaged. None the less, Alexander VI seems to have realised, even before the first invasion, the desirability of excluding foreign powers from Italy rather more than his Italian predecessor had done.

Until the start of the Italian wars, the papacy was partly insulated from the realities of European power politics, because within Italy it had sufficient influence to play a large part. Kings might try to coerce it, though support for or threats of councils, they might try to extend their influence at the Curia by securing the promotion of their subjects as cardinals, in the hope that these might have a voice in deciding policy in the Church (or even of succeeding eventually to the papacy itself), but they were usually concerned with particular problems of the Church in their own lands rather than with ecclesiastical organisation at the centre. The main problem of the popes before 1494 in relation to the princes lay in their position as administrative head of the Church rather than in politics. This included the power to collect taxes from the clergy, the claim to make appointments and the position of the pope at the head of the Church's legal system, in all of which areas the princes, who were on the spot, had considerable practical advantages. Indeed it is probably true to say that in Church-State relations during the century, it was normally the princes rather than the pope who played the more active role, while the popes had to respond to particular situations. One must therefore consider some of the problems and ambitions of the princes, and how these affected their attitude to the Church.

These varied between countries and periods, and it is important to regard ecclesiastical matters as merely one element in the policies followed by the lay powers. To overstress princely concern with Church affairs would seriously distort a proper perspective of the subject. In France for example, the Valois dynasty in the 1420s had the problem of restoring its position from a crisis no less drastic than that which the papacy had faced in the schism, arising from the Anglo-Burgundian alliance and the Treaty of Troyes with its provision for a Lancastrian succession in France. The struggle with the English remained the dominant theme of French history until the middle of the century, and even after their expulsion in 1453 the threat of renewed war was never far distant. The *rapprochement* between France and Burgundy in 1435 was a notable point in the Valois recovery, and may well have enabled Charles VII to take a harder line than he might otherwise have done against Eugenius IV when he promulgated the Pragmatic Sanction of Bourges. This action reflected increasing royal strength, just when the papacy was weakened by the Basel revolt, compared with his position in the negotiations leading to the agreement with Martin V in 1426. In the second half of the century Louis XI was involved in a struggle to the death with Burgundy as well as with asserting his authority over other major feudatories, and these matters were far more important to him than his relations with the Church, although he clearly regarded ecclesiastical support as desirable in his dealings with lay opponents. The Avignon crisis of the mid-1470s illustrates how touchy Louis was about possible papal sympathy for

Burgundy, while control of ecclesiastical appointments was also a means of increasing royal power over dissident subjects: there is little doubt that regional particularism in parts of the Languedoc could take the form of supporting local candidates for dioceses against the men whom the king wished to appoint. To secure his will in such cases, the king required papal support, which was often forthcoming as the pope also could gain from co-operation. One must remember that there was a political motive for royal action as well as the desire to reward a faithful servant at someone else's expense.

Similar political factors were at work elsewhere in ecclesiastical appointments and in Germany matters were complicated by the fact that secular and ecclesiastical boundaries did not necessarily coincide. During the Pomeranian wars in the 1470s, Albrecht Achilles of Brandenburg tried to build up a party which would favour him in the see of Cammin, but this provoked the intervention of his enemy Matthias of Hungary at the Curia, which frustrated his attempts. A papal plan to oblige the King of Poland by translating the Bishop of Ermland to Cammin also foundered on Hungarian opposition, and eventually Sixtus had to appoint, and Albrecht perforce to accept, Marinus of Fregeno, a papal protonotary and indulgence seller, who was also commendator of a Cistercian monastery in the Romagnol diocese of Senigallia. The relation between princely authority and the Church can be seen also in the way in which the Electors of Brandenburg tried to ensure that within their lands spiritual jurisdiction should be limited to bishops who were their own subjects. Similar attitudes to the Church can be seen in other principalities, where the papacy was equally powerless in resisting the gains made by rulers, who exploited major benefices in the interests of their families. At the outbreak of the Reformation, no fewer than eighteen archbishoprics or bishoprics were filled by the sons of princes.

Against the will of the secular power, the papacy could do little to reassert its control over the government of the Church in the localities. Spiritual sanctions such as interdict and excommunication had not been dropped entirely from the Church's armoury: one can see them being applied particularly in various Italian political struggles, such as Pius II's attack on Sigismondo Malatesta and the actions of various popes against Venice. But excommunication no longer could compel obedience as it had at an earlier date, because it was simply disregarded by the laity. Because the papacy could no longer have effective recourse to its spiritual authority as a weapon, it had to meet the princes more on their own terms, of political manoeuvring and financial bargaining, and in this its weakness was plain.

After the outbreak of the Italian wars, the greater political involvement of the papacy with some of the European powers tended to increase the secularity of its approach to them, and matters of spiritual authority became increasingly negotiable for political ends. This was perhaps most marked in the case of powers which were politically engaged in Italy, although as other countries of Christendom were drawn into the resulting system of power alignments, they, too, were affected in matters of Church government by the papacy's political concerns. Once the foreign powers had actually invaded the peninsula, the popes could not stand aloof from the conflicts, the more so as their own territorial rights were at stake. Even although the rivalry of Valois and Habsburg, which had replaced that of Plantagenet and Valois as the determinant of diplomatic alignments in Western Europe, originated in the Burgundian succession after the death of Charles the Bold, the alliance of the Habsburgs with Spain, which culminated in the inheritance of the Emperor Charles V, drew the popes, who had long been poised between French and Spanish interests in Italy, into the wider European power struggle.

The resulting wars imposed new strains on the papacy, at a time when it also had internal difficulties within the structure of the Church. Even before they broke out, the papacy had made administrative changes which reflect its realisation of the need to adjust its practices so as to be more effective in the changing Europe of its day. The new system of diplomatic representation and the developments in the secretariat, together with the growth of the office of cardinal protector, marked a change in attitudes towards the secular powers of Christendom and a recognition of the new importance of the nation states. The changing position of the cardinals could create problems, particularly as secular rulers sought the promotion of their own protégés to the college, though comparatively few of these latter remained subsequently at the Curia. Tensions between the pope and the college, as reflected in the election capitulations, seldom raised practical difficulties, because the cardinals were unable to assert their claims, although there were occasions, of which the revolt leading to the second Council of Pisa was the most conspicuous, when dissidents in the college allied themselves with a secular opponent of the reigning pope. The underlying pressures remained, however, and may have contributed to a reduction in the capacity of the papacy to act decisively in times of crisis, if it had reason to suspect the possible disloyalty of some of those on whom it should have been able to rely most. In one sense the popes could not win, because if they selected as cardinals men on whom they could personally depend, it would not only lay them open to charges of nepotism, but would also, and more seriously, build up a hostile faction of those excluded. On the other hand, if they attempted to balance factions, as in the case of simultaneous appointments of cardinals from rival families such as the Colonna and the Orsini, or from rival European powers, it merely created tensions in the college which led to sharp dissensions at times of conclave.

If one were to attempt an assessment of whether or not the papacy was declining in power during the century, a clear answer would be impossible. In some senses it actually gained in strength and was probably more influential among the Italian powers on the eve of the Reformation than it ever had been. It had, however, attained this position at a time when Italian politics were swamped by external intervention, and in the politics of Christendom as a whole it could count for little against much greater powers. Administratively and financially it was able to cope, at least with routine matters in the Papal States, and the willingness of petitioners to bring cases to Rome for decision does not suggest that the popular appeal of papal power had entirely gone. This, however, concealed one fundamental weakness, that access to Rome for Christians depended on sufferance, on the willingness of lay princes to permit recourse to the Curia. Clearly such permission was frequently granted, but it is also clear that the princes had made many gains in ecclesiastical matters concerning their own subjects. Nowhere is this more clearly shown than in the form of some of the agreements, which took the form of a treaty rather than that of a papal grant. The papacy was forced by circumstances to recognise that it was merely one power among many rather than an authority of a totally different nature from secular society. As the units of local political power became stronger, there was little room left for a supra-national organisation except in spiritual matters, and even there its position was vulnerable, as can be seen in its prolonged struggles against residual Hussite activity in Bohemia.

In the successive crises of the fifteenth-century papacy, the popes had retained or recovered influence through negotiations with the secular power. This descent into the market place undoubtedly weakened the moral standing of the papacy and furthermore, by allowing the kings of Christendom to come between themselves and the clergy throughout Europe, may have concealed from them the true sentiments felt by the *communitas fidelium*. Above all, one may doubt how much the popes knew about conditions in the German Church and the hostility to Rome in that country when an obscure professor at Wittenberg formulated his Ninety-Five Theses on the much debated topic of indulgences. Only subsequent events turned this apparent academic debate into an ecclesiastical revolution, and in the context of 1517–21 it is hardly surprising that the actions of Martin Luther were not the main problem in the mind of Leo X. The pope's greater concern with the forthcoming imperial election was natural in the light of his participation in European political struggles, and it is not surprising that he regarded the Elector Frederick of Saxony more as a key member of the electoral college than as the secular patron of a heresiarch.

When the historian views the Reformation, he can see it as a threefold crisis, of authority, of discipline and of doctrine. The latter two need concern us little here, except to note that the lay power had already played a part in enforcing discipline on the clergy and that it was its willingness to support doctrinal change which was the greatest innovation of the Reformation period. In many ways the issues of authority between the princes and the pope were already resolved before 1517, apart from the ultimate recognition of the latter as head of the Church, and in the sixteenth century the princes played a vital part in deciding whether or not their countries should continue such a recognition. Only one country, Ireland, remained loyal to Rome against the will of its ruler, only one other, Scotland, broke with Rome in opposition to the Crown, and in neither of these cases was political society completely normal. In Ireland, religious conservatism represented hostility to a foreign overlord, while in Scotland the weakness of the monarchy against its nobility left the latter effective power, comparable to that of the civic oligarchies in Germany which could decide for or against the Reformation. However much the Reformation had a popular basis as well as being an act of state, one cannot neglect the political implications of the crisis. If one sees, as one reasonably can, that in the fifteenth-century popes and princes had found a common interest in resisting the constitutionalism of conciliarism or of noble movements, and in the exploitation of the Church's resources to their own advantage, why did this *entente* break down, and leave the way open for the divisions in the sixteenth-century Church? The answer appears to lie in the fact that whereas in the fifteenth century these common interests were stronger than the forces dividing the princes from the popes, in the sixteenth the balance had tilted in the opposite direction. As the princes strengthened their control over their subjects within states in which national feeling was becoming stronger, an alliance with the papacy offered less practical advantage and a break from it could represent an assertion of independence. In the light of the practices which existed between the Council of Constance and the emergence to prominence of Luther, it is not hard to see the subsequent divisions of the Church as a natural evolution, and it is perhaps less remarkable that the Reformation occurred than that it affected only parts of Europe. The incompleteness of the breaks between the papacy and the lay powers of Christendom possibly requires more explanation than the fact that some countries rejected Roman supremacy, and this may be found in the political circumstances of early sixteenth-century Europe. The princes who remained in the Catholic camp were those whose political interests lay in the same regions as those of the pope, and whose revolt from Rome would almost certainly have bound the pope firmly in an alliance with their opponents. For them, it was easier to continue the system which had worked before 1517. Loyalty to Rome for a secular ruler was not an emotional attachment but a matter of self-interest, and this surely underlies the actions of the European princes throughout the whole crisis of the Western Church.

Glossary

Annates: payment of the first year's revenues made by a cleric to the papacy on appointment to a non-elective benefice reserved to the Holy See. The term was also used loosely to include services (q.v.).

Camera Apostolica: the papal financial office. This was headed by the chamberlain, to whom the treasurer was subordinate. It included accounting and judicial departments as well as being responsible for cash and for the minting of money.

Capitulations: agreements drawn up by the cardinals in the course of a papal election to try to limit the action of the new pope.

Collation: the act by which a bishop presented and instituted a clerk to a benefice in the bishop's patronage.

Commendam: the granting of a major benefice (e.g. a bishopric or an abbey) to a non-resident holder (the commendator) who drew the revenues of the office. The commendator was usually clerical but might be a layman.

Datary: the office of the Curia responsible for dealing with petitions to the pope from Christendom and for the payments made in connection with the grant of papal graces. The term was also applied to the official who was at the head of the office.

Elective benefice: a benefice which had traditionally been filled by election rather than by patronage (e.g. a bishopric or an abbey, where the electors were respectively the canons of the cathedral and the monks of the abbey).

Expectative: the grant of the reversion of a benefice by the pope on its next vacancy.

Legates/Nuncii: papal envoys. The distinctions between these are discussed in chapter 5.

Mortmain: the grant of land into the 'dead hand' of a corporate body, which, on account of its perpetual existence, could not be liable for the payment of succession dues. This was most normally applied to ecclesiastical corporations, such as churches, monasteries or colleges at universities.

Penitentiary: a priest appointed to assist a bishop in hearing confessions and enjoining penance. Also the supreme church court in spiritual matters, which had the power to deal with matters involving ecclesiastical censures.

Peter's Pence: tax traditionally payable to the papacy from various nations of Christendom (England, Denmark, Norway, Sweden, Poland, Bohemia, Croatia, Dalmatia, the lands of the Teutonic Knights, Aragon and Portugal).

Postulation: a request to ecclesiastical authority to admit a nominee to a benefice by dispensation from a canonical impediment (e.g. a chapter could postulate its bishop-elect to the pope if he were under age).

Provision: a papal appointment to a benefice normally in the patronage of another.

Regalia: the rights of a prelate held from a prince in virtue of his secular relationship to him (e.g. jurisdictional rights in connection with land) cf. Spiritualities.

Reservation: the action of the pope in claiming the right to present to a particular benefice or class of benefices in future.

Rota: the popular name for the Audience of Causes of the Apostolic Palace, the papal court of appeal from Christendom, particularly in matters relating to the collation of benefices.

Services, common (*Servitia communia*): payment made on appointment by bishops and abbots, whose benefices were assessed at more than 100 florins per annum. The level of the tax could be varied (see chapter 4).

Services, lesser (*Servitia minuta*): payment made on the same occasion to various members of the Curia. The rate was related to that of the common services.

Spiritualities: the resources of a church derived from its ecclesiastical rights, such as tithes, offerings, lands held for spiritual as opposed to secular services.

Bibliography

It is not always easy to determine the precise category into which certain works fall. Collections of source material (e.g. 17 Martène and Durand's *Veterum Scriptorum . . . Amplissima Collectio*) which contain both documentary and narrative material have been placed arbitrarily under documentary sources, as have journals. 'Literary Sources' include both chronicles and treatises. Documents which have been printed as parts of articles are noted not under primary sources but under secondary works. For this bibliography it has been necessary to include only those works which are of major importance, as a comprehensive listing of works would necessitate several volumes.

PRIMARY SOURCES: DOCUMENTARY

1 *Calendar of Papal Registers* (from 1417), HMSO, London, 1906–60.
2 *Calendar of Scottish Supplications to Rome*, 3 vols, ed. E. R. Lindsay, A. I. Dunlop (*née* Cameron) and I. B. Cowan, Scottish History Society, Edinburgh, 1934–70.
3 *Calendar of State Papers relating to Spain, 1485–1509*, HMSO, London, 1862.
4 *Calendar of State Papers relating to Venice*, Vol. I, HMSO, London, 1864.
5 A. I. Cameron, *The Apostolic Camera and Scottish Benefices, 1418–1488*, St Andrews University Publications XXXV, London, 1934.
6 *Correspondance de l'empereur Maximilien Ier et de Marguerite d'Autriche*, 2 Vols., ed. Le Glay, Soc. de l'histoire de France, Paris, 1839.
7 *Dépêches des ambassadeurs milanais*, 3 Vols., ed. B. de Mandrot, Soc. de l'histoire de France, Paris, 1839.
8 H. Hoberg, *Taxae pro communibus servitiis, 1295–1455*, Studi e Testi 144, Vatican City, 1949.
9 *Johannis Burckardi Liber Notarum*, ed. E. Celani, Rerum Italicarum Scriptores, Città di Castello, 1906.
10 *Journal de Clément de Fauquembergue*, 3 Vols., ed, A. Tuetey and H. Lacaille, Soc. de l'histoire de France, Paris, 1903–15.
11 *Journal de Jean Barrillon*, 2 vols, ed. P. de Vaissière, Soc. de l'histoire de France, Paris, 1897–9.
12 *Journal des États généraux de France en 1484 par Johan Masselin*, ed. A. Bernier, Collection de documents inédits sur l'histoire de France, Paris, 1835.
13 *Letters of James IV*, ed. R. K. Harvey and R. L. Mackie, Scottish History Society, Edinburgh, 1953.

14 *Lettres de Charles VIII*, 5 vols, ed. P. Pélicier and B. de Mandrot, Soc. de l'histoire de France, Paris, 1898–1905.

15 *Lettres de Louis XI*, 10 vols, ed. E. Charavay, J. Vaesen and B. de Mandrot, Soc. de l'histoire de France, Paris, 1883–1908.

16 E. Martène and U. Durand, *Thesaurus Novus Anecdotorum*, 5 vols., Paris, 1717.

17 E. Martène and U. Durand, *Veterum Scriptorum et Monumentorum Historicorum, Dogmaticorum, Moralium Amplissima Collectio*, 8 vols, Paris, 1724–33.

18 J. Mazzoleni (ed.), *Il 'Codice Chigi', un registro della cancellaria di Alfonso I d'Aragona re di Napoli per gli anni 1451–1453*, Naples, 1965.

19 A. Mercati, *Dell' archivio vaticano*, Studi e Testi 157, Vatican City, 1951.

20 A. Mercati, *Raccolta di Concordati su Materie ecclesiastiche tra la Santa Sede e le Autorità civili, I. 1098–1914*, Vatican City, 1954.

21 *Ordonnances des rois de France*, Vols X–XXI, Paris, 1763–1849.

22 E. von Ottenthal, *Regulae Cancellariae Apostolicae*, Innsbruck, 1888.

23 *A Parisian Journal, 1405–1449*, ed. and trans. Janet Shirley, Oxford, 1968.

24 P. Paschini, *Il carteggio fra il card. Marco Barbo e Giovanni Lorenzi, (1481–1490)*, Studi e Testi, 137, Vatican City, 1948.

25 C. du Plessis d'Argentré, *Collectio Judiciorum de novis erroribus*, Paris, 1755.

26 *Procès de condemnation et de rehabilitation de Jeanne d'Arc*, ed. J. E. J. Quicherat, Soc. de l'histoire de France, Vol. V, Paris, 1849.

27 *Rotuli Parliamentorum*, London, 1783.

28 T. Rymer, *Foedera*, London, 1709.

29 *Statutes of the Realm*, Vol. III, London, 1817.

30 M. Tangl, *Die Päpstlichen Kanzleiordnungen von 1200–1500*, Innsbruck, 1894.

PRIMARY SOURCES: LITERARY

31 T. Basin, *Histoire de Louis XI*, ed. C. Samaran, Paris, 1963.

32 *La chronique d'Enguerrand de Monstrelet*, ed. L. Douët-d'arcq, Soc. de l'histoire de France, Vols IV and V, Paris, 1860–1.

33 *Chronique de Mathieu Escouchy*, ed. G. du Fresne de Beaucourt, Soc. de l'histoire de France, Vols II and III, Paris, 1863–4.

34 *Chronique scandaleuse*, ed. B. de Mandrot, Soc. de l'histoire de France, Paris, 1894–6.

35 *Chroniques de Louis XII par Jean d'Auton*, 4 vols, ed. R. de Maulde la Clavière, Soc. de l'histoire de France, Paris, 1889–95.

36 A. Coville, *Lé traite de la ruine de l'église de Nicolas de Clamanges*, Paris, 1936.

37 *Le Débat des Hérauts d'Armes*, ed. L. Pannier and P. Meyer, Soc. des anciens textes français, Paris, 1877.

38 E. Dudley, *The Tree of Common Wealth*, Manchester, 1859.

39 T. Ebendorfer, *Chronica Austriae*, ed. A. Lhotsky, MGH Scriptores Rerum Germanicarum N.S. Vol. XIII, Berlin and Zurich, 1967.

40 D. Erasmus, *Ciceronianus*, ed. and trans. P. Mesnard, Erasme, *La philosophie chrétienne*, Paris, 1970, and ed. A. Gambaro, *Il Ciceroniano*, Brescia, 1965.
41 D. Erasmus, *Julius Exclusus*, trans. P. Pascal, Bloomington, Indiana, 1968.
42 J. Fortescue, *The Governance of England*, ed. C. Plummer, London, 1885.
43 J. Fortescue, *De Laudibus Legum Anglie*, ed. S. B. Chrimes, Cambridge, 1942.
44 *Gesta Henrici Quinti*, ed. F. Taylor and J. S. Roskell, Oxford, 1975.
45 M. Goldast, *Monarchia*, Vol. I, Hanover, 1611; Vol. II, Frankfurt, 1614.
46 *Italian Relation of England*, trans. C. A. Sneyd, Camden First Series XXXVII, London, 1847.
47 W. Lyndwood, *Provinciale*, Oxford, 1679.
48 *Mémoires de Philippe de Commynes*, 3 vols, ed. E. Dupont, Soc. de l'histoire de France, Paris, 1840–7.
49 N. Machiavelli, *Il Principe*, ed. L. A. Burd, Oxford, 1891.
50 E. W. Miller, *Wessel Gansfort, Life and Writings*, New York and London, 1917.
51 H. A. Oberman, D. E. Zerfoss and W. J. Courtenay, eds. and trans *Defensorium Obedientiae Apostolicae et Alia Documenta*, Cambridge, Massachussetts, 1968.
52 Pius II (A. S. Piccolomini) *Commentaries*, ed. and trans. F. A. Gragg and L. C. Gabel, Smith College Studies in History, Vols XXII, XXV, XXX, XXXV and XLIII, Northampton, Massachussetts, 1937–57. Abridged as *Memoirs of a Renaissance Pope*, London, 1960.
53 Pius II, *De Gestis Concilii Basiliensis Commentariorum*, ed. and trans. D. Hay and W. K. Smith, Oxford, 1967.
54 J. Torquemada, *Summa de Ecclesia*, Venice, 1561.
55 *Three Books of Polydore Vergil's English History*, ed. H. Ellis, Camden First Series XXIX, London, 1844.

SECONDARY AUTHORITIES

56 C. M. Ady, *Pius II*, London, 1913.
57 C. M. Ady, *The Bentivoglio of Bologna*, London, 1937.
58 H. Angermeier, 'Das Reich und der Konziliarismus', in *Historische Zeitschrift*, Vol. cxcii (1961).
59 H. Baron, 'Imperial Reform and the Habsburgs', in *American Historical Review*, vol. xliv (1938–9).
60 C. Bauer, 'Die Epochen der Papstfinanz', in *Historische Zeitschrift*, vol. cxxxviii (1928).
61 F. le van Baumer, *The Early Tudor Theory of Kingship*, Yale Historical Publications XXXV, Newhaven and London, 1940.
62 R. Bäumer, 'Die Zahl der Allgemeinen Konzilien in der Sicht von Theologen des 15. und 16. Jahrhunderts', in *Annuarium Historiae Conciliorum*, vol. i (1969).

63 B. Behrens, 'Origins of the Office of English Resident Ambassador in Rome', in *English Historical Review*, vol. xlix (1934).

64 W. Bertrams, *Der neuzeitliche Staatsgedanke und die Konkordate des ausgehenden Mittelalters*, Analecta Gregoriana XXX Series Facultatis Iuris Canonici Sectio B (n.3), Rome, 1950.

65 L. Bilderback, 'Proctorial Representation and Conciliar Support at the Council of Basel', in *Annuarium Historiae Conciliorum*, vol. i (1969).

66 A. J. Black, 'Heimericus de Campo: the Council and History', in *Annuarium Historiae Conciliorum*, vol. ii (1970).

67 A. J. Black, *Monarchy and Community*, Cambridge, 1970.

68 C. F. Black, 'Commune and Papacy in the Government of Perugia, 1488–1540', in *Annali della Fondazione italiana per la storia amministrativa*, vol. iv (1967).

69 C. F. Black, 'The Baglioni as Tyrants of Perugia', in *English Historical Review*, vol. lxxxv (1970).

70 M. Bloch, *Les rois thaumaturges*, Strasbourg and Paris, 1924.

71 F. L. Borchardt, *German Antiquity in Renaissance Myth*, Baltimore and London, 1971.

72 A. Bossuat, 'L'idée de nation et la jurisprudence du parlement de Paris au XVe siècle', in *Revue historique*, vol. cciv (1950).

73 A. Bossuat, 'La formule "Le roi est empereur en son royaume". Son emploi au XVe siècle devant le parlement de Paris', in *Revue historique de droit français et étranger*, 4th ser, vol. xxxix (1961). Translated in P. S. Lewis (ed.), *The Recovery of France*.

74 P. Bourdon, 'L'abrogation de la pragmatique et les règles de la chancellerie de Pie II', in *Mélanges d'archéologie et d'histoire*, vol. xxviii (1908).

75 O. de la Brosse, *Le pape et le concile*, Unam Sanctam 58, Paris, 1965.

76 D. M. Bueno de Mesquita, 'The Place of Despotism in Italian Politics', *see* J. R. Hale, J. R. L. Highfield and B. Smalley (eds.).

77 D. M. Bueno de Mesquita, 'Ludovico Sforza and his Vassals', *see* E. F. Jacob (ed.), *Italian Renaissance Studies*.

78 P. Caillet, 'La décadence de l'ordre de Cluny au XVe siècle et le tentative de réforme de l'abbé Jean de Bourbon (1456–85)', in *Bibliothèque de l'école des chartes*, vol. lxxxix (1928).

79 *Cambridge Medieval History*, Vol. VIII, Cambridge, 1936.

80 R. W. and A. J. Carlyle, *Mediaeval Political Theory in the West*, Vol. VI, Edinburgh, 1936.

81 F. L. Carsten, *The Origins of Prussia*, Oxford, 1954.

82 F. L. Carsten, *Princes and Parliaments in Germany from the fifteenth to the eighteenth century*, Oxford, 1959.

83 L. Celier, 'Alexandre VI et la réforme de l'église', in *Mélanges d'archéologie et d'histoire*, vol. xxvii (1907).

84 L. Celier, 'L'idée de réforme à la cour pontificale du concile de Bâle au concile de Latran', in *Revue des questions historiques*, vol. lxxxvi (1909).

85 L. Celier, *Les dataires du XVe siècle et les origines de la daterie apostolique*, Bibliothèque des écoles françaises d'Athènes et de Rome, 103, Paris, 1910.

86 D. S. Chambers, *Cardinal Bainbridge in the Court of Rome, 1509–14*, Oxford, 1965.

87 D. S. Chambers, *The Imperial Age of Venice, 1380–1580*, London, 1970.
88 S. B. Chrimes, *English Constitutional Ideas in the Fifteenth Century*, Cambridge, 1936.
89 H. J. Cohn, *The Government of the Rhine Palatinate in the Fifteenth Century*, Oxford, 1965.
90 N. Cohn, *The Pursuit of the Millenium*, London, 1962.
91 G. G. Coulton, *Five Centuries of Religion*, Vol. IV, Cambridge, 1950.
92 M. Creighton, *History of the Papacy*, Vols II–IV, London, 1882–7.
93 R. G. Davies, 'Martin V and the English Episcopate . . .', in *English Historical Review*, vol. xcii (1977).
94 J. Delumeau, 'Le progrès de la centralisation dans l'État pontifical au XVIe siècle', in *Revue historique*, vol. ccxxvi (1961).
95 J. Delumeau, *L'alun de Rome*, Paris, 1962.
96 H. Dessart, 'L'attitude du diocèse de Liège pendant le concile de Bâle', in *Revue d'histoire ecclésiastique*, vol. xlvi (1951).
97 J. G. Dickinson, *The Congress of Arras*, Oxford, 1955.
98 N. Didier, 'Postulation, election et provision apostolique à l'évêché de Carcassonne en 1456', in *Revue historique de droit français et étranger*, 4th ser., vol. xxix (1951).
99 K. Eckermann, *Studien zur Geschichte des monarchischen Gedankens im 15. Jahrhundert*, Abhandlungen zur mittleren und neueren Geschichte, vol. lxxiii, Berlin, 1933.
100 J. H. Elliott, *Imperial Spain, 1469–1716*, London, 1963.
101 J. Favier, 'Temporels ecclésiastiques et taxation fiscale: le poids de la fiscalité pontificale au XIVe siècle', in *Journal des savants* (1964). (No vol. number).
102 J. Favier, *Les finances pontificales a l'époque du grand schisme d'occident, 1378–1409*, Bibliothèque des écoles françaises d'Athènes de la Rome, 211, Paris, 1966.
103 R. Feenstra, *Philip of Leyden*, Glasgow, 1970.
104 K. A. Fink, 'Die Sendung des Kardinals von Pisa nach Aragon im Jahre 1418', in *Römische Quartalschrift*, vol. xli (1933).
105 K. A. Fink, 'Die politische Korrespondenz Martins V nach den Brevenregistern', in *Quellen und Forschungen aus italienischen Archiven*, vol. xxvi (1935–6).
106 K. A. Fink, 'Zu den Brevia Latenarensia des Vatikanischen Archivs', in *Quellen und Forschungen aus italienischen Archiven*, vol. xxxii (1942).
107 K. A. Fink, 'Zur Beurteilung des Grossen Abendländischen Schismas', in *Zeitschrift für Kirchengeschichte*, vol. lxxiii (1962).
108 K. Forstreurer, 'Der Deutsche Orden und die Kirchenunion während des Basler Konzils', in *Annuarium Historiae Conciliorum*, vol. i (1969).
109 L. C. Gabel, *Benefit of Clergy*, reprinted, New York, 1969.
110 L. Gallet, 'La monarchie française d'après Claude de Seyssel', in *Revue historique de droit français et étranger*, 4th ser., vol. xxii (1944).
111 J. G. Gaztambide, 'The Holy See and the Reconquest of the Kingdom of Granada, (1479–1492)', *see* J. R. L. Highfield (ed.), *Spain in the Fifteenth Century*.
112 F. Gilbert, 'Sir John Fortescue's *dominium regale et politicum*', in *Medievalia et Humanistica*, vol. ii (1944).

113 J. Gill, *The Council of Florence*, Cambridge, 1961.
114 M. P. Gilmore, *Argument from Roman Law 1200–1600*, New York, 1967.
115 M. Godet, 'Consultation de Tours pour la réforme de l'église de France, (12 novembre 1493)', in *Revue d'histoire de l'église de France*, vol. ii (1911).
116 E. Göller, 'Der Liber taxarum der päpstlichen Kammer', in *Quellen und Forschungen aus italienischen Archiven*, vol. viii (1905).
117 E. Göller, *Die päpstliche Pönitentiarie*, Bibliothek des kgl. preuss. historischen Instituts in Rom, Vols III, IV, VII and VIII, Rome, 1907–11.
118 E. Göller, 'Deutsche Kirchenablässe unter Papst Sixtus IV', in *Römische Quartalschrift*, vol. xxxi (1923).
119 A. Gottlob, *Aus der Camera Apostolica den 15. Jahrhunderts*, Innsbruck, 1889.
120 J. Guiraud, *L'état pontifical après le grand schisme*, Bibliothèque des écoles françaises d'Athènes et de Rome, 73, Paris, 1896.
121 J. R. Hale, *Machiavelli and Renaissance Italy*, London, 1961.
122 J. .R. Hale (ed), *Renaissance Venice*, London, 1973.
123 J. R. Hale, J. R. L. Highfield and B. Smalley (eds), *Europe in the Late Middle Ages*, London, 1965.
124 J. Haller, 'Die Belehnung Renés von Anjou mit dem Königreich Neapel (1436)', in *Quellen und Forschungen aus italienischen Archiven*, vol. iv (1901).
125 J. Haller, 'England und Rom unter Martin V', In *Quellen und Forschungen aus italienischen Archiven*, vol. viii (1905).
126 J. Haller, 'Die Prägmatische Sanktion von Bourges', in *Historische Zeitschrift*, vol. ciii (1909).
127 F. Harting, 'Berthold von Henneberg, Kürfurst von Mainz', in *Historische Zeitschrift*, vol. ciii (1909).
128 J. Hashagen, 'Laieneinfluss auf das Kirchengut vor der Reformation', in *Historische Zeitschrift*, vol. cxxvi (1922).
129 J. Hashagen, 'Die vorreformatorische Bedeutung des spätmittelalterlichen landesherrlichen Kirchenregiments', in *Zeitschrift für Kirchengeschichte*, vol. xli (1922).
130 J. Hashagen, 'Papsttum und Laiengewalten im Verhältnis zu Schisma und Konzilien', in *Historische Vierteljahrschrift*, N.F., vol. xxiii (1926).
131 J. Hashagen, 'Landesherrliche Ablasspolitik vor der Reformation', in *Zeitschrift für Kirchengeschichte*, vol. xlv (1927).
132 R. Haubst, 'Der Reformentwurf Pius des Zweiten', in *Römische Quartalschrift*, vol. xlix (1954).
133 D. Hay, 'Pietro Griffo, an Italian in England, 1506–1512', in *Italian Studies*, vol. ii (1938–9).
134 D. Hay, *Polydore Vergil*, Oxford, 1952.
135 D. Hay, 'Italy and Barbarian Europe', *see* E. F. Jacob, (ed.), *Italian Renaissance Studies*.
136 D. Hay, *The Italian Renaissance*, Cambridge, 1961.
137 D. Hay, 'The Church of England in the Middle Ages', in *History*, vol. liii (1968).

138 D. Hay, 'The Italian View of Renaissance Italy', in *Florilegium Historiale*, *Essays presented to W. K. Ferguson*, eds. J. G. Rowe and W. H. Stockdale, Toronto, 1971.
139 D. Hay, *The Church in Italy in the 15th Century*, Cambridge, 1977.
140 C. J. Hefele, trans. H. Leclercq, *Histoire des conciles*, vols VII, VIII, Paris, 1916–21.
141 J. R. L. Highfield, 'The Catholic Kings and the Titled Nobility of Castile', *see* J. R. Hale, J. R. L. Highfield and B. Smalley (eds).
142 J. R. L. Highfield (ed.), *Spain in the Fifteenth Century*, London, 1972.
143 H. Hoberg, 'Der Informativprozess des Rotarichters Dominikus Jacobazzi', in *Römische Quartalschrift*, vol. li (1956).
144 W. von Hofmann, *Forschungen zur Geschichte der kurialen Behörden von Schisma bis zur Reformation*, Bibliothek des kgl. preuss. historischen Instituts in Rom, Vols XII, XIII, Rome, 1914.
145 U. Horst, 'Grenzen der päpstlichen Autorität: Konziliare Elemente in der Ekklesiologie des Johannes Torquemada', in *Freiburger Zeitschrift für Philosophie und Theologie*, vol. xix (1972).
146 V. Ilardi, ' "Italianità" among some Italian Intellectuals in the early Sixteenth Century', in *Traditio*, vol. xii (1956).
147 P. Imbart de la Tour, *Les origines de la réforme*, 2nd edn, Melun, 1944–8.
148 E. F. Jacob, *Essays in the Conciliar Epoch*, 2nd edn, Manchester, 1953.
149 E. F. Jacob (ed.), *Italian Renaissance Studies*, London, 1960.
150 H. Jedin, 'Giovanni Gozzadini, ein Konziliarist am Hofe Julius II', in *Römische Quartalschrift*, Vol. xlvii (1939).
151 H. Jedin, trans. E. Graf, *A History of the Council of Trent*, Vol. I, Edinburgh, 1957.
152 P. J. Jones, 'The End of Malatesta Rule in Rimini, *see* E. F. Jacob (ed.) *Italian Renaissance Studies*.
153 P. J. Jones, *The Malatesta of Rimini and the Papal State*, London, 1974.
154 M. Jusselin, 'Remonstrances du Parlement au roi sur la situation de l'église de France', in *Bibliothèque de l'école des chartes*, vol. lxxiv (1913).
155 E. H. Kantorowicz, *The King's Two Bodies*, Princeton, 1957.
156 H. Keussen, 'Ein Kölner Traktat von c.1440–49 über das Verhalten der Glaubigen zur Zeit des Schismas', in *Zeitschrift für Kirchengeschichte*, vol. xl (1921).
157 M. D. Knowles, *The Religious Orders in England*, Vol. II, Cambridge, 1957.
158 W. Kohler, 'Die deutsche Kaiseridee am Anfang des 16. Jahrhunderts', in *Historische Zeitschrift*, vol. cxlix (1933–4).
159 Z. Kozlowska-Budkowa *et al.*, *Les universités européennes du XIVe au XVIIIe siècle*, Geneva, 1967.
160 A. Kraus, 'Die Sekretäre Pius II', in *Römische Quartalschrift*, vol. liii (1958).
161 A. Kraus, 'Secretarius und Sekretariat', in *Römische Quartalschrift*, vol. lv (1960).
162 D. Kurze, 'Nationale Regungen in der spätmittelalterlichen Prophetie', in *Historische Zeitschrift*, vol. ccii (1966).
163 C. H. Lawrence (ed.), *The English Church and the Papacy*, London, 1965.

164 C. Lefebvre, 'L'enseignement de Nicolas de Tudeschis et l'autorité pontificale', in *Ephemerides Iuris Canonici*, vol. xiv (1958).

165 G.-L. Lesage, 'La titulature des envoyés pontificaux sous Pie II (1458–64)', in *Mélanges d'archéologie et d'histoire*, vol. lviii (1941–6).

166 J. Lesellier, 'Une curieuse correspondance inédite entre Louis XI et Sixte IV', in *Mélanges d'archéologie et d'histoire*, vol. xlv (1928).

167 P. S. Lewis, 'France in the Fifteenth Century: Society and Sovereignty', see J. R. Hale, J. R. L. Highfield and B. Smalley (eds).

168 P. S. Lewis, 'Jean Juvenal des Ursins', in *Medium Aevum*, vol. xxxiv (1965).

169 P. S. Lewis, *Later Medieval France*, London, 1968.

170 P. S. Lewis (ed.), *The Recovery of France in the 15th Century*, London, 1971.

171 J. Lortz, trans. R. Walls, *The Reformation in Germany*, London, 1968.

172 P. Luc, 'Un appel du pape Innocent VIII au roi de France (1489)', in *Mélanges d'archéologie et d'histoire*, vol. lvi (1939).

173 J. Lulvès, 'Päpstliche Wahlkapitulationen', in *Quellen und Forschungen aus italienischen Archiven*, vol. xii (1909).

174 W. E. Lunt, *Papal Revenues in the Middle Ages*, 2 Vols., New York, 1934.

175 W.E. Lunt, *Financial Relations of the Papacy with England, II, 1327–1534*, Cambridge, Massachussetts, 1962.

176 K. B. McFarlane, 'Henry V, Bishop Beaufort and the Red Hat, 1417–21', in *English Historical Review*, vol. lx (1945).

177 L. J. Macfarlane, 'The Primacy of the Scottish Church, 1472–1521', in *Innes Review*, vol. xx (1969).

178 D. McRoberts, 'The Scottish Church and Nationalism', in *Innes Review*, vol. xix (1968).

179 R. Maere, 'Les origines de la nonciature de Flandre', in *Revue d'histoire ecclésiastique*, vol. vii (1906).

180 M. Mallett, *The Borgias*, London, 1969.

181 U. Mannucci, 'Le capitolazioni del Conclave di Sisto IV (1471)', in *Römische Quartalschrift*, vol. xxix (1915).

182 V. Martin, *Les origines du Gallicanisme*, vol. II, Paris, 1939.

183 G. Mattingly, 'The First Resident Embassies: Medieval Italian Origins of Modern Diplomacy', in *Speculum*, vol. xii (1937).

184 R. de Maulde la Clavière, 'Alexandre VI et le divorce de Louis XII', in *Bibliothèque de l'école des chartes*, vol. lvii (1896).

185 F. Miltenberger, 'Versuch einer Neuordnung der päpstlichen Kammer in der ersten Regierungsjahren Martins V (1417–20)', in *Römische Quartalschrift*, vol. viii (1894).

186 L. Mohler, 'Bessarions Instruktion für die Kreuzzugpredigt in Venedig (1463)', in *Römische Quartalschrift*, vol. xxxv (1927).

187 G. Mollat, *Les papes d'Avignon, 1305–1378*, 9th edn., Paris, 1949.

188 G. Mollat, 'Contribution à la histoire du sacré collège de Clément V à Eugène IV', in *Revue d'histoire ecclésiastique*, Vol. xlvi (1951).

189 E. de Moreau, 'La legislation des ducs de Bourgogne sur l'accroissement des biens ecclésiastiques', in *Revue d'histoire ecclésiastique*, vol. xii (1946).

190 E. de Moreau, *Histoire de l'église en Belgique*, Brussels, 1949.
191 H. A. Oberman, *The Harvest of Medieval Theology*, Cambridge, Massachusetts, 1963.
192 H. S. Offler, 'Aspects of Government in the late medieval Empire', *see* J. R. Hale, J. R. L. Highfield and B. Smalley (eds).
193 P. Ourliac, 'La pragmatique sanction et la legation en France du cardinal d'Estouteville', in *Mélanges d'archéologie et d'histoire*, vol. lv (1938).
194 P. Ourliac, 'Le concordat de 1472', in *Revue historique de droit français et étranger*, 4th ser., vols xx–xxi (1942–3). Translated in P. S. Lewis (ed.), *The Recovery of France*.
195 P. D. Partner, 'Camera Papae; Problems of Papal Finance in the later Middle Ages', in *Journal of Ecclesiastical History*, vol. iv (1953).
196 P. D. Partner, *the Papal State under Martin V*, London, 1958.
197 P. D. Partner, 'The "Budget" of the Roman Church in the Renaissance Period', *see* E. F. Jacob (ed.), *Italian Renaissance Studies*.
198 P. D. Partner, *The Lands of St Peter*, London, 1972.
199 L. Pastor, *History of the Popes*, trans. F. I. Antrobus and R. Kerr, Vols I–VII, London, 1906–8.
200 R. Menéndez Pidal, 'The Significance of the Reign of Isabella the Catholic', *see* J. R. L. Highfield (ed.), *Spain in the Fifteenth Century*.
201 R. Menéndez Pidal, 'The Catholic Kings according to Machiavelli and Castiglione', *see* J. R. L. Highfield (ed.), *Spain in the Fifteenth Century*.
202 B. A. Pocquet du Haut-Jussé, *Les papes et les ducs de Bretagne*, vol. II, Bibliothèque des écoles françaises d'Athènes et de Rome, 133, Paris, 1928.
203 F. Priebatsch, 'Staat und Kirche in der Mark Brandenburg am Ende des Mittelalters', in *Zeitschrift für Kirchengeschichte*, vols xix–xxi (1899–1901).
204 P. Prodi, 'The structure and organisation of the Church in Renaissance Venice', *see* J. R. Hale (ed.), *Renaissance Venice*.
205 B. Pullan, 'The occupations and investments of the Venetian nobility in the middle and late sixteenth century', *see* J. R. hale (ed.), *Renaissance Venice*.
206 F. Rapp, *L'église et la vie religieuse en occident à la fin du Moyen Age*, Paris, 1971.
207 H. Rashdall, ed. F. M. Powicke and A. B. Emden, *The Universities of Europe in the Middle Ages*, Vol. II, London, 1936.
208 A. Renaudet, *Préréforme et humanisme à Paris pendant les premières guerres d'Italie*, 2nd edn, Paris, 1953.
209 M. Reeves, *The Influence of Prophecy in the Later Middle Ages*, Oxford, 1969.
210 J. Richard, 'Origines de la nonciature de France', in *Revue des questions historiques*, vols lxxviii and lxxx (1905–6).
211 J. Richard, 'Origines des nonciatures permanentes', in *Revue d'histoire ecclésiastique*, vol. vii (1906).
212 J. Richard, 'Origines et développements de la secretairerie d'état apostolique (1417–1823), in *Revue d'histoire ecclésiastique*, vol. xi (1910).
213 J. Richard, 'La monarchie pontificale jusqu'au concile de Trente', in *Revue d'histoire ecclésiastique*, vol. xx (1924).

214 P. N. Riesenberg, *Inalienability of Sovereignty in Medieval Political Thought*, New York, 1956.

215 R. de Roover, *The Rise and Decline of the Medici Bank*, Cambridge, Massachusetts, 1963.

216 J. Rott, 'Note sur quelques comptes des collecteurs pontificaux du XVe siècle concernant la France', in *Mélanges d'archéologie et d'histoire*, vol. li (1934).

217 N. Rubinstein, *The Government of Florence under the Medici (1434–94)*, Oxford, 1966.

218 S. Runciman, *The Fall of Constantinople*, Cambridge, 1965.

219 A. J. Ryder, 'The Evolution of Imperial Government in Naples under Alfonso V', *see* J. R. Hale, J. R. L. Highfield and B. Smalley (eds).

220 J. Salvini, 'L'application de la Pragmatique Sanction au chapitre cathédral de Paris', in *Revue d'histoire de l'église de France*, vol. iii (1912).

221 J. J. Scarisbrick, 'Clerical Taxation in England, 1485 to 1547', in *Journal of Ecclesiastical History*, vol. xi (1960).

222 J. J. Scarisbrick, *Henry VIII*, London, 1968.

223 F. E. Schneider, *Die römische Rota*, Görres-Gesellschaft zur Pflege der Wissenschaft in katholischen Deutschland – Veröffentlichungen der Sektion für Rechts- und Sozialwissenschaft, 22, Paderborn, 1914.

224 P. E. Schramm, *Der König von Frankreich*, 2nd edn, Weimar, 1960.

225 R. Schwoebel, *The Shadow of the Crescent; the Renaissance Image of the Turk*, New York, 1969.

226 P. E. Sigmund, *Nicholas of Cusa and Medieval Political Thought*, Cambridge, Massachusetts, 1963.

227 L. W. Spitz, *The Religious Renaissance of the German Humanists*, Cambridge, Massachussetts, 1963.

228 A. Stoecklin, 'Das Ende der mittelalterlichen Konzilsbewegung', in *Zeitschrift für schweizerische Kirchengeschichte*, vol. xxxvii (1943).

229 A. Hamilton Thompson, *The English Clergy and their Organisation in the later Middle Ages*, Oxford, 1947.

230 J. A. F. Thomson, 'Tithe Disputes in later Medieval London', in *English Historical Review*, vol. lxxviii (1963).

231 J. A. F. Thomson, *The Later Lollards, 1414–1520*, Oxford, 1965.

232 J. A. F. Thomson, 'Innocent VIII and the Scottish Church', in *Innes Review*, vol. xix (1968).

233 J. A. F. Thomson, 'Papalism and Conciliarism in Antonio Roselli's *Monarchia*', in *Medieval Studies*, vol. xxxvii (1975).

234 B. Tierney, 'Hermeneutics and History: the Problem of *Haec Sancta*', in T. A. Sandquist and M. R. Powicke (eds), *Essays in Medieval History presented to Bertie Wilkinson*, Toronto, 1969.

235 J. Toussaint, *Les relations diplomatiques de Philippe le Bon avec le concile de Bâle (1431–49)*, Louvain, 1942.

236 R. H. Trame, *Rodrigo Sánchez de Arévalo: Spanish Diplomat and Champion of the Papacy*, Washington, 1958.

237 W. Ullmann, 'The Legal Validity of Papal Electoral Pacts', in *Ephemerides Iuris Canonici*, vol. xii (1956).

238 W. Ullmann, 'Eugenius IV, Cardinal Kemp and Archbishop Chichele', in

Medieval Studies presented to Aubrey Gwynn S.J., ed. J. A. Watt *et al.*, Dublin, 1961.
(Both of these articles were reprinted in W. Ullmann, *The Papacy and Political Ideas in the Middle Ages*, London, 1976.)
239 E. Vansteenberghe, *Le cardinal Nicolas de Cues, 1401–64*, Lille, 1920.
240 J.-M. Vidal, 'Une crise episcopale à Pamiers, (1467–1524)', in *Revue d'histoire de l'église de France*, vol. xiv (1928).
241 J. Vincke, 'Kirche und Staat in Spanien während des Spätmittelalters', in *Römische Quartalschrift*, vol. xliii (1935).
242 J. Vincke, 'Auseinandersetzungen um das päpstliche Provisionswesen in den Ländern der aragonischen Krone', in *Römische Quartalschrift*, vol. liii (1958).
243 P. de Vooght, *Les pouvoirs du concile et l'autorité du pape au concile de Constance*, Unam Sanctam, 56, Paris, 1965.
244 A. Werminghoff, 'Neuere Arbeiten über das Verhältnis von Staat und Kirche in Deutschland während des späteren Mittelalters', in *Historische Vierteljahrschrift*, N.F., vol. xi (1908).
245 W. E. Wilkie, *The Cardinal Protectors of England*, Cambridge, 1974.
246 J. Wodka, *Zur Geschichte der nationalen Protektorate der Kardinäle an der römischen Kurie*, Publikationen des Österreichischen Historischen Instituts in Rom, Bd. iv, t. ii, Innsbruck and Leipzig, 1938.
247 B. L. Woodcock, *Medieval Ecclesiastical Courts in the Diocese of Canterbury*, London, 1952.

REFERENCE WORKS

248 D. Baker (ed.), *Bibliography of the Reform 1450–1648*, Oxford, 1975.
249 L. E. Boyle, *A Survey of the Vatican Archives and of its Medieval Holdings*, Pontifical Institute of Medieval Studies, Subsidia Mediaevalia, 1, Toronto, 1972.
250 I. B. Cowan, 'The Vatican Archives, a report on pre-Reformation Scottish Material', in *Scottish Historical Review*, vol. xlviii (1969).
251 C. Eubel, *Hierarchia Catholica Medii Aevi*, Vols I–III, Münster, 1913–23.
252 F. R. Goff (ed.), *Incunabula in American Libraries*, New York, 1964.
253 L. de Mas Latrie, *Trésor de Chronologie*, Paris, 1889.
254 G. Moroni, *Dizionario di Erudizione storico-ecclesiastica*, Vol. XIII, Venice, 1842.
255 *Short-title Catalogue of Books printed in the German-speaking Countries and German Books printed in other countries from 1455 to 1600, now in the British Museum*, London, 1962.
256 *Sussidi per la consultazione dell'archivio Vaticano*, Vol. I, Studi e Testi, 45, Rome, 1926.

This bibliographical survey is concerned primarily with the works specified in the above list and will attempt to indicate both what were the major primary sources employed in writing the book and the more important secondary works used. After a brief survey of bibliographical material, primary sources will be considered under the two general categories of documentary and literary. The consideration of the secondary material will follow roughly the structure of the book; the themes studied in the first six chapters are to some extent self-contained, and the bibliography for each of these will be dealt with in the same order as the chapters in the book. The themes studied in Chapters 7 to 10 are more closely interwoven with each other, so the works relating to these will be discussed together, and will, as far as possible, be grouped by the countries with which they are concerned.

The important part played by the Church in medieval society makes it inevitable that almost any work dealing with the period concerned will throw some light on the subject. The older standard bibliographies for medieval history, such as those by Potthast and Paetow, are therefore of some value. In the sphere of ecclesiastical history, there are two recent books which deserve particular notice, Rapp's volume in the *Nouvelle Clio* series (206), and Baker's *Bibliography of the Reform* (248) for material dealing with the British Isles. The range of these is wider than the topics covered in this present work, but they provide substantial reference material. For up-to-date bibliographical references, the annual survey in the *Revue d'histoire ecclésiastique* is indispensable, and the *Revue d'histoire de l'église de France* also contains bibliographical material. Other journals which are specially concerned with ecclesiastical history and which are of particular importance include the *Römische Quartalschrift*, the *Zeitschrift für Kirchengeschichte* and the *Journal of Ecclesiastical History*, but a substantial number of papers on matters of ecclesiastical interest appear also in general historical periodicals.

The most useful guides to the central archives of the Church, as far as the English-speaking reader is concerned, are the works by Boyle (249) and Cowan (250), though the latter deals only with Scottish material. Among the records of the central government of the Church, much still remains to be printed for this period, but the historian does have the volumes of Chancery ordinances and regulations edited by Tangl (30) and Ottenthal (22), and for part of the period, the records of payments of common services collected by Hoberg (8). For relations between popes and princes, Mercati's edition of concordats between the Holy See and the secular powers (20) is a source of prime importance. Otherwise, much of the material has been printed in connection with particular national churches, such as the English *Calendars of Papal Registers* (1) and the Scottish records of both supplications to Rome (2) and payments made to the Apostolic Camera (5). These do, however, illustrate the working of papal government as well as the affairs of the Church in particular countries. For the late fifteenth century, there is a useful collection of letters of Cardinal Marco Barbo (24) and the important diary of Johann Burckard, the papal master of ceremonies (9). Although neither of these are official records, they show the working of papal government and of the Curia.

When one considers the working of ecclesiastical administration and the concern of the secular power with how this might affect its own interests, one can have recourse to collections of documents that do not deal exclusively with ecclesiastical matters. One country where the interaction of politics and church government was particularly complex was France, so among the important sources are the collected letters of Louis XI (15) and Charles VIII (14), and the large collection of French royal ordinances (21). The external policies of the French kings in relation to Italy, where they were most likely to impinge on papal interests, are illuminated by the letters of the Milanese ambassadors to the French court (7). From France there also come a number of journals which reflect contemporary attitudes to the Church: for the early fifteenth century there are those of Clément de Fauquembergue (10) and the Bourgeois of Paris (23); for the meeting of the Estates–General of 1484 there is Jean Masselin's (12), and for the early sixteenth century, including the period of the Concordat of Bologna, Jean Barrillon's (11). The English Parliament rolls (27) and statutes (29) also contain a number of references to ecclesiastical matters. One country where the relationship between the papacy and the Crown was particularly complex was the kingdom of Naples because it was a papal fief; fortunately these complications can be illustrated in the *Codice Chigi*, a chancery register dating from the mid-fifteenth century (18).

Material relating to other countries can be found in some of the older documentary collections, notably in the two massive series of volumes edited in the early eighteenth century by the Maurists, Martène and Durand, the *Thesaurus Novus Anecdotorum* (16) and the *Veterum Scriptorum . . . Amplissima Collectio* (17). These volumes contain both documentary material and chronicle sources, many of which are not available elsewhere. Indeed, this is one of the problems with a number of important sources, that no modern editions are available. The most important fifteenth-century treatise on ecclesiology, Torquemada's *Summa de Ecclesia*, is available only in a sixteenth-century edition (54), and number of other writings on political and ecclesiological theory, published by Melchior Goldast (45), have not been reprinted since the early seventeenth. Also from the seventeenth century dates the only edition of the most important English work on canon law of the fifteenth century, William Lyndwood's *Provinciale* (47). Some authors are available in more recent editions, such as Nicolas de Clamanges, writing in the period of the schism (36) and Gabriel Biel, who defended papal authority around 1460 (51).

The best collection of fifteenth-century chronicles available is that published by the Société de l'Histoire de France, and many of the chronicles throw light on ecclesiastical matters, including those of Monstrelet (32) and Escouchy (33), the *Mémoires* of Commynes (48) and the *Chronique scandaleuse* (34). All these editions were printed in the nineteenth century; another chronicle of the period which has been re-edited more recently is Basin's *Histoire de Louis XI* (31). For seeing the politics and government of the Church from the inside, a valuable source is the writings of Pope Pius II. His history of the Council of Basel is available in a good modern edition (53), but his autobiographical *Commentaries* have been badly served by historians. The original Latin edition of 1584 was severely bowdlerised and the complete text is available only in an English translation. This itself is not easily accessible and the work is best used in an abridgement (52). For attitudes in the Church in northern Europe, the writings of Wessel Gansfort provide useful evidence (50) for the late fifteenth century, and for the early sixteenth century there are numerous editions of the works of Erasmus (40, 41). For English-speaking readers, the forthcoming Toronto edition is likely to supersede any existing versions, but at the present moment only a limited number of volumes in this series have appeared. For Italian statecraft, in which the papacy was so closely implicated, Machiavelli (49) is a basic text.

When one turns to secondary writings, the most marked development in recent historiography has been the willingness to study the fifteenth-century Church in its own right, and not merely as a precursor of the Church in the period of the Reformation. Most notably, this has meant 'getting behind Trent', and trying to avoid criticising the fifteenth-century Church for not attaining the standards which were stipulated (though not always attained) by both Catholic and Protestant reformers. In this context, the substantial attention which has been paid to the conciliar movement and its aftermath has been able to avoid strong denominational attitudes. There have been probably two main factors in this widespread interest, the influence of the second Vatican Council and the increasing amount of work that has been done in the last generation by canonist scholars. This is not to say that conciliarism had been completely neglected previously – a mid-fifteenth-century German treatise of considerable interest was printed and discussed by Keussen (156) as early as 1921, and the most comprehensive history of the councils, that of Hefele and Leclercq (140) is even older. Jedin's study of Gozzadini (150) was a notable contribution to the study of conciliar survival into the sixteenth century, and the most important paper on the interaction of conciliar thought with national sentiment and with politics is that by Stoecklin (228). This paper has probably not received the attention which it deserves, probably because it appeared during the Second World War in a periodical which is not widely circulated. One characteristic of most writings on conciliarism in the period before Vatican II is that they tend to contain an element of apologetic – this is particularly true of Jedin's *History of the Council of Trent* (151) and there are traces of it also in Gill's work on the Council of Florence (113) and Trame's study of the papalist writer, Arévalo (236). Since the early 1960s, closer attention has been paid to the views which contemporaries held of the fifteenth-century councils, notably in the articles by Bäumer (62), Fink (107), Horst (145) and Tierney (233), and the books by de la Brosse (75), Sigmund (226) and de Vooght (243). One consequence of this has been to turn the attention of historians to some of the minor writers of the period, who are perhaps more representative of contemporary opinion than such dominant figures as Torquemada. Black's paper on Heimeric de Campo (66) and Thomson's on Antonio Roselli (233) typify this approach.

Compared with studies of the nature of the Church, there has been less recent debate on historical views of the nature of secular authority. Here, however, there have been advances through increasing studies of legal sources, both treatises and court proceedings. This is clearly shown by Gilmore (114) in his study of how Roman law was applied in political thought, and by Riesenberg (214) in his examination of ideas of sovereignty. Individual legal writers who contributed to the discussion of secular power were found in various countries, the Dutchman Philip of Leyden, discussed by Feenstra (103), the Englishman Fortescue, studied by Gilbert (112), and the Frenchman Seyssel, examined by Gallet (110). The records of the Parlement of Paris have proved a fruitful source for ideas of royal power and of nationhood in the fifteenth century, and have been analysed in two papers by Bossuat (72, 73). Other writers who have contributed to our knowledge of French political and popular sentiment have been Lewis (167) and Schramm (224). If one turns to England, one sees that Chrimes developed his views on English constitutional ideas in the fifteenth century (88) largely from legal sources, whereas le van Baumer drew mainly on treatises for his examination of kingship in the early Tudor period (61). Attitudes to monarchy and sovereignty were not, however, always based on such rational sources; kingship also had a strongly mystical element in it, as was shown by Kantorowicz (155), and might possess thaumaturgical powers, as described by Bloch (70). Even more tending towards the irrational in the expression of political ideas was recourse to vaticinatory writings, such as those studied by Kurze (162) and these may represent a tradition of Joachimist prophecy so brilliantly surveyed by Reeves (209). It is perhaps worth noting that some of the stranger political ideas found their home in the unstable political conditions of the empire, although there is evidence, collected by Kohler (158) for the continued development of ideas of empire as late as the early sixteenth century. This may well have been connected with attempts at imperial reform, either brought about from below by the diet and the electors, of whom one of the most important was Archbishop Berthold of Mainz, studied by Hartung (127), or encouraged by the imperial house, as described by Baron (59). At the same time, and distinct from such ideas of empire, there was a developing sense of German self-consciousness; Borchardt (71) has shown how this was cultivated by the humanists, but also percolated down to a more popular level. A parallel sense of national identity may be seen in Italy, at least among the writers considered by Ilardi (146) and Hay (135).

When one comes to examine the forces operating within the Church, the study of the college of cardinals has on the whole been neglected. The important paper by Mollat (188) does not go beyond the time of Eugenius IV, although it must be taken as the starting point for any analysis of the composition and activities of the cardinalate in the later period also. There are various useful studies of individual cardinals, perhaps most notably of the most distinguished of them, Nicholas of Cusa, although the best single study of him from the historian's point of view is still Vansteenberghe's (239). He also has attracted the attention of philosophers, and there is probably scope for considerably more work on him with the publication of the new Heidelberg edition of his works. Other cardinals have been studied in particular circumstances, such as in Chambers' book on Bainbridge (86) or Mohler's article on Bessarion (186). One important institutional development affecting the cardinals was the development in this period of the office of cardinal protector of individual national Churches. The basic work on this is still Wodka's (246); for England this can be supplemented by Wilkie's recent book (245), although much of the ground covered by this lies beyond the period of this study. The role of the cardinalate in diplomacy is well illustrated by Fink (104). As far as the position of the cardinals in relation to the popes is concerned, the crucial question of authority hinged on the pacts made at the time of conclaves, and the fundamental paper on this is still that published in 1909 by Lulvès (173). Only slightly later than this, and supplementary to it, is Mannucci's detailed examination of the pact of 1471 (181). The only recent contribution to the topic has arisen out of the development of canonist studies, in Ullmann's examination of the legal validity of the pacts (238). The same author in another paper (237) has considered one of the other significant developments of the century, the distinction being drawn between the curial cardinals, who played an active part in the central government of the Church, and those for whom the cardinalate was a dignity rather than an office, as they remained in their country of origin, where they might play an important part in the life of both Church and State.

The earliest major work on papal finance in this period is Gottlob's on the cameral records (119), and the best general introduction is the paper by Bauer (60). For English readers, Lunt (174) provides a useful survey of the various forms of papal revenue. Other valuable older works are those of Göller on cameral records (116) and on indulgences (118), of Miltenberger on the problems of reorganising the Camera immediately after the Great Schism (185), of Rott on the activities and accounts of papal collectors in France (216), and of Guiraud on the condition of the Papal States after the schism (120). Guiraud can be supplemented by the more recent works of Partner on the papal lands, both in a general study (198) which covers the period from the end of the sixth century to the middle of the fifteenth, but does not include the half-century immediately before the Reformation, and in a detailed study of the pontificate of Martin V (196). The same writer has also made useful contributions to the more general problems of papal finance in the period (195, 197). The most important recent work on papal revenues is that of Favier (101, 102), but unfortunately this is concerned with the period before that of the restoration of unity in the Church, and can be used only as background for it. It is to be hoped that his studies can be extended into the later period, for there is no doubt that a comparable detailed examination of papal financial problems would illuminate the working of ecclesiastical administration in general and its effect on politics. Two works which throw useful light on aspects of papal finance in the fifteenth century are Delumeau's on the exploitation of the alum revenues (95) a new source of income to the popes from the middle of the century, and de Roover's history of the Medici bank (215), which considers, *inter alia*, the role played by loans and credit arrangements in the finances of the Church.

There is no general introduction to the governmental machinery of the Church in the fifteenth century. Mollat's study of the Avignon popes (187) can provide a basis for the later period, supplemented by the general papers by Richard (213) and Delumeau (94). The history of individual departments within the Curia is rather better covered, although none of the important works on these are of recent date, such as Celier on the Datary (85), Göller on the Penitentiary (117) and Schneider on the Rota (223). The older work of Richard on the Secretariat (212) can be supplemented by the two more recent papers by Kraus (160, 161), and by the detailed studies of the diplomatic of particular groups of documents by Fink (105, 106). For the composition of the Curia and records of holders of particular offices, Hofmann (144) is still of fundamental importance. One of the major changes of this period was the development of a more formal system of representation of the papacy at the courts of the European princes, but little work has been done on the system of nunciatures since the time of Richard (210, 211) and Maere (179), except for one detailed study by Lesage (165). Representation of the papacy in the countries of Christendom was matched by the growing custom of sending envoys to Rome; for this there is a general article by Mattingly (183), while the development of the English resident embassy is covered by Behrens (63). The complexity of the Church's administration led, not surprisingly, to demands for reform, an issue examined by Celier both for the century between the Council of Constance and the Fifth Lateran Council (84) and in the particular circumstances of Alexander VI's reign (83). An earlier attempt at reform, in the time of Pius II, was examined more recently by Haubst (132).

The general political history of the papacy is inextricably involved with that of Italy and indeed with that of Christendom as a whole. Here there has been no attempt at a modern general history, with the result that one still has to have recourse to older works such as those of Creighton (92) and above all of Pastor (199). Despite his conservative bias, and despite the fact that no modern historian would accept his views on the Renaissance, Pastor still is the historian whose knowledge of the documentary sources makes his book indispensable. These general works can be supplemented by more recent studies dealing either with particular areas of papal concern or with individual periods or pontificates. Attitudes to the Turks and relations with the Eastern Church in the period before 1453 are covered by Gill (113) and Runciman (218), while the response of the West after the fall of Constantinople is studied by Schwoebel (225). Partner's study of the Papal States under Martin V (196) is illuminating also for the general history of the pontificate, but other periods have not received such thorough examination. It was probably Pius II's own voluminous writings and his colourful character, which has attracted historians to his life and reign, but the best study of him is still probably Ady's of 1913 (56). Other popes have tended to be neglected, with the exception of the Borgias, whose notoriety has given them undue prominence, although Mallett's book (180) provides an excellent study of the papacy in the early period of the Italian wars, both in its position in European diplomacy and in its internal governmental concerns. A major desideratum is a comparable study covering the pontificates of the Rovere popes, Sixtus IV and Julius II; the former's pontificate saw crucial developments in both papal politics and administration, while the latter's saw some of the major crises of the Italian wars.

Because the popes were Italian princes as well as heads of the Church, it is possible to explain their policy more clearly by studying individual states in the peninsula. This is particularly important for towns which lay within the States of the Church; here there are useful books or articles by Ady on Bologna (57), Black on Perugia (68, 69), one of these being particularly concerned with the respective roles of the papacy and the commune in town government, and Jones on Rimini (152, 153). For the way in which the independent states affected papal policy, the church historian can make use of works such as Rubinstein's on Florence (217), Chambers's and Hale's on Venice (87, 122) and Bueno de Mesquita's on Milan (76, 77). Recently Hay has reminded historians that there was an Italian Church (139), which needs to be studied independently of the history of the papacy, and that the individual dioceses of it might stand in a similar relationship to Rome as those elsewhere in Christendom.

When one turns to the relations between the papacy and the powers of Christendom outside Italy, one can usually draw useful introductory material from individual national histories. Books which deal with the issues at stake between popes and princes tend naturally to discuss all the matters which might be in dispute, although individual articles probably concentrate on the issues which predominated in particular disputes. Such examination of individual episodes, and the factors which affected them, has probably been the main line of work on this subject in recent years, and there have been comparatively few attempts to provide a synthesis of it, even in relation to particular countries, still less considering Christendom as a whole. For France, Martin's book (182) does provide such a synthesis for the period down to the pragmatic sanction, and some of the issues of the later period, and particular episodes within it, are taken up in the articles by Bourdon (74), Haller (126), Ourliac (193, 194) and Salvini (220). A common feature of many of these is that they show how the principles of Church government contained in the pragmatic were regarded by the secular power, not as an absolute system but as negotiable bargaining counters which could be employed in negotiations with Rome. Nowhere is this brought out more clearly than in another paper by Haller (124), where he shows how the political problems of the succession to the kingdom of Naples could affect the extent of influence which the king and the pope might exercise over the Church in France. For later in the century, two major articles concerning disputes over benefices illustrate the complexity of factors which operated in Franco-papal relations, which cannot be seen simply in terms of royal and papal interests but must also pay heed to the concerns of the local clergy and nobility and to pressure from the cardinals; these are Didier's on Carcassonne (98) and Vidal's on Pamiers (240). On the fringes of France, the semi-autonomous state of various duchies added a further factor in a complex situation; for Brittany there is a comprehensive survey of relations between the dukes and Rome by Pocquet du Haut-Jussé (202) and for the lands of the dukes of Burgundy there are works by Dessart (96), Moreau (189, 190) and Toussaint (235). The political involvement of the French crown in Italy is brought out also in the papers by Lesellier (166) and Luc (172), while de Maulde la Clavière demonstrates how Alexander VI was able to exploit his jurisdictional powers as pope for his own and his family's advantage in the matter of Louis XII's divorce (184). A good general study of conditions in the French Church in the second half of the fifteenth century and the first half of the sixteenth is that by Imbart de la Tour (147), but the outstanding book on this period is undoubtedly that by Renaudet (208), whose comprehensive study of the pressures of politics and government, ecclesiastical reform and intellectual developments illuminates every aspect of church life in the years from the 1470s down to the eve of the Reformation.

No other country was so closely involved with papal politics over so long a period as was France, so the interaction of political and administrative matters was perhaps less conspicuous elsewhere. Nevertheless it is clear that the papacy had to make similar concessions to the secular power on a number of matters; several of these are discussed in a series of papers by Hashagen

(128–31), although these are marred by inadequate documentation. Werminghoff (244) also looked at the German lands as a whole, and a useful recent summary of the state of the German Church is provided by Lortz (171), although this does show signs of a rather old-fashioned theological bias at some points. Within Germany, of course, most power lay with the territorial princes rather than at the centre, and there is a useful study of the relations between the spiritual and secular powers in the Mark of Brandenburg by Priebatsch (203). This covers far more than merely papal relations with the princes, but touches on a large number of important points which did concern the popes. Aspects of Spanish relations with Rome are covered in various papers in the volume edited by Highfield (142) and in the articles by Vincke (241, 242).

The appropriate chapter in Lawrence's book on relations between the English Church and the papacy (163) provides a useful introduction to Anglo-papal relations, and it can be supplemented by Hay's article (137), which brings out both the national character of the Church and some aspects of its external relations. It seems fairly clear that in many matters the English Church was able to go its own way with only limited reference to Rome, after the failure of Martin V to reassert papal influence in the 1420s. This particular controversy, originally examined by Haller (125), has recently been reconsidered by Davies (93), who has stressed the particular issues involved in it, especially those concerned with provisions to benefices, and has argued convincingly that the wider issues of authority were of less importance than the more immediate ones. Attitudes to the authority of Rome were essentially practical, and it was recognised that there were jurisdictional rights which the pope could exercise. This might involve recourse to Rome on a local matter such as a tithe dispute in London, examined by Thomson (230), or on a major issue such as the question of Henry VIII's divorce. Scarisbrick's life of this king (222) gives a valuable assessment of the canon law issues involved. The same writer also has a useful paper on the taxation of the English clergy (221), and financial relations between England and Rome are studied in the book by Lunt (175). Elsewhere in the British Isles, the developments in the Scottish Church discussed by Macfarlane (177) and Thomson (232) show that similar factors could operate in relations between the secular power and the papacy in remote parts of Christendom as in lands nearer to Rome.

When one tries to set developments in the Church against the wider intellectual background of the age, the crucial question concerns the relations between the Church and the world of Renaissance humanism. Hay's book (136) sets the papacy in its Italian cultural context, while Spitz, through a series of case histories of individual humanists (227), illustrates religious attitudes in Germany. In the book already mentioned Renaudet (208) does the same for the Church in France. The papacy cannot, however, be seen only in the context of a society which was undergoing cultural change, it needs to be seen also as a factor within the diplomatic and political structure of Christendom, a characteristic which is well brought out in Dickinson's book on the Congress of Arras (97). This political role of the papacy in a world of developing nation states had to find a new form of expression, and it took the form of a system of concordats, usefully covered by Bertrams (64).

Notes

CHAPTER 1

1 *107*, 341. *Attendentes, quod a tempore obitus felicis recordationis Gregorii pape undecimi predecessoris nostri, nonnulli Romani pontifices aut pro Romanis pontificibus se gerentes et in suis diversis obedientiis reputati* . . . In 1440 John XXIII was still described as *fel(icis) rec(ordationis)* in cameral records. *8*, 249.

2 *125*, 283 n.2. *Nos quidem ipsi sumus ab omnipotenti Deo Iesu Christo super vos et universalem ecclesiam constituti* . . . *Si quis nos spernit Christum spernere convicitur.* (1427).

3 *51*, 12. The authors point out that the agreement avoids the use of the term 'pre-eminence' in relation to councils.

4 One might note that Jakob had been connected with the University of Cracow, which had had a strong conciliarist tradition from the time of the Council of Pisa onwards.

5 *151*, I, 68. Jedin's gloss on this, 'We need not stop to show the untenability of these arguments: they dash themselves in vain against the rock of papal supremacy by divine right', must be understood as an affirmation of doctrine rather than as a historical judgment.

6 *228*, 23. Although one can see in retrospect that Zamometič's attempt had little hope of success, contemporaries may have regarded it more seriously than later writers. Certainly there are a number of references to the episode in the correspondence of Cardinal Marco Barbo. *24*, see index under Zamometič.

7 *7*, II, 146–7. *et non patire ch'el papa governa el mondo a suo modo, et cha se staga tanto tempo senza concilio.*

8 For example, the Dominican Jean Sarrazin (1430), the Augustinian Nicholas Quadrigarii (1443), and the Franciscan Jean l'Ange (1483). Some German universities, such as Erfurt, Vienna and Heidelberg, also maintained a theoretical adherence to conciliar doctrines.

9 One may wonder how far More's attitude was influenced by that of Erasmus. Certainly the latter, in his *Julius Exclusus*, makes the late pope take up an extreme papalist position and allows St Peter to criticise his attitudes and actions in terms moderately favourable to the assembly at Pisa. *41*, 61–70.

CHAPTER 2

1 One should note particularly the statement of E. Kovacs, *159*, 39: *Die Gründung der Universität diente unter den mitteleuropäischen Verhältnissen auch der Einheit und der politischen Unabhängigkeit des Landes.*

2 It is noteworthy, however, that at least two of the Scottish bishops who founded universities, Turnbull of Glasgow and Elphinstone of Aberdeen, were connected with the king as royal officials.

3 A literary manifestation of this national self-consciousness may be seen in a French

treatise, *37*, written between 1453' and 1461, in which two heralds debate the distinctions between their countries.

4 *45*, I, 421. *Nam clarum est quod rex Franciae de facto non recognoscit superiorem*.

5 Bertrams, *64*, 72, suggests that the territorial state was replacing the earlier association of people under a leader (*Völkergemeinschaft*). This whole movement developed with the reception of Roman law in many parts of Europe, because this contributed to the growth of the idea of public power. In the mid-fifteenth century a French writer clearly envisaged a territorial state when he wrote that the King of Scotland was king in his realm as the King of England was in his, and that he was not the subject of the English king but only his neighbour. *37*, 21. On the other hand, the formula was not always accorded the same significance: the fourteenth-century Dutch jurist, Philip of Leyden, rejects the idea that the count of Holland could be regarded as *imperator* or *princeps in partibus suis*.

6 One might note particularly Torquemada's stress on the unifying role of the head in any society. *54*, II, chap. 23 (p. 136v).

7 *10*, I, 63. A similar assertion had been made on the previous day, *ibid.*, I, 59. A. Bossuat, *73*, 374, states that the proceedings against the university resulted from its recognition of Martin V as pope without awaiting the decision of the king, but Fauquembergue's journal shows that, although the question of recognition was being considered at the same time, the proceedings against the university arose from the question of the right of appeal to Rome. This misunderstanding goes back to contemporary writing, in the Journal of the Bourgeois of Paris, *23*, 108.

8 *72*, 59. The Parlement did not go as far as the bloodthirsty rhetorical patriotism of the Florentine Salutati, who declared that he would be prepared to sacrifice father, brother, wife or unborn child, for the sake of *amor patriae*. *155* 245.

9 *21*, XIII, 267. *Inscrutabilis divine altitudinis providencia, per quam Reges regnant, rerumque pulicarum gubernacula possident . . .*

10 When the Cardinal of Lyons refused to confirm the election of a bishop of Angers, Louis instructed Parlement to favour the latter, *car, si autrement vous le faictes, nous vous montrerons par effect que nous ne serons pas contens de vous*. The king had been much concerned with the appointment of this bishop for over a year. *15*, VII, 293–4, VIII, 6–7, 58.

11 There was some disagreement among commentators as to the precise nature of *merum imperium*, and concerning who had the right to possess and exercise it, but the view of Accursius in the Gloss on the Corpus Juris Civilis, that it comprised cases which concerned a man's person, citizenship or liberty, is a useful general guide to the traditional view. *114*, 30.

12 Once in the dative form *nostre Germanice nationi* and once in the genitive *nationis nostre Germanice*.

13 *158*, 48–50. Kohler quotes, without identifying his source, the affirmation: *Dz volk macht den kaiser, und der kaiser macht nit dz volk*. According to Baron, *59*, 301, Maximilian was the centre of the humanist circles in which modern national thought first developed in Germany, but nationalist feeling seems to have existed in the country earlier. One of the earliest chroniclers to see Germany as a separate entity from Rome was the anonymous author of the *Koelhoffische Chronik*, published in 1499. *71*, 91, 95–6.

14 The earliest German edition of the *Germania* seems to have been published by F. Creussner at Nuremberg about 1475, and a new edition by Conrad Celtis was printed at Vienna in 1500. *255*, 847. Cf. F. R. Goff, *252*, 580, who dates Creussner's edition to 1473–4 and suggests that it may antedate the Rome edition of the work published by Schurener.

15 Used by M. Steinmetz in *159*, 115.

16 The text of the introit was: *Venite benedicti Patris mei percipite regnum quod vobis paratum est ab origine mundi*. *178*, 7.

17 Vergil wrote this in the context of the latter stages of the Hundred Years War, but was clearly referring to his own time. *55*, 82.

18 *46*, 21–2, 23–4. The pride of the English and their contempt for other nations had been asserted also earlier in *37*, 5, 51. It can be seen, too, in the anti-French tone of *44*, written about 1417.

19 An example of this can be seen in the role of the Baglioni family in Perugia, discussed by C. F. Black, *69*. Even when the papacy was comparatively weak, it could provide a focus for other families which resented Baglioni influence, if the latter became too dictatorial. The Baglioni themselves had benefited from papal favour in their rise to power.

20 *17*, VIII, 988. *Quid enim Deo acceptius, quid sanctius, quid honorificentius agi aut excogitari potest, quam suo studio & diligentia ecclesiae unitatem & animorum salutem quaerere aberrantium, ut reducantur ad ovile Christi? Hoc opus regium est.*

21 *47*, 217a. (Gloss (e) on *Foro regio*). A French parallel to this is a treatise by Bernard Lauret, president of the Parlement of Toulouse, who declared that secular judges in France had cognisance in certain cases of possessory suits concerning benefices. *45*, II, 1, 650.

22 During the Great Schism a similar split had occurred in the Carthusian order, with Seitz, in Austria, as the head house of the Roman obedience.

CHAPTER 3

1 One might note that in 1484 Richard III tried to secure the promotion of Bishop Shirwood of Durham, who was a curialist.

2 This overstated the case: only some two and a half years had elapsed since the death of Morton's predecessor, Cardinal Bourgchier.

3 Richard Pace, who had been in Bainbridge's entourage, thought that the king should have one or two resident cardinals in Rome, *86*, 1. Henry may have felt the same a few years later when he unsuccessfully sought the promotion of the curialist Bishop of Worcester, Silvestro Gigli. *17*, III, 1,304–5, 1,306–7.

4 Evidently Rodrigo Borgia was regarded as Italian rather than Spanish because of his long residence at the Curia.

5 *31*, I, 300. There is no need to dismiss this statement as biassed because of Basin's hostility towards both Louis and Balue. The king's role in Balue's promotion is mentioned also in the *De Gestis Ludovici XI* of Amelgard of Liège. *17*, IV, 762. The pope yielded to Louis in the hope that the king would suppress the Pragmatic Sanction of Bourges.

6 It may be noted that Gonzaga, Sansoni and Medici were all appointed only to the grade of cardinal deacon.

7 The crisis originally broke out in 1467 and since then there had been a series of disputing claimants. *240*, 304–64, esp. 333–5, 343–4.

8 *180*, 77, 85–6, 97. Borgia obtained the vice-chancellorship on 1 May 1457, and Rovere the post of grand penitentiary in 1476. Borgia's predecessor as vice-chancellor, Francesco Condulmiere, was also the nephew of the pope who appointed him. *144* II, 69.

9 *151*, I, 87. Marco Barbo (Paul's cousin) particularly was a man of noted piety and generosity. While Jedin's contrast is reasonable as far as numbers are concerned, one should not apply it indiscriminately to the quality of men chosen – after all Rodrigo Borgia had been appointed in 1456.

10 For examples, Domenico Capranica (1426), the Greek humanist Bessarion and the Spanish theologian Juan Torquemada (1439), the austere and upright Juan Carvajal (1446), the philosopher Nicholas of Cusa, perhaps as an intellectual and a reformer the greatest figure in the fifteenth-century Church (1448), and the vigorous

reformer Carafa (1464). For learning one might also add Tommaso Parentucelli (1446), who became Pope Nicholas V and, with perhaps some reservations as to suitability, the future Pius II, Aeneas Sylvius Piccolomini (1456).

11 The promotion is discussed in detail by Pastor, *199*, VII, 200–7. This attempt to strike a balance between Roman noble families had a precedent under Sixtus IV, whose promotions to the college in May 1480 included representatives of the Orsini, Colonna and Savelli families. Cosmo Orsini died after eighteen months, and another member of the family, Giovanni Battista, was made a cardinal at the next promotion, in November 1483. *251*, II, 19.

12 Figures from *251*, I–III and *199*, IV, 200, n. The excess of French appointments under Nicholas was partly due to the promotion of three former cardinals of Felix V, all French, and of Felix himself after the end of the Basel Schism. There is an analysis of the composition of the college for 1480–1534 in *86*, 6.

13 Each of these countries had over thirty cardinals in the period between Martin V and Julius II, whereas no other country's representation even attained double figures.

14 The absentees were two Frenchmen, two Germans and one Hungarian.

15 Lulvès summarises the situation tersely in his comments on the capitulation of 1458. The cardinals were to have the right to warn a pope who failed to observe the pact, up to three admonitions *Blieb aber diese fruchtlos, ja, was dann?*.

16 The former declared that the cardinals must not enter into pacts during an election, and the latter that they did not exercise papal power during a vacancy, in virtue of which they might issue a decree defining the terms of their participation in the election.

17 The basis of the belief in a divine origin goes back to a gloss on the decree *Per venerabilem* of Innocent III, in which the cardinalate was derived from the Levites.

18 *45*, II, 1778 (*recte* 1678). Earlier Decio had indulged in a piece of ingenious special pleading on behalf of the minority of cardinals for having called the council without the approval of the majority, *45*, II, 1774 (*recte* 1,674). A similar view was put forward by Zaccaria Ferreri, *45*, II, 1,657.

19 There had been one in 1431, but in 1447, when the Basel Schism had not yet been completely resolved, the cardinals seem to have been willing to leave the new pope unfettered by their demands.

20 There does not appear to have been any reference to the need for unanimity if the Curia was to be moved outside Italy, and one suspects that there was a general assumption that the new pope would be an Italian who would not contemplate such a move. In both these conclaves there was an overwhelming majority of Italians, fifteen out of eighteen in 1471 and twenty one out of twenty-five in 1484, but possibly some of those present at the earlier conclave could recollect a time when the non-Italian element was more prominent. *199*, IV, 199, V, 232–3.

21 The desirability of a council meeting was also stressed in the conclave sermon. *16*, II, 1759.

22 *9*, II, 383–4, 400. Burckard does not give details of the capitulation. Pastor notes that the pope promised to summon a council within two years, and that general councils should then meet every third year. *199*, VI, 194.

23 *1* (1417–31), 18–19, 170. The appointment of a replacement would suggest a development of procedure since the Avignon period; cf. *187*, 466. By the end of the century one sees cases being heard by a succession of cardinals, *13*, 34.

24 Earlier examples of warlike cardinals may be seen in Vitelleschi under Eugenius IV and Scarampo under Calixtus III. Even a cardinal without military inclinations might be assigned to warlike duties, as when Marco Barbo was sent on a mission to report on the state of defences against the Turks on the Adriatic coast in 1480. *24*, 215–8.

25 A good example of a cardinal whose family benefited from his influence was Vitelleschi, although he predeceased Eugenius IV, who appointed him. His family, which had been increasing in power since the thirteenth century, made notable gains during the cardinal's period of dominance. *120*, 139–40.

242 POPES AND PRINCES

26 The draft reform bull (clause 36) laid down *ipso facto* excommunication for cardinals who obtained favours on account of the protection of a prince.

27 A protector was named for the Duchy of Savoy in 1507, for Poland before 1511 and for Denmark in 1513. The town of Ragusa had had a protector under Alexander VI, in 1500, while the earliest mention of a Spanish protectorate came surprisingly late, in 1516, the same year as that of the Marquisate of Montferrat. A Scottish protectorate was certainly established by 1505.

28 Examples of this may be seen in lobbying for support for a provision to an abbey or a bishopric, and for favour in the appointment of a royal councillor as senator of Rome, *18*, 128–30, 267–8, 326–8, 344–7 (nos 122–5, 267–8, 322–8, 344–9). A letter to Cardinal Colonna of 27 October 1451, requesting support for a provision was followed a day later by an instruction to royal officials to allow the cardinal to export six horses from the realm, an action which suggests attempted bribery. *18*, 146, 151–2 (nos 142, 150).

29 In his first letter after his appointment, he subscribed himself as the king's obedient subject, *193*, 427.

30 For example, the arrest of the pro-French cardinals by Alexander VI in 1494 and of Cardinal Clermont by Julius II in 1510. On this latter occasion other cardinals who sought his release were themselves threatened with imprisonment. A precedent for such arrests can be seen during the pontificate of Sixtus IV, when Cardinals Colonna and Savelli were arrested for treason in 1482, because of their conduct in the struggle in Naples.

CHAPTER 4

1 Such making of pledges in return for a loan was not unusual. John XXIII pledged a mitre with the Medici, and it was recovered by Martin.

2 In 1421 Carlo and Pandolfo Malatesta paid the *census* for their vicariates for the coming year as well as for the past one. *196*, 69–70.

3 The fault might lie with a sub-collector who failed to account to his superior, as in the diocese of Aosta, which was five and a half years in arrears in 1416. *119*, 35.

4 Between 1427 and 1429 the Malatesta at Rimini paid only 5,000 florins of the annual *census* of 8,000. At Perugia, the papal share of the profits from the city fell from 12,000 florins in 1424 to 8,000 under Eugenius. *196*, 172, 189–90. Similar problems in collecting taxes occurred during the schism, when the popes conceded tax reductions to their secular allies. *102*, 637.

5 Between October 1431 and January 1434, the *Introitus* and *Exitus* books record fourteen separate payments to him, totalling 13,886 florins. It is worth noting that institutional continuity was preserved between the two pontificates, despite changes in papal policy. *120*, 131–3.

6 *95*, 17, 19–20. The fall of Phocea was not the only cause of increased alum prices. The Turkish advance before 1455 had already led to some interruptions of supply and increases in price, and these were not checked by the discoveries at Tolfa. Delumeau estimates that in the fifteen years after 1453, alum prices in the West rose between 400 and 500 per cent.

7 The figure of 100,000 florins given by Lunt, *174*, I, 60 as the annual income from alum seems too high in the light of Delumeau's detailed calculations, as indeed does the estimate of 50,000 ducats in a document of 1480 quoted by Partner, *197*, 269. This seems to have been the sum hoped for rather than that actually obtained. (At this date the ducat and the cameral florin may be regarded as equivalent in value.)

8 *126*, 24–5. It was not only in lands owing direct obedience to the king that one sees conciliar politics affecting payments to Rome. When Duke Jean V of Brittany

adhered to the Council of Basel in 1440, there was an interruption in the series of annate payments to Rome. *202*, II, 570.

9 *174*, I, 88, II, 291. Lunt cites a tax book, dating from after 1470, in which France is described as a 'reduced country'. The reductions in payment are borne out by the figures in *8*, *passim*.

10 The *census* always appears to have been well under 2 per cent of the sum payable in services.

11 *116*, 150, 166. *175*, II, 305, 433, 439. The matter was complicated by alterations in the exchange rate between the £ and the cameral florin. Similar difficulties existed in the financial relations of the papacy with other nations, particularly in periods of monetary instability. *5*, lxxxvii, *203*, xxi. 62–3. The figures in *8* suggest few changes had occurred before 1455, the date at which this work ends. The published figures for Scotland continue to 1488, and suggest that service obligations altered little, although there were certain fluctuations in annates paid by lesser benefices. This can be seen in two parishes north of Glasgow, New Kilpatrick and Cadder. *5*, 122, 125, 132, 151, 187, 194–5.

12 *5*, 16 (balance remitted to Bishop of Glasgow in 1432 after monitions to pay in each of the two previous years, *ibid*., 315–6), 31 (remission of balance to Bishop of St Andrews, 1433), 45, 53 (delay in paying balance after initial part payment, Glasgow, 1455–62), 49 (absolution of Bishop of Caithness for irregularity incurred through delay in paying, and remission of debt).

13 One must remember that there were also occasions when the papacy was able to insist on obtaining its share, as from the indulgences to the College of St Salvator, St Andrews, in the early 1460s. *5*, 326.

14 *216*, 316–7. This account also shows how indulgence money was absorbed into meeting routine administrative expenses, with one-third going to the collector for his own needs. In Brittany, however, the pope seems to have stipulated that indulgence money should go to crusade funds. *202*, II, 743.

15 Attempts to levy a share for the pope were unsuccessful, *111*, 359–60. The popular appeal of crusading may be seen also in Paul II's establishment of a fraternity to raise money to resist the Turkish advance, with membership fees on a sliding scale. This body, however, incurred the suspicions of Louis XI. *15*, IV, 137–40 and note.

16 Probably one reason for the concern of the reform commission with compositions was their excessive exploitation by Alexander VI's unpopular datary, Giovanni Battista Ferrari. *85*, 60, 100.

17 *197*, 266–8.

18 The figures of income and expenditure are tabulated in *119*, 259–65.

19 The *Introitus* and *Exitus* books, though limited in detail, bear out Tornabuoni's judgments.

20 There was a deficit in the *Introitus* and *Exitus* books for 1506–7, but this was probably balanced by income that did not pass through the main cameral accounts.

CHAPTER 5

1 One might note as examples Martin V's regulations 30, 38 and 62. (*22*, 193, 195, 200). These derived respectively from Boniface IX's regulations 37 (*22*, 65), Urban V's regulation 17 (*22*, 17) and Benedict XIII's regulation 94 (*22*, 138), which was itself a modification of Gregory XI's regulation 67 (*22*, 38–9).

2 *2* (1423–8), 98–9; (1428–32), 49–50. Cf. the suit relating to the vicarage of Haddington which was reopened after representations to the pope. *2* (1428–32), 190–1.

3 The dispute continued intermittently over some eight years, though its undue length may have been partly due to the detention of the city's orators at Köln for over a year, and their consequent failure to present a case before sentence had been given

in favour of the parish clergy. When the orators reached Rome, they were able to have the case reopened.

4 This does not appear to have been successful, judging by the reappearance of a demand for it under Pius II, and from the list of laymen who held office in the Penitentiary later. *144*, II, 5, 193–4; *30*, 370.

5 *249*, 133; *256*, 150–69.

6 The relationship between these series is examined by Fink, *106*, 260–6.

7 Nicholas Bock, Bishop of Kulm, Gregory XII's nuncio to Germany, later received the humbler post of collector for the provinces of Bremen and Riga.

8 The embassies of men such as Francisco de Toledo and Rudolf of Rudersheim in 1461 were more long lasting than that of Nicholas of Cusa in 1450.

9 *133*, 118–28, esp. 120–5. Griffo was in the service of the Camera, but the main aim of his first visit to England was essentially the political task of interesting Henry VII in plans for a crusade.

10 After the end of the mission of Stefano Nardini, from April 1467 to June 1468, the main Roman representative in France was the principal collector of the crusading tenth, Falco de Sinibaldi.

11 Hofmann, *144*, gives a list of offices obtained by Colonna dependents under Martin V, by Spaniards under Calixtus III, by Sienese (including members of the Piccolomini family) under Pius II, by Rovere relations under Sixtus IV and by Cibò relations under Innocent VIII.

12 The only break in this series of papal relatives was Alexander VI's appointment of Ascanio Maria Sforza in 1492, and this was certainly a reward for services in the conclave when Alexander was elected.

13 *45*, I, 322. *cum hodie non conferatur hoc officium homini sanctae vitae, sed potius sanguini et consanguinitati.*

14 Not more than twelve minor penitentiaries, twenty-five lesser abbreviators of chancery and eight referendaries. (Articles 53, 85, 95.) *132*, 215, 217, 220–1.

15 *151*, I, 128–30. Nor should one forget that there were others who urged curial reform as a necessity if the loyalty of Christendom was to be retained by Rome. *144*, I, 328 n.2.

16 These all occur frequently in the registers, e.g. dispensation for marriage to Sir Alexander Forbes and Elizabeth Fraser (1421), commutation of a vow of pilgrimage (1426), permission to hold benefices in plurality (1422). *1* (1417–31), 174, 223, 439–40, 468.

17 For involvement of ecclesiastical courts in debt litigation, on the grounds that failure to pay implied a breach of faith, cf. *247*, 90–2.

18 Various long series of such grants are noted: e.g. *1* (1417–31), 299–343, 412–22, 428–32, 446–51, 532–7, 548–57, 560–3. The total number of beneficiaries from these grants amounts to several hundred, and these represent requests for favours from only one small part of Christendom during part of a single pontificate.

19 These figures are given in *250*, 232–3.

CHAPTER 6

1 Two years later the French king was still talking about furnishing a crusade contingent only when he had Genoa in his hands and the Angevins in Naples. 7, I, 153.

2 The disturbed condition of Naples was regarded as normal. In August 1485 Giovanni Lorenzi reported to Cardinal Marco Barbo, *Res Regni consueta turbatione variantur*. *24*, 119.

3 For the territorial power of the Colonna, see *120*, 50–9. Martin also sought gains for his relatives in Naples, a policy already followed by Boniface IX during the schism.

4 In Perugia after the death of Braccio, Domenico Capranica was far more influential than Pietro Donato. *196*, 170.

5 There had already been a possible clash in 1441, when Ravenna, *de jure* a papal city, passed into Venetian hands.

6 Jones, *153*, 234–8, shows that it was largely due to the diplomatic intervention of Venice, alarmed at increasing papal power in the Romagna, that Sigismondo saved any part of his state.

7 From their strategic control of important Appennine passes, the Montefeltri of Urbino were among the most powerful fifteenth-century signorial families.

8 Pastor, *199*, 300–12, defends the pope from being implicated in the proposal to murder the Medici, but his argument seems specious: Sextus could hardly have been so naïve as to believe that the Medici could be overthrown without bloodshed. He can probably, however, be exonerated from any acquiescence in the details of the plot.

9 The best summary of the political situation on Innocent's death is in *180*, 110–12.

10 *180*, 112–8. This modifies the traditional view of the conclave in *199*, V, 377–85. During Innocent's illness in 1490, twenty months before his death, Sforza was already identified with Borgia and his little private court of bishops (several of whom later became cardinals), in lobbying for votes in the expected election. *24*, 211–3.

11 Of the Italian powers only Florence, which since the fall of the Medici was virtually a client state of France, was not involved in the league.

CHAPTER 7

1 The rules of Eugenius IV and Nicholas V also began with sections on papal reservations.

2 One might note that in academic circles some men saw freedom of election during the schism as temporary. In 1412 Guillaume Roussel, the rector of the University of Paris, declared that the return to freedom of election could not survive the existence of a pope with an incontestable claim.

3 There were complex struggles over the filling of bishoprics, with the pope, the duke and the chapters all trying to advance their own interests. Attempts were made to conciliate rival claimants by translating them to vacant sees, or even by creating an additional bishopric in the duchy, possibly to accommodate a man who had received episcopal orders but had failed to obtain a see. At St Brieuc, troubles between rivals persisted for more than decade, until one of them died in 1462.

4 The distinction between Normandy and the rest of France was still remembered in the early sixteenth century. *11*, II, 60.

5 The pope also sent the duke an illuminated manuscript of the decree of union, decorated with the arms of Burgundy. *235*, 173–4.

6 Philip's bastard half-brother Jean was elected Bishop of Cambrai in 1439 and received papal confirmation, although he did not possess any of the holy orders. He appeared in his see only once in forty years and also left a large progeny of bastards. *190*, 68; *235*, 175. Philip's bastard son David set aside a canonically elected candidate by papal provision to Utrecht in 1455, and overcame the citizens' resistance with his father's support. The rival candidate had to be content with a pension. *33*, II, 315–7; *17*, V, 490–1. For a similar pensioning off of a freely elected abbot, see John of Ypres' continuation of the Chronicle of St Bertin. *17*, VI, 625–6.

7 It was probably as a favour to Martin that faculty was granted in 1426 to his nephew Prospero Colonna to obtain benefices in England to the value of 500 marks. *28*, X, 354. Compare a similar grant to Eugenius IV's nephew in 1435. *28*, X, 629.

8 *45*, I, 525. The contemporary English canonist, William Lyndwood, noted that English kings conferred deaneries and prebends by lawful prescriptive right, but he also attempted to reserve papal rights by distinguishing between the conferment of *temporalia* and *spiritualia*. *47*, 126a.

9 Such were the views attacked by the papalist writer, Arévalo, in the 1440s, when he was the King of Castile's orator at the imperial court. *236*, 45–6.

10 When the cardinal died in 1485, a year after Peckenschlager's translation, the see was granted to another Italian, Ippolito d'Este, and was not held again by a Hungarian until 1497. Matthias Corvinus, despite his activity in curial diplomacy, was less successful in securing the removal of an unsatisfactory prelate than James III of Scotland, who had William Scheves appointed first as co-adjutor and later as successor to Archbishop Patrick Graham of St Andrews.

11 *19*, 47–8, 49–50, 59–60. These are only examples of Rossi's search for benefices; others may be found elsewhere in the correspondence.

12 Christian also obtained the bull of foundation for a university at Copenhagen.

13 In the 'political testament' of Ludovico il Moro, probably dating from 1497–8, there is a passage dealing with promotions to benefices, which illustrates the extent of ducal power. *35*, II, 315–6.

14 In 1481, however, the doge was prepared to lobby the Curia for an abbacy for his nephew. *24*, 26.

15 The republic continued to appoint the Patriarch of Venice and to submit a list of four candidates for the archbishopric of Crete, from whom the pope could choose.

16 For example, four letters of 16 October 1451 seeking an abbacy for the 17-year-old Pietro Aiossa. *18*, 128–30, (nos 122–5).

17 In this the king could draw on support from the Parlement, which presented him with a lengthy remonstrance against the abolition of the pragmatic.

18 *15*, VII, 137–8. This letter, of 10 August 1478, is couched in exceptionally strong terms.

19 In 1496 Charles VIII revoked powers to confer benefices, granted to his officers, on the grounds that the privilege had been abused, and a decree of Louis XII in 1499 concerning judicial administration laid down that the pragmatic be observed on various matters connected with collations.

CHAPTER 8

1 The recognition that some support should be given to the papacy was repeated in another declaration in the following spring. *10*, I, 104.

2 In Spain and Germany the first half of any payment of services had to be made within a year and the second half within the following year. In France the periods were only eight months each, perhaps in an attempt to compensate the popes for reductions in the scale of the dues. There were no provisions concerning annates and services in the English concordat.

3 The reference to 'the laws of the kingdom' probably reflects resistance to Martin V's attempts to secure the repeal of the Statute of Provisors.

4 In the 1460s there were further complaints about the drain of money to Rome for various payments, probably in the period between Louis XI's abrogation of the pragmatic and Pius II's death. *21*, XV, 204–6. About the same time Louis issued ordinances against Roman exactions through the papal rights to *spolia defunctorum*. *21*, XVI, 160–3, 217–9.

5 Frederick continued to receive such grants later in his reign, from Paul II in 1469 and Innocent VIII in 1487. *119*, 186.

6 *96*, 690. It is not quite certain that it was the pope who granted this exemption, but he seems the most likely person to have authorised it. The conclusion is unverifiable because the source document is missing; Dessart thinks that it may have been destroyed during the Second World War.

7 Nicholas V confirmed this tax grant in 1447.

8 It should be stressed that the German clergy were as opposed to the Italians as were the lay powers. The Bishop of Bamberg was associated with the three electoral princes in opposing Innocent VIII in 1487, and Archibishop Berthold of Mainz attacked the greed of the Italians. *127*, 535.

9 In the imposition of the tariff on alum, no specific mention was made of supplies from Tolfa and all foreign alum was affected.

10 A reservation might be inserted in the grant, such as the stipulation that certain military services, due to the king, should still be performed. *21*, XVII, 95–7.

CHAPTER 9

1 *88*, 393. *Mes, Sir, l'act de Parliament ne peut faire le Roy d'estre person; car nous per nostre ley ne pouvons faire ascun temporel home d'aver Jurisdiction spirituel; car nul poit ces faire sinon la supreme teste.*

2 The question of appeals was complicated by the council's claim that it, rather than the pope, possessed ultimate jurisdiction.

3 The subjection of Calais to the jurisdiction of Canterbury was cited as a parallel. *28*, XII, 740–1. In general, friendly relations prevailed between Henry VII, Archbishop Morton and the pope, and these probably facilitated this transfer.

4 *4*, I, 183–4. Earlier in the century, Martin V, Eugenius IV and Nicholas V had laid down rules concerning the transfer of mendicants to other orders. *22*, 246, 257.

5 *231*, especially chapters 1, 9; *17*, II, 1,506–7. (Letter to Louis XI, 1 July 1475). The pope was involved in a campaign against the Waldensians at this time, because shortly afterwards he wrote to the Archbishop of Turin on the same matter. *17*, II, 1,510–11.

6 *125*, 272. Haller states wrongly that Anne was the *daughter* of the Earl of March.

7 One notes the cases of Archbishop George Neville of York in 1471 and of Bishop Morton of Ely and others in 1483. Admittedly Morton's original detention in June may have been primarily a precautionary move by the Duke of Gloucester during his usurpation, and the bishop's attainder followed his participation in Buckingham's rebellion in the autumn. At this time, Morton, and one of the other rebel bishops, Peter Courtenay of Exeter, escaped overseas, while the third, Lionel Woodville of Salisbury, reached sanctuary. As a result it is impossible to say how ruthlessly Richard III might have acted against clerical politicians who fell into his hands after crossing his path.

8 It took fifteen months before papal emissaries could secure custody of the bishops of Le Puy and Montauban, arrested in January 1487.

9 Melchior von Meckau, who was made a cardinal in 1503.

10 Some criminal cases were taken to Rome and heard in the Rota. *223*, 70.

11 *10*, I, 338–9, II, 93. The latter case actually concerned the author of the journal, who was involved in litigation over a canonry. One of the other litigants, Robert de Saint-Ligier, was forbidden to proceed against him at the Curia or in any other Church court, until Parlement ordained otherwise.

12 *202*, II, 490. There was still Gallican resistance to papal hearing of such cases in 1430. *154*, 522.

13 *98*, 39–78. A further complication was that Bazillac also had support from his relative Cardinal Pierre de Foix.

14 It is an interesting comment on the legalism of French public attitudes that while the kings were never prepared to accept papal action against the pragmatic, they appear to have accepted that the decrees originally approved by the Council of Basel could be annulled by another general council, even although the latter was dominated by the pope.

CHAPTER 10

1 Bilderback, *65*, 149–51, attempts to differentiate between the motives of Brittany, Aragon and Savoy, which are seen as being specifically national, and those of other countries which regarded the council as an 'ecclesiastical agency'. While different rulers had different motives, this distinction seems too clear cut, because in Brittany and Savoy at any rate the issues cited by the author are ecclesiastical.

2 *97*, 78–9, 87–97. A similar mission of pacification was undertaken on the council's behalf by the Bishop of Parma between the Teutonic Order and the Poles, *108*, 127. Half a century later, Cardinal Marco Barbo still regarded the preservation of peace between Christian princes as the Church's responsibility. *24*, 182.

3 One may wonder how far this remained a problem among later popes. Nicholas V was certainly aware of some conditions in northern Europe, having been at the Congress of Arras in the suite of Cardinal Albergati, and Pius II was the most far travelled of all Renaissance popes. Even those aware of the problems of some countries outside Italy, such as Calixtus III with his Spanish background, or Julius II, who had visited France when a cardinal, might have only limited knowledge of others. Furthermore even a well-informed pope might easily find that his knowledge of the political scene in a particular country had gone out of date.

4 Professor Denys Hay has suggested to me that there is further evidence for this breach between the Italians and even the humanists of northern Europe in the attack which Erasmus made in the *Ciceronianus* on the Italians, who claimed for themselves a virtual monopoly of Ciceronian standards of Latin style.

Index